FIGHTING BACK

FIGHTING BACK

The Chris Nilan Story

Chris Nilan

TRIUMPH
BOOKS

For the people I love most on earth, and for whom I would gladly give my life.

For Jaime; if it were not for her, I would not be here to write this book.

For my mother, the best and coolest mom; and for my dad, the number-one hero in my life.

For my beautiful children—Colleen, Christopher, and Tara— whom I love fiercely, and for whom there is nothing I wouldn't do.

For my siblings—Susan, Stephan, and Kim; and for all my nieces and nephews.

For the Honorable Judge Paul H. King, a great coach and close friend, and a man without whose guidance, caring, advocacy, and support I would have never come close to achieving my childhood dream of playing in the NHL.

CONTENTS

FOREWORD

Chris Nilan lives by a motto: "Never back down. Never stay down." That motto describes the man through and through.

I have known Chris for close to thirty-five years, and over that time, I have grown to respect him as a teammate, a player, and a person. We became and remain close friends.

I first heard about Chris Nilan, though I didn't yet know his name, early in May 1979 when I was playing for the Montreal Canadiens. We were in Boston for games three and four of an epic seven-game Stanley Cup semifinals series en route to the finals, in which we beat the New York Rangers four games to one. We took the first two games in Montreal. Boston evened the series with wins in the next two games at Boston Garden.

The day after Game 3, with Game 4 set for the next night, we had a skate around at the Garden. Later that day, I was talking with Gilles Lupien, our six-foot, six-inch, 205-pound defenseman, whom we relied on heavily for his physical play and toughness. He told me an interesting story about something that had happened after practice. He, Guy Lafleur, and Jacques Lemaire, having showered and changed into street clothes, were leaving the Garden to grab a cab to our hotel. We were staying in the bordering city of Cambridge, across the Charles River from Boston.

As they reached the sidewalk, a long boat of a car pulled up. In the front of the car were the driver and passenger: two kids, maybe in their late teens or early twenties. They offered my teammates a ride to the hotel. Gilles, Guy, and Jacques, always adventurous, jumped into the backseat.

In no time, the kid sitting in the front passenger seat turned around and started to babble. He said that he and the guy driving the car had sneaked in to our practice that morning and watched all of it. He then started yapping about how he had been drafted by the Canadiens, and that he would be on the team the next season. This information got the three Canadiens, who were already on the team, looking at one another. Then Guy leaned forward and peered closely at the "draftee." With incredulity and great curiosity in his voice, he asked, "And who are you?" Well, the name the young man provided didn't register with anyone, but the kid maintained that the Habs had drafted him the previous year. He also explained that he was a forward who played for Northeastern University in Boston. During that ten-minute trip to the hotel, the occupant of the front passenger seat had much to say.

You meet all types, especially if you play hockey.

It most certainly was a funny story, one worth retelling—and we believed that, for sure, this young man, the one with the incredible and fanciful tale, would never be heard from again by any Montreal Canadien.

Except he would be heard from again. In a major way.

A few months later, in early September, it was the first day of training camp. We were all there in the locker room at the Forum—veterans, rookies, draftees, minor leaguers in the Canadiens system—pulling on our equipment and getting ready for the inaugural skate of the new season.

I heard Gilles and Guy laughing, and I saw that they were talking with a fresh-faced kid who had a head of curly dark brown hair and intense eyes. The kid was sitting down and fully dressed for practice, save for his skates.

Gilles and Guy were calling him, whoever he was, "Boston."

Guy said something like, "You said you would be here, and you are here."

So he was.

Chris "Knuckles" Nilan—the college boy from Boston, the one who had told my teammates the incredible yarn about being drafted by the Canadiens, asserting that he would soon be one of us—had arrived. The 231st player of the 234 selected in the 1978 NHL draft, he would be around for a while.

Right from the get-go, Chris exuded attitude and confidence and enthusiasm, and a bit of craziness . . . but a bit of craziness in a good way. His hockey skills were rough and in need of polishing, but he also possessed a rare mix of focus, guts, determination, physical and mental strength, and work ethic, which the Montreal Canadiens needed. Truth is, from the first days of training camp, even before Chris was sent to our AHL affiliate, the Nova Scotia Voyageurs, for seasoning and development, the Canadiens coaches and management took notice of him.

There are very few NHL players who would eventually do what Chris did for us—protect and stand up for the high-scoring stars, score twenty or more goals a season, and defend against the opposition's top offensive threats and throw them off their game.

Now, let there be no doubt: Chris Nilan came into the league and earned his roster spot as an enforcer. But being an enforcer alone would not satisfy him. He needed to become a total hockey player; indeed, the Montreal Canadiens needed him to become a total hockey player. And Chris responded by working exhaustively, inviting coaching and advice, watching, listening, learning . . . and getting better.

He established himself as a well-rounded defenseman integral to the success of the franchise with the most wins in NHL history. And he teamed with Guy Carbonneau and Bob Gainey to form one of the most effective checking lines in the annals of hockey.

What most of the public most commonly associated with Chris Nilan were his physical play and his fighting, paired with a no-holds-barred and brutally frank personality. Yet those who knew him best saw his extraordinary generosity, his loyalty, and his empathy for those who were hurting and in a bad way.

When Chris was playing for Montreal, as he still does today, he gave considerably of his time in visiting children in the city's hospitals. He not only visited with young people, but he made an effort to get to know them and to understand the specific challenges they faced. Chris forged strong bonds with the patients—and they adored him, as did their families and the hospital staff.

Yes, Chris is giving and generous. He will give you his final dollar if he believes you need it.

When I was general manager for the Habs, I made the painful decision to authorize trading Chris following his prolonged disagreement with Coach Jean Perron. I admired and respected Chris, but for the good of the team, I had to back Jean. Chris loved being a Montreal Canadien, and being traded away hurt him immensely. But Chris never held my decision against me on a personal level.

A few years later, when Chris was at the end of his playing career, it gave me and the Montreal Canadiens organization, and the Canadiens fans, tremendous happiness, and an opportunity to show our gratitude for all he did for the team, to be able to bring him back to Montreal. It was the only proper way for Chris to go into retirement—wearing, in his final game in the NHL, as he did in his first game in the league, the Montreal Canadiens tricolor.

Well known are the challenges and difficulties that Chris went through when his playing days were over. What he faced and endured is horrendous; he suffered from chemical addiction, which destroys lives across all socioeconomic demographics. It could be said, accurately, that opioids destroyed his own life, but only temporarily. Chris Nilan—employing great effort and discipline, and the fighting spirit that so many had witnessed in hockey arenas in North America—emerged from the ashes.

How Chris battled and continues to battle that terrible foe, and how he is beating that nemesis, has only increased the admiration I hold for him. Highly estimable, also, is the responsibility Chris acknowledges for the pain he caused others, and for which day after day he seeks to make amends.

After so much difficulty and tribulation, Chris is again doing well.

Chris lives just outside of Montreal with his girlfriend and soul mate, Jaime, and their two dogs, who are very much like children to the couple. Chris is busy. He hosts a popular radio show on the Montreal sports station TSN Radio 690. He has a "Knuckles" clothing line, articles from which are sold in stores in Quebec and through KnucklesBrand.com. His company's maxim echoes his own: Never back down. Never stay down.

Chris also frequently makes appearances to address bullying and chemical dependency. Enlisting his powerful personality and his life experience, he helps people deal with and defeat these societal scourges. (He can be booked through KnucklesNilan.com.) In speaking and advising on countering and guarding against bullying, this former NHL enforcer, who protected so many, so many times, brings high-level credibility and a valuable message to individuals of all ages. As someone who knows intimately and firsthand the relentless grip of opioids and alcohol, Chris has the authority and insight to steer those with a chemical dependence toward, and help keep them on, the path of sobriety.

Fighting Back, the name of this book, nicely encapsulates and symbolizes so much of what Chris Nilan is about. He never stopped fighting, whether with his knuckles on the ice, or to become a hockey player, or as he clawed out of the abyss of suffering and saved himself. He continues to save himself, while saving others.

Whether as consequence of his own choices and decisions or accidents of fate, Chris Nilan got knocked down, repeatedly. But as his character and his soul demands, he could never back down and never stay down.

True winners and true champions never do.

It is an honor and privilege for me to introduce the remarkable life story of a great friend and a special person.

—Serge Savard

1

KNUCKLES

PEOPLE CALL ME "KNUCKLES."

If you know about my NHL career, you may think the nickname
was earned during those thirteen seasons I was in the league, ten
of which were with the Montreal Canadiens. While playing for
Montreal, I established franchise records for most penalty minutes
in a career (2,248) and most penalty minutes in a season (358).
Actually, those 358 record-setting minutes, which I tallied during
the 1984–85 season, were tops in the NHL that year. And whose
Canadiens record did I break? Well, that would have been mine, set
the previous season with 338 minutes, a total that was also the most
in the league. Yep, I led the NHL in penalty minutes in two consecutive seasons.

Oh yeah, here is another stat: in my time in the NHL, I got into
222 on-ice fights. I don't begin to know how many off-ice fights I had
during that period.

The Canadiens won the Stanley Cup in 1986, and in the eighteen
games in the postseason that year, I posted 141 penalty minutes.

I spent a lot of time sitting in the penalty box. So much time that, to be honest, part of me was really hoping that when they closed the old Montreal Forum, the penalty box bench would somehow find its way back to me. After all, the Boston Bruins' great player and tough guy, Terry O'Reilly—with whom I had some good scraps—was given the Bruins' penalty bench when they closed the Boston Garden. I mean, really, c'mon. I heard the bench from the Forum was auctioned off.

Anyway, people were calling me "Knuckles" before I ever showed up for my first day of training camp in Montreal. It was a nickname I earned while I was in college—and it was inspired not so much by my aggressiveness on the ice as my frequent brawling off of it. In college hockey there isn't much fighting, because if you do fight you are suspended for at least a game. So I didn't do much fighting on the ice in college.

But when I was at Northeastern University and playing for the Huskies, when I was out at night with my teammates or guys from the old neighborhood, or other kids I knew from Boston, and if someone mouthed off to my friends or to me, well, that was an invitation to start throwing punches. And I was a very good fighter. Not trained in boxing or karate or kung fu or any of the martial arts—just a guy who liked, and knew how, to fight and who, most of all, was fueled by a deep and resonating anger that stemmed from the way I grew up (which I'll talk about later).

Of course, I started using my knuckles and fists long before I got to Northeastern. I was fighting in the streets of Boston when I was in grade school. I fought in self-defense, and when I was insulted—or merely felt I was insulted. What I didn't do, though, is look for someone to pick on. In fact, I stood up for the kid who was picked on. I was never a bully.

But I could punch. I could always punch. I can still punch. And if you talk to any of the top mixed martial arts coaches—you know, those guys who teach the ultimate fighters—they will tell you that the physical foundation of fighting is balance . . . and punching. I really liked to fight. I knew my job and I was dedicated to doing it. I took pride in what I did.

I can't speak for anyone else, but for me, I loved every minute of my job. Did I have fear before a game, when I knew I had to go out there and fight guys twice my size—once, twice, sometimes three times a night? Sure I did. But it was that fear that motivated me and that kept me prepared and ready.

Listen, fear is a funny thing. It can affect a person in one of three ways: it can paralyze you, make you turn and run, or it can motivate you to stand and face it. Fear is what inspires me to stand and fight.

But my dream was to become a hockey player, not just a fighter. I wanted to be a great hockey player. Fighting was the easy part for me—the *hard* part was becoming a well-rounded player. Being a good fighter opened the doors of the NHL for me—someone who didn't have great passing, skating, or nose-for-the-puck skills in the beginning. Fighting might have gotten me to the NHL, but it was my unrelenting and diligent work and perseverance that enabled me to develop into an effective full-time hockey player and to have a thirteen-year career doing what I loved.

But the reality is that an enforcer wears down physically and emotionally. Hockey beats the hell out of you even if you are an offensive artist who rarely gets involved in heavy contact. If you are a grinder, a scrapper who fights frequently, you are just pounding yourself into early problems. I've had more than thirty surgeries, including eleven operations on my right knee and one on my left knee. Both of my shoulders have been operated on twice. I've had four surgeries on my hands. I've had several dental surgeries.

Today, I walk slowly, with a very dedicated limp.

I had my four front teeth knocked out by a punch in an off-the-ice fight, but I was able to get to the hospital in time to save them. Yet it wouldn't be a permanent reattachment, because a few years later, during a game, a puck smashed into my mouth and took out those same four teeth.

I am finally getting dental implants. It will be nice to have a smile again—you know, the type of smile where you want to actually show your teeth.

There's a price to pay for playing hockey the way I did, and I guess you could say I'm paying it. But I have no regrets whatsoever, and if I could, I'd do it all over again. Wouldn't change a thing. Swimming in alcohol and burying myself in pills is how I handled the physical pain that resulted from hockey. It just so happened that it also started to work pretty well at numbing the emotional pain I was feeling.

When I chew on all of this and think it over, I understand that a guy like Alan Stewart is a smart guy. You might not know the name Alan Stewart. His career and mine had some tight parallels. He is about my age, and he was tough and could fight with the best of them. During the 1980s, which was the bulk of my years in the NHL, Alan bounced around the American Hockey League and occasionally would get brought up to the majors to do the dirty work and to fight.

During the 1991–92 season, I was on the Boston Bruins but inactive because of an injury. We also lost the services of other tough guys to injuries and to trades. So the Bruins acquired Alan "Beef Stew" Stewart from the New Jersey Devils to provide some of the figurative and literal punch we needed. Alan played four games for us that season, and then he retired and went home to Canada. He said he was sick of fighting. Alan played another season of hockey, in the AHL, but I don't think his heart was in it.

Sure, I have my thoughts on what effects fighting and getting hit have in the short term, and in the long term, on enforcers in hockey. But I know my thoughts may not match up with those effects others feel. So I prefer to focus on my own hockey career.

I do believe strongly, though, that getting hit in the head is never a good thing. And getting hit repeatedly in the head is a bad thing that happens repeatedly. The trauma has to do lasting damage.

For example, Derek Boogaard was one hellish fighter, one of the best. In one fight, Derek slammed a punch with such force into the side of the helmet of his opponent that the helmet cracked.

Derek died young, at twenty-eight, from an accidental overdose of medication, while recovering from a concussion. His family donated his brain for medical research. What did the researchers find? That Derek had a form of brain disease called chronic traumatic encephalopathy—or CTE—which can be caused by repeated trauma to the head. Is anybody surprised?

Of course, before the next NHL season would start, another of the league's players was dead.

NHL enforcer Bob Probert came from a family in which there was a lot of heart disease among the men. Bob died young, at the age of forty-five. His family did what Derek Boogaard's family did: donated Bob's brain for research. They found evidence of CTE. No kidding.

In a way, I fit a stereotype that Hollywood and the publishing industry have leveraged and put to work to make a lot of money over the past fifteen years—that of the hard-edged, tough Irish kid from a hard-edged, tough Irish neighborhood in Boston.

Shoot, I mean, wow . . . let's see . . . what do we have for movies? There is *Good Will Hunting*, *The Town*, *The Departed*, *Boondock Saints*, *Boondock Saints II: All Saints Day*, and *Monument Ave.*—and three movies based on popular novels written by master storyteller Dennis Lehane: *Mystic River*, *Gone Baby Gone*, and *Shutter Island*.

Then there are the books that haven't been made into movies yet, including *All Souls*, *Brutal*, and *The Brothers Bulger*.

It is said that an Irish baby in Boston comes into this world with his chin jutted out and fists balled and looking for a fight. That might be true—sometimes. I think that my Irish brethren also find this generalization demeaning and insulting. Then again, some of my brethren think this is as funny as all get-out.

I do have to say that hockey, a game that is the love of my life, gave me the opportunity to put that scrappy Irish kid in play and keep him active.

Every part of the game, including fighting, allowed me to channel all my energy and release it from my system in a healthy way. Well, sort of in a healthy way; you might argue that all the fighting wasn't healthy—especially if you look at the injuries I sustained. But when hockey was no longer in my life, there was an emptiness I did not know how to fill—and that void contributed to my making choices that were dangerous and life threatening.

When hockey was gone, I think the tough and scrappy kid, and all that emotion that was bubbling inside of me all the time, had no release, and it just stayed in me. There, it fed an animal that was emotionally and physically in pain and needed something to kill that pain.

I found that something—actually a few somethings—and it almost deep-sixed me. Indeed, there was a stretch in which I was about as dead as I was alive.

And I didn't only hurt myself; I hurt those who loved me. That is the biggest sin. If, when you fuck up your own life, you can do it without fucking up other lives, then go right ahead. But that is rarely the case. You almost always hurt others as well.

Today I am clean and sober. I have been clean for three years. For three years, I have stayed away from the booze and the pills, the poison I used to shoot into my arm on a daily basis. In my quest to get right, I had the help of so many who could have given up on me but didn't.

I owe a lot to my family, my friends, my former teammates, and substance abuse professionals who worked with me and truly consider what they do to be a mission, one that is as much about making a life as making a living.

I give my girlfriend, Jaime, credit over and over—credit she deserves totally—for saving my life. I met her when I was getting clean, and we've battled our addictions together. She supports and loves me, and when I messed up, she let me know that she wouldn't be there if I kept going that way.

Love is often tough.

What is my outlet now? How do I try to stay clean? What will support me staying clean? How can I stay healthy?

These questions bring me to this room in a beautiful retreat center and resort—Centre touristique La Petite Rouge—set in the hills about a hundred miles to the north of Montreal.

It is late in the morning on a weekday in early October 2012. In front of me are sixty students from Holy Trinity Catholic High School in Ontario. I am speaking to the students as part of a two-day retreat they are taking part in at the center. They have been selected on the basis of their leadership qualities and essays they wrote.

I would assume that most of these kids, but not all, come from fairly solid financial and family circumstances. I share with them the experience of being educated in a Catholic high school. I share with them the experience of being young and excited about the future— and also being somewhat apprehensive about the road ahead of me. I can relate.

This is also Canada. In Canada, everyone pays attention to the NHL and former NHL players.

Administrators at the school asked me to address these young people and talk to them about bullying. Speaking about bullying and advising how to counter and deal with it is one of the ways I make a living today. I also speak to corporate groups about tenacity and not giving up. I speak to a variety of audiences about my ongoing battle with addiction—about my victories and my losses in this fight, and how the fight continues every day.

And every weekday, from 1 to 3 p.m., I host a live call-in radio show called *Off the Cuff* on TSN Radio 690, an all-sports English station based in Montreal.

(Here, I would like to say thank you to TSN's Mitch Melnick, a longtime radio journalist in Montreal and one of Canada's most talented and popular media personalities. He gave me many opportunities to appear on his show through the years, and he consistently advocated for me with the station. I owe him a lot.)

On the show, I am honest, give my opinions and insights in a straightforward way, and don't try to pussyfoot around where I stand—on anything.

An issue I discuss on the show, and which I talked about frequently when I was a guest on Mitch's show, is fighting in hockey.

I believe that the NHL wants to take fighting out of hockey. They have implemented so many rule changes that it makes it harder for two guys to drop their gloves. I disagree with what the league is doing. I feel there is a place for fighting in hockey and don't think there is anything wrong with two guys spontaneously dropping their gloves and going at it.

I don't believe in "planned" fights—situations in which two guys discuss having a fight before a game, with the intent of getting the crowd hyped up. This type of fighting is almost a farce and detracts from the sport—it cheapens it.

But fighting is part of hockey; it always has been and always will be. Enforcers allow the "greats" like Gretzky, Lafleur, and Crosby to be great; enforcers make room for the scorers to do what they do best.

I also talk about bullying on the show. I take advantage of whatever outlets and opportunities that are available to me to address bullying.

I particularly value and enjoy standing directly in front of grade-schoolers and teenagers when talking about this major social problem. It is the best way to connect with these young people and to emphasize and push the message—to transfer the urgency and energy I feel about the issue. And in these situations, I am there to answer questions—and to pose questions—and afterward speak one-on-one with kids.

Speaking in front of big groups is not a natural thing for me. I have had to work at it, and practice and practice and practice—even though I am primarily of Irish descent, and the Irish are known for being glib and storytellers. Yes, the Irish can talk; in fact, the Irish say that a writer is a failed talker. Growing up, I heard from my parents about the Blarney Stone in Ireland—legend has it that if you kiss it, you will be given the gift of gab. Truth be told, I don't think anyone of Irish descent needs to kiss the Blarney Stone to be able to tell a tale or spin a yarn.

So I am thinking that, after the time and effort I have and continue to put into public speaking, my inner Irishman enables me to deliver in an interesting and engaging fashion the message I want to put across to audiences.

It's funny—I sometimes got nervous playing hockey in front of 16,000 people. For a while, I got more nervous speaking in front of sixteen people. I've heard that people's number-one fear is public speaking; it is even ahead of the fear of death. So I guess, as it has been said, people would rather be in the box than delivering the eulogy.

Today, I am far more comfortable speaking than I was even two years ago. I have my own straightforward way of talking, and I don't pretend to be a loud and poetic and flowery orator. I am not an arm-waving preacher at the pulpit. In fact, I don't like to stand at a lectern or podium when I speak. It isn't me. I stand in front of the crowd and I talk and I am direct, and I have an even cadence, and I tell the truth—sometimes the painful truth. And while I won't use vulgar language, I most certainly do use—as necessary and where appropriate—hard and harsh language, and sometimes language that makes people feel uncomfortable.

I tell stories that aren't pretty. And I get across what I want to get across, and I teach the lessons I want to teach. People tell me they remember what I say.

This is good—for I definitely need the kids I'm speaking to today to remember what I'm saying about bullies and bullying.

There have always been bullies. There were bullies when man still lived in caves and had just discovered fire and still walked with his knuckles dragging on the ground. The need to assert power and gain confidence and control by picking on the weaker—or, at least, perceived weaker—person is hardwired into our biology and psychology. In the animal kingdom, we see bullying as well.

I guess you can figure that I am not in agreement with a lot of what we are doing in society in terms of becoming more sensitive and caring and holding hands and making sure we are having more Kumbaya moments. I think that in not letting our kids wipe their asses for themselves—and in having parents hover around their kids all the time—we are raising wimps and pussies and pushing young people along the road to a day in which they will become full-fledged adult babies.

Yet heightened awareness about bullying and adult intervention to prevent it are good things. They are good things through and through. Even if we did not have the mobile and online and instantaneous electronic communication that has taken bullying to new levels and new extremes, adults and young people who are leaders would still need to step up and become more involved in anti-bullying measures.

Bullying is just so injurious, destructive, and soul destroying that society has to punch back at it. And this should have been the case even before the Internet, texting, Facebook, and mobile phones.

Exhibit A: Phoebe Prince.

I tell the kids from Holy Trinity Catholic High School about this beautiful and lovely young woman, an immigrant from Ireland and a student at a high school in Massachusetts, who was bullied unmercifully—and while, sure, some of it was cyberbullying, a whole lot of it involved bullying tactics as recognizable and prevalent in 1950 as they are today.

In fact, the final day—the final afternoon—of her life, as Phoebe walked home from school, a car full of her tormentors drove past, and one threw a soda can at her and yelled "whore." We will never be sure if that action was the one that made her decide what she would do that day. It surely increased whatever pain Phoebe was feeling.

We know this: when Phoebe got home, she went into a closet and looped a scarf around her neck—a scarf that her younger sister had given her as a gift—and hanged herself. Her sister, the same one who had given her the scarf, found her.

Throwing a soda can at someone and calling that person a whore. Those actions were available as bullying devices in the days before color TV.

I talk about Phoebe Prince because bullying can destroy a person figuratively and literally. Especially if the person who is being bullied has other issues in his or her life—and that is often the case, and is often directly connected to why the person is being bullied— the taunts and torment can push someone into a very lonesome and dark place. If the bullied person suffers from underlying depression, the pain can become too much; it can become unbearable.

I talk to the kids about where the bullying starts, its roots and all that. Bullies are created close to home—either within the family unit in which they grow up, or in something within them that is lacking and insecure and sometimes hostile. Yet, like everything in life, what starts a kid down the path toward being a bully and what sustains a kid in being a bully are not always easy to identify. If only life were that simple.

Even good kids from good homes who have a sound set of values can get involved in bullying. All kids want to belong, and kids like camaraderie, and it is all too often in the buddy-building process that kids find comfort in getting together to pick on someone. I know it is mean and all that—and the good kid usually figures this out fairly quickly—but it is a fact. A simple fact.

There are other kids, not bad kids, who themselves might have been or might understand that they can become the target of bullying, and they head this off by joining up with and supporting a bad element. This is a defense mechanism—and they become "hangers-on" and bolster their own sense of confidence. What often happens in these situations, though, is that the hanger-on can become bullied within the group of his so-called friends. Believe me, any protection these kids enjoy with the group of punks is short lived.

One of the most difficult ways for the bullied to handle the bully is to stand up to him or her. Sometimes it is a matter of just standing there and saying right out, "Stop. Leave me alone!" And if that doesn't make it stop, use the "I" phrase, as in, "I said stop. Leave me alone!"

When the bully gets called on to think about the merits of being an asshole and a shithead, it can—not always, but more often than most would think—result in the bully backing up and laying off.

I can't emphasize enough—and I share this with young people—the importance and value for a kid who is being bullied of having people come to his or her defense and having student leaders in a school who will get together and intervene. If kids can't handle and stop bullying on their own, they need to tell teachers, coaches, school administrators, and other adults in positions of authority about the problem. This isn't being a tattletale; it is about maybe saving a life.

And okay, I am not going to bullshit you—do I see value in standing up to the bully, even if it requires a physical fight? Yes, I do, although I would never advise a child to fight. Even if the bullied person gets his ass kicked—and quite often, the opposite is true—it inspires the bully to stop and find easier prey. But I also know that for some kids, fighting back in this way is something they just can't do. It isn't them.

Still, I gotta tell you—and, again, I'm not going to bullshit you here—there is nothing, absolutely nothing, more satisfying than seeing the tables turned on the bully.

Adults need to act like grown-ups and be responsible—because, oftentimes, even the most grounded, best intentioned, and self-sufficient kids can't resolve bullying themselves. Parents, on both sides of the bully aisle—that is, parents of bullies and of the bullied—can step in and put an end to the problem. Teachers and coaches, directors of youth groups who know about bullying and don't do something about it are in the wrong line of work.

I can relate to people who intervene, because coming to someone else's defense was my role in hockey. Contrary to what some of you may think, I was not a bully on the ice—I was a protector.

I hear this comment a lot: "How come you go around advocating against bullying when you were one of the biggest bullies when you played?" Here is what I say to that: it was my job to protect my teammates, among them some of the best who ever played the game. If another team was messing with Guy Lafleur, Bob Gainey, Chris Chelios, or another one of our goal scorers, then I had to make sure that I messed with whoever was messing with them. I was actually the guy who took on the bully.

Jamie Hubley could have used a protector. I would have been proud to stand up for Jamie Hubley.

I talked to those sixty kids from Holy Trinity Catholic High School about Hubley, a fifteen-year-old young man who lived in Ottawa and was a figure skater. He was openly gay. He also battled depression—

severe depression. I can only imagine how being bullied and having depression mixes. I can't see how that would ever end up good.

Hubley had a supportive family, and adults did get involved and tried to help. Still, it must be tough to shake the experience of getting batteries shoved into your mouth, which some bullies did to him. One more case of it all becoming too much. Hubley went online and posted a video about the pain and torment he felt. On Friday, October 15, 2011, he posted these words on his blog: "It's so hard, I'm sorry, I can't take it anymore."

The next day, Jamie Hubley did what Phoebe Prince did: he hanged himself.

Would it have mattered if I had been there for Jamie Hubley like I was there for Art Lucie?

I will never know.

Funny thing—for years I didn't think about what I did for Art Lucie. But apparently it stuck with him.

It was the spring of 2012, and I was in Lake Placid, New York, for a benefit event. I was in the hotel lobby, checking in, and who walks out from the room behind the desk but Art Lucie. He had a big smile on his face, and I recognized him immediately—even though it had been more than thirty years since we had last seen each other.

Art yelled, "Chris Nilan! This is great!" And he quickly walked around to where I was standing and we gave each other a big hug. I came to find out Art's family owned the hotel. The Lucie family went way back in Lake Placid; the family was very successful and prominent in the area.

How did Art and I know each other? We met in the late 1970s, when I did a post–high school grad year at Northwood School, a college prep school up in the Adirondacks. Art was a classmate of mine. He was a good kid. I liked talking and hanging out with Art when we attended Northwood. He always had good stories. He, of course, knew Lake Placid inside and out; he was someone who helped you get the lay of the land. He had all the inside scoops on Lake Placid and Northwood School.

Anyway, that day we were talking, and he brought something up that happened at Northwood School when we were students. It was something that I did remember, even if it hadn't been front and center on my radar screen in the years since. It seemed, though, to mean a lot to Art Lucie. It seemed to be something that was prominent on his radar screen.

What he remembered was being outside a classroom one day, by himself, with no one around other than a kid who was a lot bigger than him—and who had been giving him some trouble over the past few days. The kid pushed Art against the wall, and he was acting all menacingly.

And that is what I saw when I came around the corner and into the hallway.

I yelled, "Hey, leave him the fuck alone!" I ran toward the two, and the big kid backed away from Art, but turned to me and made like he was going to have it out with me. Okay, so bring it on.

I said, "Listen, you asshole, you wanna fuck with someone, you can fuck with me." And this punk was like, "Oh yeah?" And I went, "Yeah," as I got in his face.

It took only a few seconds—him and me, eyeball to eyeball—before he muttered, "Fuck this," and walked away.

He never bothered Art again.

Therein lies an important lesson—a fundamental lesson—in learning how to handle bullying and the bully.

Handling the bully, sticking up for my teammates, was a major part of my life; it was a major part of how I made a living. My ability to handle the bully was a cornerstone of the earliest years of my life, and is at the root of the value and support I offer in advising others how to deal with bullies.

Knuckles is more than my nickname; it is also a summation and descriptor of my life—a life of having a chip on my shoulder, of clawing and chasing for acceptance, of battling to reach a level of hockey that so many thought was unattainable for me, of struggling with internal and external demons, of fighting to achieve extraordinary personal and professional highs, and of letting down my guard and not fighting back and allowing addiction to almost kill me.

I'm still fighting. I fight every day to stay clean and live smart and be responsible.

So this is my life story.

It is a story about a fight that never ends.

2

WEST ROXBURY— THE EARLY YEARS

HENRY, MY DAD, WAS BORN in Boston in 1935, in the middle of the Great Depression. He grew up in the blue-collar and very hard-working, ethnic, mostly Irish neighborhood of West Roxbury. My mom, Leslie, was born in Illinois in 1936; she moved with her family to Boston, to the neighborhood of Roslindale—or "Rozy," as it is commonly called—when she was two years old.

West Roxbury and Roslindale, equally Irish in makeup, border each other.

Mom and Dad met and soon started dating when they attended Roslindale High School. When my mom was seventeen and my dad was eighteen, they found out they had a baby on the way. In that they both were from Irish-Catholic families, and in that this was Boston in the early 1950s, this meant they were going to get married. Which they did. Both also graduated from high school before the baby was born.

Of course, my dad was already working when my mom became pregnant. And Mom and Dad lived for a while with my mother's parents. Then they got themselves an apartment in the town of Dedham, which borders Boston (specifically, the Boston neighborhoods of Roslindale, West Roxbury, and Hyde Park) to the south.

So the baby, Susan, arrived in 1953. She was the first of four Nilan children. After Susan came Stephan in 1955, then me in 1958 (on February 9, in the middle of hockey season), and Kim in 1961.

Four kids is a decent-sized family, but it was unremarkable in size for an Irish clan in Boston. Indeed, while it was not widely broadcast or discussed among polite society, there was a sort of unspoken strategy among the Irish in our city to boost our numbers and then take control. It was a game plan that worked very well.

The legendary Boston Irish politician, James Michael Curley—who once got reelected mayor of Boston while serving a prison term—told a WASP power broker, "We are going to outfuck you now and outvote you later."

In 1955, my dad got a job at Draper Laboratory in Cambridge. He started out in a sort of draftsman apprenticeship program there. He also was taking night courses in engineering at Northeastern University. A tough schedule. Then again, neither of my parents was ever afraid to work.

Draper Laboratory started as a part of the Massachusetts Institute of Technology in the 1930s. And when my dad began working there, it was still a part of MIT and would be until it became independent of the university in 1973. Draper is renowned for all the technology it has developed and contributed to our national defense, the US space program, and the medical field. That place is and always has been full of some scary-smart people doing some very important work.

Today, most of the graphics of system and technology design never leave a computer screen, but when my father started at Draper, everything was still plotted and laid out on paper. So for a young guy just out of high school, getting hired into a training program to become a draftsman was a very nice fortune.

My dad worked on some impressive projects and technology, including the Deep Submergence Rescue Vehicle that Draper developed for the US Navy.

So my dad had himself good and steady work. Mom and Dad were super providers. None of us wanted for anything. When the Nilan kids got a bit older, my mother went to work as well, on the help and customer-service desk at Marshall's, a department store.

Dad found yet another way to make money to support his family, as well as serve his nation. In 1955, with a wife, an infant, and a toddler, he enlisted in the US Army Reserve. After basic training, he chose to become a Green Beret. Dad would stay in the reserves for twenty-five years, putting in one weekend a month and two weeks a year over that period.

His annual two weeks took him all over the world. He did jungle training in South America and jumped out of planes over fjords in Norway. He went to interesting places and did interesting things. Yet with five kids and a wife at home, for whom he was the primary source of support, he was never sent into a combat zone. He didn't serve in Vietnam. But if World War III ever erupted, he would be ready—and if any nation were stupid and suicidal enough to trespass on our shores, he would be in action as well.

The first school I attended was the Ames School in Dedham, starting in kindergarten. When I was in third grade, my father's mother died, and my parents—who had saved enough money and were secure enough financially—bought the house my dad grew up in in West Roxbury.

That home, the same one Mom and Dad live in today, was a small single-family house built in the 1920s and located on Gardner Street, a narrow thoroughfare about a quarter-mile long that was lined with similar small single-family homes. I guess you could use the term "postage stamp" to describe the plot of land on which our home sat. No real front yard—like all the other houses on Gardner Street. From the sidewalk to the front door of our house was fewer than ten yards. As well, only about ten yards separated each house on the street.

We were a tight-knit community. And I suspect that not one family that lived on that street had a lot of money, but all were hard-working and had civic pride and kept their small places tidy and pre-sentable. You might have been able to find a candy wrapper on the sidewalk alongside Gardner Street, or on Gardner Street itself, but if you returned in ten minutes, it wouldn't be there.

In third and fourth grade, I attended the Joyce Kilmer Elementary School in West Roxbury. It was about a mile away, and I walked to and from school.

The Nilan family was a traditional American Irish-Catholic family. Mom and Dad worked hard and stayed together, they saved and were frugal, and if we were not exactly God-fearing, we were all definitely God-reverent and religiously observant. We went to church—Saint Theresa's, in West Roxbury—every Sunday. We observed all holy days. We didn't eat meat on Fridays.

As much as possible, we had dinner together every night. And on Sundays, we had a big family dinner. My parents empha-sized family unity. My dad was, and remains, a tough, hard-edged Irishman. He enjoyed his daily highball or two; sometimes he had a couple of beers instead. He did not tolerate lip from anyone. He also was not reluctant to smack his kids if he thought they needed it. I got smacked frequently—and I think the experience hardened me and made me tough and inclined to fight outside the house. I had to take it inside the house, but I sure wasn't going to take it outside the house.

When I got to West Roxbury, I met some guys who became life-long buddies: Bobby Moritz, Eddie Kenney, Pat O'Brien (one of eight kids), Larry Jackson, twin brothers Ronald and Donald Harrington, and Paul "Bubsy" Dinozzi. They were my age and also attended school in West Roxbury.

We walked together to and from school. Back then, we did not have all the activities and scheduling that you have today, so we had to find and create our own fun—and mischief. After school, during the fall, we played tackle football on a field around the corner from Gardner Street. We and some other guys who lived nearby would go at it—without pads—and not infrequently, fights would break out. It wasn't a big deal. We got over it.

Early on, I disliked most organized sports; then again, I disliked most organized things. Yep, I sometimes "bristled" at authority. I will say this, though: if I respect the authority, I will listen to and accept that authority. I played a year of Pop Warner football, for the Cowboys in the West Roxbury league—but I only lasted that one year. I didn't like it. I played a year or two of Little League baseball, but that was that as well—I didn't like the game and was bored.

The first winter the Nilans lived in West Roxbury was when I found the love of my life. Her name was hockey.

At the end of Gardner Street, just around the corner a bit and running alongside the road, was an area—maybe thirty yards by twenty yards—that had a sandy, cracked tar surface that dipped a bit; it abutted a scrub of grass and trees. That little sunken area often became flooded during rainy periods or when large amounts of snow melted and drained into the depression. And when it got cold enough, the water froze and we had ourselves a micro-pond and micro-rink.

That oversized puddle is where I learned to skate—and where

I first started pushing and slapping at a puck. Bobby and Pat and Bubsy and I would go down there after school and on weekends. Our parents bought us skates and sticks and pucks, and I am fairly confident that none of the equipment was of standout quality, but we didn't care—not a bit. We had a blast, skating and scrambling for the puck, shoving and checking each other. Once I got the hockey bug, I never lost it.

We put in a lot of skating on that frozen puddle—and what was nice about it was that we could skate into the evening because street-lights and lights from nearby houses kept our urban rink bathed in just enough of a glow that we could figure out where the puck was and where we were going.

Not long after we adopted and took over that puddle, we found even more ice—and a far bigger area of it—about a half mile away from our puddle. It was a swamp next to West Roxbury High School. The guys and I did a lot of skating up there—and were joined by kids from other neighborhoods. Let me tell you, there are skills that are developed when playing on shallow pockets of, I'll call it *natural,* ice, that you don't learn on smooth, man-made rinks or even the flat ice of ponds.

You see, when you skate on big puddles, on swamps, or on the overflow that weaves in and around woods, you almost always have to negotiate around rocks and sticks and roots and sprouts of grass. You have to keep your wits about you—and those obstacles are training devices that help you along and improve your skating agil-ity and passing ability.

In fifth grade, I got involved in organized hockey for the first time. I played in the Charlie Doyle League, a youth hockey league in West Roxbury. Charlie Doyle was a local state representative who cobbled together the money and community support for a six-team league. I was nine years old, and it was the beginning of the 1967–68 hockey season. Bobby and Pat and I were on the same team. Eddie and Bubsy didn't take up hockey.

We played at the "squirt" level, which was the level nine- and ten-year-old kids played at in the US youth hockey system. If you have been around youth hockey in America for a while, you know the levels well. You've got the mini mites (ages five and six), mites (seven and eight), squirts (nine and ten), peewees (eleven and twelve), and bantams (thirteen and fourteen)—and then there are the older kids, the midgets and the juniors.

We had a good coach; his name was Steve Curtin. Coach Curtin worked for the phone company and loved and knew hockey. He emphasized the basics, gave a lot of individualized attention, and didn't play favorites. He had a balanced perspective and had his priorities in order. My father also helped out a bit with the coaching.

Hockey leagues and programs were sprouting up all over New England. And along with them, the state of Massachusetts, city of Boston, and other cities and municipalities commenced a big ice rink–building phase. There were indoor rinks and outdoor rinks, and rinks that had roofs yet were open on the sides—so I guess you would call them hybrid indoor/outdoor rinks.

What set off and fueled this hockey boom was the emergence in the late 1960s of an era of Boston Bruins hockey in which the team came to be known as the "Big Bad Bruins." Yes, the Bruins were building at this time, bringing in the players who provided a mixture of high-level skating, passing, scoring, checking, mouthing off, and punching out necessary to win a Stanley Cup. And the Bruins needed to win a Stanley Cup. In fact, the last Cup the team had won was in 1941.

When I started to play hockey, the Bruins were a long-established institution in Boston, having been founded in 1924, and the team was one of the "Original Six"—along with the Chicago Blackhawks, Detroit Red Wings, Montreal Canadiens, New York Rangers, and Toronto Maple Leafs—that comprised the NHL from the 1942–43 season until the league expanded in 1967.

It had been a long time since the Bruins—or the Bs, as they are also known in these parts—had hoisted the big trophy. But it looked like the components were in place for things to change. Perhaps the biggest catalyst came in the form of an eighteen-year-old kid from Parry Sound, Ontario, who first stepped onto the ice for the Bruins at the beginning of the 1966–67 season. His name was Bobby Orr.

Also that year, the Bruins made Gerry Cheevers their starting goalie. Orr and Cheevers joined a team that had a hard-hitting offensive star in Johnny "Chief" Bucyk, an Edmonton native of Ukrainian ancestry, who was in the middle of a remarkable twenty-year NHL career.

Later that season, the Black and Gold acquired winger John "Pie" McKenzie from the Rangers. Things continued to come together for the 1967–68 campaign, when Boston signed the immensely talented, and even more flamboyant, center Derek Sanderson. And in what can only be regarded as a blockbuster trade, it acquired Phil Esposito, Ken Hodge, and Fred Stanfield from the Chicago Blackhawks.

The Boston Bruins were starting to win—but almost as important to the people of Boston, they were starting to win with a lot of scoring and beauty and artistry combined with large doses of machismo and physical hockey and a willingness to brawl and intimidate. These Bruins were very good and very tough, and Boston—heck, all of New England—loved it.

When the Bruins won the 1970 Stanley Cup, things got really hockey crazy in the region. For sure, you could see those bumper stickers around there that read JESUS SAVES. ESPOSITO SCORES ON THE REBOUND. No small thing, this type of sacrilege; remember how religious and Catholic it was in the Boston area back then.

I was totally caught up in watching the Bruins on TV and listening to them on my transistor radio. These guys were giants in my eyes—bona fide superheroes. In some ways, I think that not having the Internet and all the cable stations and all that contributed to my holding the players in even higher esteem than young people do today with pro players. Oh sure, kids nowadays have every type of memorabilia and all sorts of images of their favorite players all over their walls. They have all that promotion and publicity hitting them all the time. But this removes the mystery and the aura from the players. The fans and those they cheer for are almost too close.

I didn't know everything there was to know about the Boston Bruins—and even though they played, and some resided, in the same city in which I lived, they were far-off and remote and legendary figures. I saw them on TV and caught their pictures in the newspaper—but I didn't have immediate, 24/7 access to visuals and information about them like kids do today. Orr and Sanderson were people of myth, larger than life; they lived in another stratosphere.

I already loved hockey prior to the Bruins' ascendance. And my affection for the game soared along with the fortunes of the team.

I get asked what it was about hockey that drew me to it, as opposed to other sports. People can understand how I am not a baseball guy, but they surely see in me something of a football guy. I mean, really, since I was coordinated and enjoyed contact and had a nose for where the play was heading, don't you think I had "undersized inside linebacker" written all over me? I can see people wondering about that. I think what was, and what remains, appealing about hockey for me is that, on the ice, there is the flow of the game, and the alternating few minutes of energetic explosion, and then a few minutes of rest—over and over.

Plus, I enjoyed skating. I felt a sense of freedom every time I'd step onto the ice. When you skate—especially if you do it well—you glide. And you can glide fast—very fast. There is skill and elegance in skating. Imagine me, Knuckles Nilan, talking about skating as elegant. But it can be.

In the summer of 1968, Boston built a community ice rink at the end of Gardner Street, alongside the Charles River and across the street from a Veterans Administration hospital. It was of the mixed variety—open to the elements on the sides, yet having a roof. When that rink opened in December of '68, its number-one patron—far and away—was Chris Nilan.

The team I played on in the Charlie Doyle League had one practice a week, at night, on one of the many rinks in the area. We played our games on the weekends, on Saturday or Sunday afternoons. Sometimes we would have a game on both days. I played wing. I was not a standout, but I surely was one of the better players in the league, and my hustling and physical play were already evident.

After school, the guys and I would go up there and pay a buck or whatever it cost to use the ice, and we would skate for about three hours. The rink had lights, so darkness wasn't an issue. Indeed, on Friday and Saturday nights, and on the eve of some holidays, the rink would be open until eleven. I knew the rink manager, a guy named Paul Hynes, and he would let us skate even after the official closing time, for another half hour or so, until he had gotten through his end-of-day paperwork and receipts and all that. Sometimes my buddies and I would even sneak into the rink in the early-morning hours, like at twelve-thirty or one o'clock, and skate for a couple hours.

I am not so sure how unusual it was for kids in the Boston area to be as addicted as we were to skating and hockey back then. It was a contagion that affected the entire region.

For fifth grade—that would be the 1968–69 school year—I enrolled at St. Theresa's School, on the same grounds as St. Theresa's Church, where the Nilan clan went to Sunday Mass. The school was run by the Archdiocese of Boston. My mom and dad didn't have a lot of money, but they believed strongly in a Catholic education, and they would do what was needed to make sure we could attend St. Theresa's—which went from fifth through eighth grade—and then go to a Catholic high school.

I was young for my grade. Again, I was born February 9, so I wouldn't turn ten for another five months. Most kids in my grade had had their tenth birthdays the previous school year.

My sister Susan had already gone through St. Theresa's and was attending the Ursuline Academy, a Catholic high school in Dedham. Stephan was in eighth grade at St. Theresa's. By the time I got to St. Theresa's, my sister and brother had established a track record of disfavor with the nuns who ran the school. Because of that history, one of the school's chief disciplinarians, Sister Ida—always stern-faced, stout, and unsmiling—didn't like me from the get-go. This was not fair.

Soon enough, though, I gave the sister justification for disliking me.

Sister Ida taught English. I was in her class and quickly became a problem. I couldn't help myself. I liked to joke and get the other kids going in class—mischief that would invite different types of responses from Sister Ida. She often walked up to my desk and grabbed my cheek with her thumb and the side of the knuckle of her index finger and then gave the cheek a sharp tug. She also jabbed me in the chest with her knuckle. Sister Ida was sure I had it coming and just as sure that what she was doing was in the right.

Sometimes I got sent down to the office of the principal of St. Theresa's—her name was Sister Maruna. When that happened, I had to stay after school or clean up certain rooms in the school. Sometimes my parents would receive a call, and then I was in for it at home, with Mom and Dad reading me the riot act, and Dad also giving me a slap or two.

But I did need discipline. I think I have always had an overactive mischief and joker gene in me.

One day while in seventh grade, and still attending St. Theresa's, a nun tossed me out of class. No problem for me; standing in the hall was preferable to sitting in class. So there I was, standing there—and it was wintertime and there was a lot of snow on the ground outside—and what did I see lined up along the walls in the hallway but all the boots and galoshes the students had worn to school that day. I got an idea—an idea inspired by Derek Sanderson's auto-biography, *I've Got to Be Me,* which I had just read and I loved.

In the book, Sanderson tells how, as a kid in Niagara Falls, Ontario, he had been in an empty hall of the school he was attending, and he saw something similar to what I now was looking at—pairs and pairs of winter footwear belonging to students who were in class. The young Sanderson rearranged all the boots and galoshes, mixing and matching them, strewing them this way and that way. And, you know, I was so impressed with reading what my idol did when he was about my age that I had to do it as well.

I thought it was cute and harmless. What it did was earn me another trip to the principal's office. Mom and Dad got a call as well.

I was growing—and still acting—up.

The Nilan family never went on any big trips or did much traveling. My dad would get to see exotic places during the summer when he did his two weeks of Army Reserve training. But the Nilans as a family, I don't believe, ever made it out of New England. Not that it mattered to me—most of the guys and girls I knew who lived in West Roxbury never made it out of New England either. Heck, getting out of Boston was a big experience.

But my father and mother did think it was important that we have a vacation every year. The summer following my birth, for the first time in what would be a Nilan custom, my parents rented a cottage for a week near the ocean in the neighborhood of Brant Rock in Marshfield, a coastal town south of Boston, about twenty miles north of where the peninsula of Cape Cod starts. Marshfield is quite ritzy now—a lot of money there—but in the 1960s and into the early '70s, it was still a good bit blue collar and had a sizable population of fishermen.

So every summer, on a Sunday afternoon, the Nilans would jump into our American-made station wagon—we never had two cars, just one, and always a station wagon made in the USA—and take the twenty-mile trip to Marshfield, where we stayed until the following Sunday afternoon. It was a lot of fun, those seven days. Mom and Dad and the kids would hit the beach for several hours. My father taught my brother, Stephan, and me how to scuba dive. The family might go out to eat a couple times at local seafood restaurants. And Mom and Dad could relax with a cocktail and the smell of salt air and the sound of surf and waves nearby—a most deserved break from their hardworking lives at their jobs in and outside of the home.

That week in Marshfield was a luxury.

When I got into junior high, and Mom and Dad had a little bit of money put away and were a bit more settled, the summer got even more luxurious because, in addition to that week down in Marshfield, they rented a cabin up at Lake Sunapee in New Hampshire for another week. Summer was awesome. We stayed up at Lake Sunapee in early July, and in early August we went down to Marshfield.

It took me many years to understand and get my head around the sacrifice my parents made in taking us on vacation and paying to send us to Catholic school. Not much money was left over for them. But they didn't want it any other way. Mom and Dad had a strong sense of right and wrong, and of commitment, and of good, solid values, and of the responsibility they had to each other and to their children. In some blessed way, the hard work they put in for the family, and whatever sacrifices they made, and whatever privations they experienced, assured them they were living the right way and being good Catholics and good Americans. I think all this made them happy as well.

When I was in seventh grade, I was on a peewee hockey team that played in the Boston Neighborhood Hockey League, or BNHL, as it was commonly known. This team was different than the one I had played on the past few years, because it had players from all over the city. Steve Curtin again was our coach.

We had talent, and Coach Curtin got the most out of us. Some of the players were Bobby Cotter and Mark Fidler, two of the best players to come out of Charlestown, another hard-nosed, blue-collar Irish Boston neighborhood. There were the Harrington twins, Tom and Peter, who lived in the Beech Street housing projects in Roslindale. We had Phil Bowers, Michael Keeley, Mike Crisp, and one of the best defensemen in Massachusetts, Billy Mahoney.

Again, we had talent and we could play.

And we were tough.

Steve Curtin made sure we had fun, and he also thought it was important to win. We liked playing for him, and we wanted to do well for him. We also wanted to win for ourselves.

Sometimes our enthusiasm and drive to compete got out of hand—like the game we played one night at Ridge Arena in Braintree, a town ten miles south of Boston. I don't know who started it; maybe it was me. But one player got checked, hard, and the guy who got checked threw a punch—and the brawl was on. Talk about the height of ridiculousness—here you have eleven- and twelve-year-old kids throwing down. Players from both teams left the benches and joined in the fray. Players were punching, wrestling, falling onto the ice, and rolling around. Coaches, referees, and a few parents were among us, trying to get everyone separated and establish some order.

I'm thinking that this thing lasted for a good five minutes or so. Finally, it got broken up. And of course, that was that—the game was over. Parents and coaches helped sequester the teams from each other, and the adults held our team inside the building while the other team and coaches left.

It was a lot of fun.

We ended that season in the best way possible—beating Charlestown in the BNHL final at Watson Rink in Cambridge, on the campus of Harvard University. We won 9–5, and I scored a goal. My team, Hub City, was the peewee champion of all of Boston. Coach Curtin, our parents, and all the players went out for pizza afterward. I thought it was just about the best night I could ever have on earth. Man, even the Boston Bruins just might find out about our big win, I thought.

Even at the age of twelve, I already had a lot of fights behind me. When you live and play on the streets of a gritty and ethnic section of any city, anywhere on earth, you are open to more opportunities to fight. And believe me, as I said earlier, the Irish have a fighting impulse in them. Then again, I had far more scraps than most kids my age who lived in those neighborhoods. I just wouldn't and couldn't let things go.

Amid all those early fights, there was one that kind of stood out and which was something of a harbinger of the hockey enforcer I would be so many years later. It happened the spring after Hub City won the league crown.

It was after school, and I had been walking down to the end of Gardner Street to meet up with some of the boys. And as I was walking, I heard my friends Pat and Bobby yelling. They were urging Bubsy on. I knew what was up: there was a fight happening. I ran full bore to the action, and when I got there I saw Bubsy on his back and this older, bigger kid—he was fifteen (so three years older than us) and outweighed Bubsy by a good thirty to forty pounds—on top of him, throwing punches. I knew who this kid was—he lived over near the West Roxbury–Roslindale line.

Bubsy was doing a good job of blocking some punches, but only some, and he was still managing to fight back a bit.

I started yelling for Bubsy to try to get up—and incredibly, Bubsy broke free and got to his feet. But only for a few seconds, before the bigger kid threw him down and started pounding on him again. At this point—and Bubsy wasn't surrendering—Pat and Bobby and I were telling the kid to stop it and leave Bubsy alone; we said the fight (if you could call it that) was over. The kid didn't listen and threw a couple more shots at Bubsy.

This infuriated me—very fast.

I tackled the bully and pulled him off my friend. We rolled on the ground and jumped up and faced each other, and I saw that he was not only a lot bigger than Bubsy, he was a lot bigger than me as well. He had hate in his eyes, and he called me "motherfucker" and said, "I'm going to beat the fuck out of you." Adrenaline and fear and anger all coursed through me.

I didn't wait for him to throw a punch; I just went at him.

Something snapped in me. I lost it. I was one vibrating wire of fury.

I was throwing everything at him as fast and as hard as possible. I punched and clawed. I got him down, and I was like this feverish, manic machine, and this prick was caught up in its churning gears and mashing and cutting parts.

He didn't have a chance. It took all of thirty seconds or so before he was screaming for me to stop. He was begging for me to stop. And, you know, I did stop. I got up. Something got switched off. The bullied bully crawled away from me and then stood up and looked at me. His nose was bleeding, he had scratches on his cheek and forehead, and his eyes were wide with fear and astonishment. He spun around and ran.

Then I turned to my friends.

Funny thing—their eyes were wide with fear and astonishment as well.

3

FEARING HENRY

I'VE SAID THAT WHATEVER was residing in me that inclined me to be a fighter and brawler might have had its roots in having to take some smacks from my dad. I also think the experience made me tough and resilient and able to withstand a punch and a beating and not get beaten—if that makes sense to you.

There is a lot of Henry Nilan in me. I guess it all gets passed down. My father feared his father, and my dad was sure as hell going to make sure that when he had sons, those sons would fear him.

It surely worked out that way. I feared—sometimes borderline hated—my dad. I also admired and loved him fiercely.

One thing is for sure: Henry Nilan is a major reason that Chris Nilan came to be known as Knuckles.

It may be kind of tough to believe, but there was a long stretch in which my parents did not like the Boston Bruins. My brothers and sisters didn't like the Bruins. And when I played against the Bruins, I didn't like the Bruins, either.

After all, when I was playing for the Montreal Canadiens in Boston, the fans didn't care that I grew up in the same city where they were sitting and standing, hooting and hollering. They only cared that I was wearing the wrong jersey—and even worse, that I was a brawler throwing down with guys wearing the Black and Gold.

Yeah, during that period, I wasn't liked in Boston.

Early on, though, when I was with the Canadiens, my parents would come to the games at Boston Garden. And when they were there, and I was wearing a Habs sweater, it was largely not a fun experience for them. This can't surprise anyone.

Now, it is a given that, if you are any type of sports fan, you know that Boston fans are just about, across the board, across all pro sports, the loudest, most intense, and most devoted anywhere. They adore and provide fervent, throaty support for their Bruins, Celtics, Patriots, and Red Sox—and they give equal emotion to detesting the opposition, especially longtime rivals; hence, the popular bumper stickers in the Boston area that read YANKEES SUCK!

So anyway, as I said, it wasn't good for my parents at those games.

And there was this one game. It was in the early 1980s, and I was in uniform for Montreal, and we were in Boston. So Mom and Dad were in the stands, and there was the basic hollering and yelling around them. Nothing too bad. The fans knew who they were.

But then someone threw a piece of pizza from a few rows behind my parents, and it hit my dad off the shoulder. My dad—a former Green Beret—would have been about fifty years old at the time. He turned around and yelled up into the crowd, "If whoever threw that has the balls, why don't you come down and see me right now?"

No one came down. No one even spoke up.

Not smart to mess with Henry now, when he is seventy-seven years old. You surely didn't want to do it twenty-seven years ago.

I guess you can figure by now that my father had maybe more than an edge. Yes, he was downright feisty and tough as bare knuckles. And, again, he enjoyed a daily cocktail or two, preferably highballs—and sometimes he opted for a couple beers instead of the mixed drink.

My father was, as they say, a strict disciplinarian. He didn't take shit from anyone. Life was never easy for him, and as he sought to make things better for his family, he took on more responsibility and stress. It must have all bubbled within him—he was angry and "pissed off" and all that. Then again, his disposition was similar to that of so many of the fathers of the Irish kids I knew. Still, to this day, there remains in the people of Irish descent in America an awareness of a widespread perception that is held in Europe of the Irish—that the Irish are, just maybe, perhaps, of a lower class than all the others on the continent.

When the Irish got to America—and as they made Boston the most Irish of American cities—they knew a lot of prejudice. That term, "paddy wagon"—know where that comes from? It's linked to the denigrating name the WASPs had for the Irish; they called them "Paddys." And when the Irish got to drinking and being rowdy, the WASP cops would throw them into their traveling lockups—and the lockups took on the name of paddy wagons. Nice, huh?

So the Irish—with the men being protectors and advocates for their families—just had to be tough and willing to "get their Irish up" as needed.

Henry Nilan frequently got his Irish up with me, and with my brother, Stephan. He left disciplining the girls more to my mother. The boys got dealt with by Dad. And Dad was not about to spare the rod and spoil his boys.

Henry did not shrink from confrontation—and he was inclined

to use his fists. I'll give you an example. My sister Kim had just been born; it might actually have been the day she was born, because my dad was visiting my mom and their newborn at Faulkner Hospital (commonly called "The Faulkner") in Boston. My mom had a craving for a hot fudge sundae, so my father left the hospital and walked down the street to Brigham's to get one.

Now, I don't know if it was while he was on the way to Brigham's, or on the way back to the hospital with the ice cream, but a couple guys, each of whom had a few in them, were out in front of a bar and they saw my father, who was wearing his heavy, dark-framed eyeglasses. So they started giving my dad a hard time, calling him "Four Eyes."

My father walked right up to them and within seconds it started, and both of the loudmouths ended up in a bad way, with one belted right through the big window that was in front of the bar—really, he ended up on his back and inside.

The cops showed up and evaluated the situation, and they kind of figured out that justice had been served, albeit in a bit of a frontier fashion.

I was scared shitless of Henry. All my friends were scared shitless of Henry. If any of the guys were in front of the house at night and making noise, just messing around—and maybe smoking and having a few beers—it wouldn't last long. My dad would either open up the window in the house or step outside the front door and start yelling, "Get the hell out of here. If you want to make noise, go home to your houses and make noise. Don't cause problems here."

That's all it took—the kids would scatter. Yet we all respected my father, and he did love kids. When my friends were over and supper time arrived, my father would invite one or two or even three to have dinner at our house. When I was in grade school and into junior high, my buddies and I, and most of the other boys our age in the city, had wiffle haircuts—you know, buzzed down almost to the scalp; people also call them crew cuts. Well, my father made getting and maintaining the wiffle a community event at our house. Yep, on a Saturday afternoon we would all line up—my brother, myself, my brother's buddies, and my buddies—and Henry would go to work with his shears. Dad would be laughing and enjoying himself immensely—and getting our hair into military trim.

Henry wanted things orderly, everywhere and all the time—and definitely in our house and our neighborhood. One night, some punks kicked over the trash barrels in front of our house, and my dad—still a reserve Green Beret and very fit and always training—chased one of the punks down, grabbed him, marched him back to our house, and made him pick up all the trash, put it back in the barrels, and set them up properly.

My father's need to keep things calm, under control, and in order was evident one night when some guys and girls stopped in front of our house and started yelling and saying a lot of nasty shit about my sister Susan. Susan was probably a senior in high school, and I was fourteen and Stephan was sixteen, and we were heading for the door to at least go after the guys. But my father told us not to do anything—he was going to handle it. Or, rather, Susan was going to handle it.

You see, this had been going on for a few nights now. One of those stupid, hormone-crazed things in which Susan had started dating this guy, and the girl who used to go out with the guy—well, she and her friends and some of their guy friends were saying nasty stuff about Susan, walking past our house and yelling shit. I guess you would call this bullying. My dad was going to make sure it all stopped. So he and my sister got into his car (he wouldn't let my brother and me come along), and Henry asked Susan where he thought those kids had just gone. Susan told him they were probably hanging out at the rink at the end of the street.

My dad told my sister they were going to find these punks and the girl who had a problem with her, and it was going to be taken care of. So they drove over to the parking lot, and sure enough, the crew was all there.

My dad pulled in, and he and Susan got out of the car. These girls and guys, assholes all, were nervously snickering. They didn't like what they saw in front of them. My father shouted, "Okay, which one of you has a problem with my daughter?" There were a few seconds of silence, and my father shouted again, "Which one of you has a problem with my daughter?" So this girl sauntered forward, trying to act all badass. My father said, "Good," and with his arms crossed and setting his steely eyes on all the guys and girls across from him, he said, "Susan, get over there and settle this."

Susan settled it, all right. She put one thorough ass-whooping on this girl, tearing her hair and her blouse and throwing her down hard on the ground. When Henry saw that this big-mouthed chick had learned her lesson, he walked over and grabbed my sister's arm and told all the guys and girls, "It is over, and it is settled. And if anyone comes by my house again and starts yelling or causing trouble in any way, then you are going to deal with me." With that, he and Susan got in the car and went home.

We didn't have a bit of trouble ever again with any of those kids.

It was this attitude, and the fortitude and strength my father showed, that caused me to admire him so much. He was my hero. But, as I said, I feared him as well. A big reason I feared him is because he hit me. He slapped me on the back of the head, and he hit me with a cuffed palm on the side of the head, and sometimes, yes, he punched me—sometimes in the head.

It got him pissed if I was goofing off, just hanging out and not doing anything constructive. He didn't want me hanging around the street corners—that upset him. One warm summer night, I was at the end of the street with a bunch of my friends. We were laughing and shouting and all that. We were next door to one of the residences of the Christian Brothers, who taught at and were administrators of Catholic Memorial High School. Windows were open in the neighborhood and voices carried, and my mom and dad, both of whom had to work in the morning, were being kept up by the racket. Now, you know that Henry wasn't going to let this stand—so he got up and walked out the front door and up the street to where we were. And he started in with a version of his boilerplate "If you want to make noise, go to your own homes and make noise—and get the hell out of here, and let people sleep."

My father was pissed, and then one of my friends, Patrick Kenney, giggled. So Henry's eyes lit up, and he got more angry, and he smacked the back of Patrick's head with an open hand. That shut Patrick up. He got in his car and left.

I was always fiercely loyal to my friends, and as Patrick drove away, I said to my dad, "What are you doing, hitting my friend?" Not smart. Henry went up to me and punched the side of the head. I fell backward, and as I was breaking my fall, my hand was ripped open by a sharp edge of metal in a fence. So I grabbed my hand and pulled myself up.

Then I heard someone saying, "Hey . . . hey . . . what is going on out here?" It was Brother Heren, who lived next door. And my father said, "No big deal, Brother, just some kids making a bunch of noise, and I'll take care of it." Brother Heren kind of shook his head, turned around, and went back to the residence.

My father cuffed me upside the head and told me to get home. I walked the two hundred yards back to our house, with him a stride behind me—and he pushed me a couple times. We got back inside the house and my mother was up, and she asked, "What the heck happened?" And my father said, "No big deal, everything is fine." So my mom went back upstairs. My father wasn't done, though, because as I was standing in front of the bathroom sink, washing my hand, he hit me again. And that was that; he went to bed. And then I went to bed.

There would never be an apology from him. He never apologized for any time he hit me.

While Henry Nilan had a temper, and I did a lot of stupid things that got him angry, what really set him off was if I disrespected elders or people in authority.

In writing this book, I got to thinking about when I was the most scared of my father. I was always kind of scared of him, but I have to think that it was during the situation with the Chinese restaurant at the end of the street, when I wondered whether he was going to take his whooping to a new level.

I was a junior in high school. Down the street and around the corner was a Chinese restaurant where some of the guys and I would hang out. The drinking age in Massachusetts was eighteen back then, and depending on who was behind the bar, you might be able to get served a beer or some cocktails with your food. We did act up there and cause some trouble—mostly mischievous stuff, but we would irritate and piss off the owner, a woman whom we unfortunately called "Momma Gook." We didn't call her that to her face—but we were assholes enough anyway that she would kick us out, saying, "You no good boys—get out of here." After getting booted, we would stay away for a couple weeks and then find a way to be allowed back in.

So there was this night that I wasn't even in the neighborhood, but some guys I knew were in the restaurant and they all got tossed. One of the guys, Donny, a tough kid, walked across the street, picked up a brick, and threw it at the big window on the front of the restaurant. It smacked against the window, and it didn't break through, but made a spiderweb across all of it. Everyone ran.

Donny and the other guys didn't think anyone saw him do this. He was wrong. The next night, the lady from the restaurant called our house. My mom and dad were away. Stephan answered the phone, and he put two and two together fast, because I had heard about what had happened and had told him about it, and as soon as he heard her voice, he kind of figured she was calling about the window—and that she thought I had something to do with it. Stephan tried to pass himself off as my father, but she was smart, and it didn't fly. My parents got home within a couple days, and she got my dad on the phone and told him I had thrown the brick. She said she saw me do it.

I am not saying she was lying—for Donny, even though he was shorter than me, had a similar build to me and also had curly hair like I did. Still, she was wrong. It wasn't me. None of this mattered to my father; he went ballistic. I told my father I wasn't even in the neighborhood that night. He didn't believe me. He slapped and whacked me hard, yelling, "You disrespectful asshole—did we bring you up to act like this, huh? These people work hard and you cause them problems and insult them and vandalize their business. What the hell is the matter with you?"

It was late morning, and Henry marched my ass over to the restaurant, yelling and pushing and slapping me. He told me I was going to apologize to the owner, and then I was going to work to make the money to pay for a new window. I would not let up, though, in denying I broke the window. When we got to the restaurant, I told her I was sorry for the window and that I would pay to have it fixed—but I also said that it wasn't me who had broken it. She wasn't happy— yet she figured this was about the best resolution to the matter. She was okay with it.

My father was less than okay with it. He walked me back home, still shouting and whacking me. It was bad. And it was a breaking point.

That day, I left the house with the intention of running away. But Dad caught up with me that afternoon in the parking lot of the Veterans Administration hospital in West Roxbury, about a mile from where we lived. He seemed more concerned than mad, and he asked me why I had left home. I said to him, "I don't want to get hit anymore. I am sick and tired of getting hit. You hit me, and at school the brothers hit me. I was gonna run away because I was sick of getting hit."

And, you know, my father never hit me again.

❖

To this day, I remain sensitive to any type of slap—even to what people might intend as playful slaps to the head. First of all, slapping anyone on the head is not playful, no matter how lightly and how much in jest you do it. However, there are still people who think it is funny—and I think they also like to get a charge out of being rough, even in a friendly way, with a tough guy.

That is all-out stupid, of course.

Maybe five years ago, I was at a charity event down Cape Cod. I was sitting at a table and this guy I know well, a guy who owns a food company that sells products to restaurants and supermarkets, came up behind me and gave me a slap on the head, saying, "Hey, Chris . . ."

He didn't get another word out because I caught him short, standing up fast and turning around and throwing a light jab into his midsection—nothing hard, but enough to take a bit of the wind out of him. So he stepped back, shocked, doubled over a bit, and said, "What the hell did you do that for?" And I was like, "What the fuck do you mean, 'Why did I do that?' Don't slap me on the back of the fucking head. Do I slap you on the back of the head?"

There was also this time, about ten years after I retired from hockey, I was warming up for a spinning class—just lightly pedaling away. (By the way, I am a big spinning fan; sometimes I do two classes a day.) No one was in the spinning studio yet. Then I heard someone walk into the studio behind me; I figured it was probably someone else who was taking the class. Next thing I knew, whoomp—I got slapped on the back of the head. What the fuck . . . ?

I jumped off the bike—I was seeing red—and spun around, and who was facing me but this guy I really liked and had known for years. He knew he had totally fucked up; he saw it all in my eyes. And I saw it in his.

"What the fuck are you doing?" I said to him. "Don't ever come up behind me and put your hands on my head."

He was stammering, "What is the big deal? I was just fooling around. I didn't mean anything by it. I'm sorry."

As he said this, I got hold of myself a bit, and I said, "Listen, I know you were fooling around—but it just doesn't go over well with me. Getting hit in the head, even in a fun and fooling-around way, sets me off. Growing up, I got hit at home—and I got hit by the brothers at school. It just stays with me; I never got over it."

We got over that, he and I. He made sure he never did that again.

I felt a little bad about jumping at him like that. Poor guy probably shit his little bike shorts.

4

CATHOLIC MEMORIAL

IN THE SPRING OF 1972, as my eighth-grade year was coming to a close at St. Theresa's, plans were finalized about where I would begin high school in September. Of course, there was only one option, and that was Catholic Memorial—"CM"—the all-boys' Catholic school where my brother was a sophomore. If I could do well enough on the CM entrance exam to gain acceptance, then that was where I would be going.

All the Nilan kids were destined to go to a Catholic high school—just like we all went to a Catholic junior high school. My sister Susan was in her junior year at the Ursuline Academy, an all-girls' school in Dedham. Financing our education was difficult for my parents, but for them there was no other choice. Having three kids in Catholic school the following year, as was the plan, was just the way it was.

And when it came time for my sister Kim, three years younger than me, to attend high school, it would be the Ursuline Academy for her as well. Again, that was just the way it was.

There were excellent public schools in Boston, but my parents' determination to send us to Catholic Memorial and Ursuline Academy was based on culture, religion, values, and a desire for their kids to get a quality education. Then again, within a couple years, most of the Boston public school system would be weakened and tattered from forced busing (a subject I will touch on briefly later), but this was not the case in 1972.

Catholic Memorial was founded in 1957 by the Christian Brothers of Ireland. The Christian Brothers still ran the school, and many members of their order, along with priests, taught and served in the administration. CM had an excellent reputation for academics and athletics. Indeed, there was a large measure of prestige attached to attending CM, for both the student and his parents.

What made attending CM particularly attractive to me was that it was literally a stone's throw away. Well, not really—it was two stones' throws away, and only if you had a good arm. You just walked to the end of Gardner Street, across Baker Street, and onto the CM campus.

I did well enough on the entrance exam to get in. I was excited and felt privileged to be going to the school. I knew the course work would be demanding, but I wasn't nervous about it. Through my brother, and in living so close to the school, I already knew many kids at CM, and in a way I already felt a part of it. I was already enmeshed and comfortable in its culture.

Early on, I struggled a bit with my studies, but I plugged away and did my homework and established myself as a C and B student. I wasn't setting the world on fire, but I was advancing and doing the work and establishing that I could make it at CM. What was good for me was that the Christian Brothers, the priests, and the lay staff were staunch disciplinarians, and they had a firmly established and enforced code of conduct. I was kept in line—for the most part—which I am not so sure would have been the case in a public school.

Since CM was all guys, I didn't have the on-site distraction of girls, which spared me the effort, energy, and emotion of chasing them. That was good for my academics and my athletics. In that the student body was, at the time, about 90 percent white, I wasn't left feeling out of place.

At CM we also had many super role models and mentors, from the Christian Brothers to the priests, lay coaches, and faculty; we had adults to admire, emulate, and respect. One of my favorite people at the school was Father Frederick Ryan, a young priest in his mid-twenties whom you could talk to about anything. He was also a big backer of CM sports; he went to just about every Knights athletic event, and he would be the first to congratulate an athlete on something he had done in a game, race, or match.

There was much to recommend about CM. It was the right fit for me.

Every year I was at CM, I played only one sport. When people learn about my prep-school hockey experience, they are surprised at just how inauspicious and undistinguished I was as a player. Let's forget about me showing any pro promise, because when I was in high school, right through to my senior year, I exhibited little potential for even Division II college hockey. I worked hard, and I improved a lot from season to season, but I just wasn't a blue-chipper.

Still, I loved hockey, even though I sometimes felt it didn't love me back. No, I was not one of those hotshots who make the varsity team as a freshman. Hell, I wasn't even on the junior varsity roster as a freshman. I did make the CM Knights freshman team, but I sat on the bench, rarely getting off of it. This got me pissed. It was also a bit embarrassing.

My freshman coach was John "Bad Eyes" Glynn. We called him Bad Eyes because he was always squinting. As the season wore on and I continued to sit on the bench, I said that the nickname was because Glynn couldn't see talent. I would say that talent could be right in front of him and he would be totally unaware of it. Now, I will concede that maybe I shouldn't have been starting, but I should have been seeing a hell of a lot more playing time than I was receiving.

Not only was the situation ticking me off, which was no big deal, but it also was ticking my dad off—and that was a big deal. In fact, after one game—and this was just off the ice, on the other side of the glass at Boston Arena, where we played our home games—my dad deliberately bumped into Glynn. Hard. Glynn stumbled back with an expression of surprise on his face, and my dad barked, "My kid isn't good enough to get off the bench? Huh?" Glynn scurried away fast, and my dad gathered himself and just left the building. If that happened today, my father probably would be arrested.

Then again, everything is relative. I was playing hockey for Catholic Memorial, and the school attracted many good athletes, in all its sports. At another school, I might have been one of the better players.

This same year that I was playing—or rather, not playing—for CM, I was playing midget hockey with a team called Hub City. Coaching the team was the Honorable Paul King, presiding judge of the Dorchester District Court, a court in the Massachusetts judicial system. Judge King's younger brother was Ed King, a former football star at Boston College who also played briefly in the NFL and who later rose in the Massachusetts government and served a term as governor of the state from 1979 through 1983. Judge King also graduated from Boston College and from BC's law school.

A curious thing about Judge King: he was a Montreal Canadiens fan. How do you figure? In fact, when the Canadiens were in town, he would often meet after the game, for dinner or drinks or what have you, with two former Habs greats and Hockey Hall of Famers, Dickie Moore and Doug Harvey. As Montreal teammates, during a stretch than ran from 1952 through 1960, Moore, a winger, and Harvey, a defenseman, were part of six Stanley Cup–winning squads. Moore retired from playing pro hockey at the end of the 1967–68 season, and Harvey retired as a player after the following season, but both stayed close to the Habs organization and attended games at the Forum and on the road. Both held influence in the Montreal front office.

Judge King gave me plenty of ice time, and I enjoyed it immensely. That Judge King believed in me, and that he advocated for me, continued to pay dividends in my hockey career and my life for a long time.

I also held a job when I wasn't playing hockey. Tony's Pizza (now Tony's Place) was around the corner from my house—no more than a quarter mile away. Tony's was, and is now, a cantina with not high-end, but very good and inexpensive, Italian food. I bused tables at Tony's and washed dishes. During the fall, spring, and summer, I took a few weekday shifts at Tony's and at least one shift on the weekends.

In my sophomore year in hockey, there were no fireworks either, but I had more fun. The JV coach was a guy named Ed McElaney. I liked playing for him better than for Glynn. I got a lot more ice time, even if I wasn't starring. Being out there was what mattered, because I felt that, given the chance, it was all up to me; I couldn't blame anyone else if I didn't perform.

As I said, I wasn't much of a discipline problem at CM—and this was largely because I wasn't allowed to be a discipline problem at CM. But I was a discipline problem on the streets of Boston. I had that edge, always—and while I didn't pick on people or start fights, I had an extra-sensitive antenna to someone slighting me or looking at me or my friends the wrong way. I looked for a problem, even when one wasn't there. Of course, if someone said something insulting to either me or my buddies, then it was time to fight. I had a very good record in street fights. Not unblemished, for sure—I took my lumps and lost some bouts, which didn't stop me from getting into another one. You aren't going to be any type of fighter if you can't lose and bounce back.

While I was a student at CM, I got into some very serious trouble with the law outside of school. I also got into a bit of not-insignificant trouble while on the school grounds at CM, which had repercussions tied to race and an ugly episode in the history of Boston.

5

CONTINUING EDUCATION—
IN SCHOOL, OUT OF SCHOOL,
AND ON THE ICE

I HAVE TO ADMIT, when I entered high school, my life to that point had been fairly insular in terms of direct interaction with, and exposure to, people of different color than me.

In fact, I knew only white, Catholic, and European (mostly Irish) people, and that was it. I sure didn't grow up in a home or neighborhood that promoted understanding and relationship-building among blacks and whites. And let me just say this—ah, well, my parents weren't ever going to put their hands up to volunteer to march in a civil rights parade, if that means anything to you.

Out and about, I surely heard racist terms for blacks, Asians, Mexicans, and Jews. I was seduced into an attitude, which I embraced, of not liking people of color.

My prejudices increased in the summer of 1974, when a federal court order was issued that called for a radical desegregation plan that would affect the children, teenagers, and families of Boston.

Most of the nation knew it as busing or forced busing. We called it by those names as well.

Black children would be bused to schools that had almost exclusively white student populations and were in white neighborhoods—and white children would be bused to schools that had almost exclusively black student populations and were in black neighborhoods.

Forced busing in Boston was a mistake. It solved nothing, and it made matters worse. And what really upset a lot of people in the city was that it was imposed on the families of Boston by a federal judge who didn't live in Boston itself, but rather in the wealthy and tony suburb of Wellesley. That judge's name was W. Arthur Garrity Jr. The W in his name stood for Wendell, so it might make sense he didn't tout it.

Judge Garrity didn't seem to care that, the previous May, Boston residents had voted by a 15–1 margin against forced busing.

And I will tell you right out, in the neighborhood I lived in, and in the small society in which I ran, the opposition to busing was fierce and loud and angry and emotional. Did the opposition take on a racist tone at times? It sure did.

At least the National Association for the Advancement of Colored People (NAACP), which brought the lawsuit to which Garrity was responding when he issued his order, had Boston residents in its organization who were advocating for it. They lived in the city and would be directly affected by the enactment of the policy. The NAACP's position had merit and was worthy of respect.

And, for sure, back in the early 1970s, black public schools across the nation were, for the most part, inferior in terms of resources and the overall strength of educational environment to white public schools.

But shoving things down people's throats, especially when you don't give people time to get ready for something to be forced down their throats, is just wrong. Again, it made things worse—and in some ways, Boston never recovered from it.

It hurt the image of Boston, and it cast my home, and a city I love—which is also the birthplace of the American Revolution and the foundation of the abolitionist movement in the nation—as mean and bigoted. It painted good, hardworking Irish as toothless troglodytes.

Anyway, as soon as the news hit that, when school started in a little more than a month, this busing of schoolkids would be enforced, it created big problems in the city. White parents said they were going to keep their kids out of school, and many put plans in motion to move their families out of the city. Interestingly, black parents were largely not opposed to the busing, because it allowed their children to go to schools that were considered better than the ones they had been attending.

Boston in August is hot and humid, and as the first day of school approached, the weather supported tension. There were protests and scuffling among white and black youths. Politicians from the white neighborhoods of South Boston and Charlestown were very emotional and very public in their opposition to busing; they were in the streets and speaking at events and getting in front of as many TV cameras and microphones as possible.

Young white kids, and white teenagers like myself, watched and heard all the anger, and it fed and supported in us a dislike for blacks. I didn't get involved in any violence or intimidation against black people, but I know white kids who did. Also—and let's set the record straight here—there were many black kids who didn't like white kids and who visited violence and intimidation on them.

In the broader spectrum of my life, this period was educational and instructive, for I now know that a visceral reaction, one not based on facts or supported with knowledge, can steer one to bigotry. You see, I didn't know any blacks, but I was easily seduced into believing they were the problem in the busing fiasco. It was only when I was in college that I began to be disabused of my prejudice—and in all the years after, I became more enlightened and prejudice was kept at bay.

Both blacks and whites were pawns in a social experiment.

No matter how well-meaning the intent, forced busing proved to be terrible, even before one kid had been bused. And when the buses actually started rolling in September, the nation saw, on their TV screens, white hooligans throwing rocks at buses transporting black kids. A country watched as National Guardsmen on motorcycles formed a protective gauntlet for those students. Broadcast to America were images of US military sharpshooters stationed on rooftops in South Boston.

Busing riled whites and blacks, and for several years there was concerted and aggressive opposition to the policy. But what eventually happened was that white people just left the public schools, and many moved out of neighborhoods in the city altogether. In 1984, there were 80 percent fewer white kids in Boston public schools than there had been ten years earlier, on the eve of the start of forced busing. As for the academic opportunity for black kids, well, if you can show me one study that proves black public school students have benefited academically from busing, I would be interested in looking at it. Let me save you some effort, though, and tell you this: you won't be able find one.

In the end, both black kids and white kids got screwed.

In March of 2013, almost forty years after the grand experiment of forced busing began, the Boston School Committee voted to do away with it.

I guess it took them that long to find out it wasn't working.

❖

My junior year at Catholic Memorial coincided with the start of forced busing.

Not long into the school year, I managed to run afoul of the rules of the school, and my misadventure, while serious, was judged even more severely because it was set against the racial violence and problems going on around us.

It was in October, and I was hanging around in front of CM after school. Some black kid who didn't go to CM, but who had a buddy there, was in front of the school too. He was talking to some of the guys, and I looked over at him, but didn't say anything. He must have thought I was trying to start a problem (and I'm not so sure whether I was or wasn't), because he mouthed off to me. Well, that was all the invitation I needed, and I ran over to him and punched him, and we went at it. I quickly took control and was laying a good beating on him. From my way of thinking, if he said he'd had enough, then I would stop. But he kept resisting, somewhat.

A small crowd of guys surrounded us—most rooting for me.

I threw the kid down and got on him to deliver some more punishment, and then I heard the yelling of a couple of the Christian Brothers. They had been inside the school and, seeing what was happening, ran outside to put an end to it. As soon as I heard one of the brothers shouting for me to stop, I stopped; you didn't even think about defying the brothers.

So the kid I had been pounding on, and I, both got up. He was hurt and a bit glassy-eyed. I was fine. Brother Henry, who was furious, barked at me, asking, "What the hell happened here?"

I talked right back to him, as I pointed at the kid I just been fighting, "He started it, and I finished it."

I gotta give the kid credit: he didn't try to contradict me. He just stood there looking at me with pure dislike.

"I don't want to hear this," said Brother Henry, still pissed. "Chris, you get out of here. Go home."

So I headed toward my house, but I didn't go home; I hung out with a few of my pals at the end of Gardner Street. It was around six o'clock when I got home for supper, and my father was there, and he was not in a good mood. He said that Brother Henry, the headmaster of CM, had called and told him what I had done was very serious—that this wasn't just another fight among the students, but it was a white kid beating on a black kid. Brother Henry said my actions could be considered racially motivated. And with racial tension so high in Boston, and with the city under the microscope of not just the local media but the national media as well, what I had done could incite further violence, as well as injure the reputation of Catholic Memorial.

Brother Henry told my father that I might be expelled.

Naturally, my father made a plea on my behalf. In response, Brother Henry said he would think of something for me to do to make things right and to keep myself enrolled at CM.

My dad said to me, "When you get to school tomorrow, you are to go directly to Brother Henry's office and talk to him. You can't screw around with this. It is serious."

I didn't dare argue one bit. I nodded my head and told my father I would do whatever I had to do to save myself and ensure that all the money my parents had paid for my tuition, which they had worked so hard for, would not be wasted.

And there I was the next morning, at eight o'clock, sitting in a chair in front of Brother Henry's desk, with Brother Henry looking straight across at me with his head bent forward, his hands folded as if in prayer and pressed against his pursed lips and unsmiling mouth. He gave a good effort—allowing about five seconds of silence while he was in this pose—to make sure I recognized that the weight of the world was on his shoulders in figuring out what to do with me.

Brother Henry let me know I had done something awful, and that he had given a lot of thought to the matter, and that he had come close to expelling me. But he was willing to give me another chance—and I would earn that chance by performing a sort of detention and penance. I was ordered to return to his office at four o'clock that afternoon—a couple hours after the school day ended.

Okay, I know you might think you know where this whole thing is headed—you know, alone after school with a man of the cloth, in his office. But that wouldn't happen. Believe me. I don't care how much respect I had for the church; if a priest or brother ever touched me, he would be beaten to within an inch of his life.

Then again, that's not to say things didn't get a bit weird. Because they did.

After school, at four, I was in Brother Henry's office. All the secretaries and other administrative staff had gone for the day. What took place next was some sort of weird mixture of penance and writing a hundred times on the chalkboard, "I will not beat up people anymore." Brother Henry told me to start doing push-ups and sit-ups; all the while he stood there, not quite over me, but nearby and close enough to make it feel strange. Then he took out a camera and started photographing me doing these exercises. Brother Henry had me stand up and hold a book in each hand while I extended my arms sideways and then in front of me for several minutes. He took photos of this activity as well. I didn't protest; I didn't say anything. I did as I was told. I think this ridiculousness went on for something like forty-five minutes—this after-school session of exercise, calisthenics, and photography.

Brother Henry said I had done enough, and that I would not be expelled. He also said that he would develop the photos he had taken, and he would make one copy of each photo and throw away the negatives. On graduation day, he said, when I received my diploma, attached to the diploma in a packet would be the photos. I couldn't figure any of this out.

❖

I was saved for now, able to continue at Catholic Memorial. I knew, even then, that getting booted from CM would have been a disaster in my life. I would have squandered a great education—and the opportunity to play hockey for the Knights.

As a junior, I was a full-timer on the varsity squad. I was not a star. I made no all-anything teams. But I was a solid contributor for a school that played in one of the more competitive prep leagues in the US, so I felt confident that I could continue playing competitive hockey for many years. I just knew I could play in college—and I held on to that crazy notion of being able to make it to the NHL

As for those photos Brother Henry took of me, where are they now? I couldn't tell you. You see, in early June of 1976, when I proudly walked on stage at CM's commencement ceremonies, and Brother Henry handed me my diploma, that was all he handed me—there was no packet and there were no photos attached. I never found out what happened to those photos. I never asked.

6

MESSING UP

A YEAR AFTER MY RACE INCIDENT that really wasn't, I was one of the perpetrators of a violent attack that really was. It was a Saturday night in late September, and it was mild out. Barry Milan was driving, Tommy Gleason was in the passenger seat, and I was behind Tommy in the backseat. We had been drinking a bit of beer; we were all cradling a can. Not hammered, but definitely feeling it.

We were just tooling around South Boston. Remember, Boston is not a big place in land area—you might have seen and heard that famous tourist slogan, "Boston: America's Walking City," or whatever—so it doesn't take long to get from anywhere to anywhere else.

Barry had been kind of seeing this girl from the neighborhood of Dorchester—or "Dot," as we sometimes called it. It wasn't a serious relationship, just some dates and messing around. He did like her, though. So he said he was going to drive over to Dot to see if he could find her. No cell phones, no texting, back then. And since it was about eleven o'clock, he figured either she wasn't in, or if she was, he didn't want to piss off her parents by calling that late. Not sure how he figured he was going to run into her—but he thought he might. We were game, and we said let's go.

Within ten minutes we were in a section of Dorchester called Fields Corner, where this girl lived. Fields Corner was all white Irish working-class, just like our neighborhood. It was a neighborhood of triple-deckers alongside triple-deckers. Not much commercial activity in the neighborhood—it was mostly residential. Well, we drove up in front the house where this chick lived, and all the windows were dark, so we just kept going. And up ahead, about fifty yards along, there was an intersection. It was fairly well lit by the streetlights, and standing there were some guys, about seven of them.

We got closer, and we could see they were our age. We didn't know who they were; we had never met them before. Tommy had the window down, and he said to no one in particular, "Hey, what's up? Have you seen," and whatever her name was.

You know, as soon as he said that, and these guys all looked at us, I knew there was going to be a problem. These guys were of the same ilk as us—white Irish kids with chips on their shoulders who felt the neighborhood they lived in was theirs and that anyone, Irish or not, from another neighborhood who dared come into their territory, especially at night—well, it was understood you were looking for trouble.

Except we weren't really looking for trouble; not on this night. It didn't matter. Whoever was their big-balls leader chuckled and said, "We don't know where the fuck she is, and we don't know who the fuck you are, so get the fuck out of here, you dickheads." They all laughed, and one kicked the front right quarter panel of Barry's car, right in front of me. Another kid spit on the hood of the car.

We were furious, of course—and without saying a word, we had resolved that these punks would pay, and pay big. They were saying shit like, "C'mon, you fucking tough? You're fucking pussies—let's go." I was reaching for the door; I couldn't take it. I would go after 'em all at once if I had to. But Barry shouted, "Nah, fuck, stay in the car," and he revved the engine while lightly releasing the foot brake. The rubber on the wheels started to screech a bit, and we jumped forward. No one stood in front of the car—if he had, I'm sure that Barry would have run right over him, and then maybe backed over him for good measure. But Barry peeled out, and as we did, a bottle hit the back window of the car. Tommy was screaming for Barry to pull the car around in the street so we could do . . . something to them.

Then I got an idea. I said we should go over to West Roxbury and get ourselves some recruits and then return and pound those guys out.

Barry had had sort of the same feeling, in that he wasn't about to call it an evening without getting payback.

All three of us were ready to erupt; the only question was in what manner. Barry drove up about two blocks and then took a right so that we were out of sight of those guys down the street. He pulled the car to the side of the street and put it in park; he was rocking back and forth, slamming the steering wheel with his palms, shouting, "Motherfucker, motherfucker, motherfucker. Those cocksuckers are gonna die." I was swearing up a storm as well; I punched the back of the seat.

We then arrived at what we were going to do. We weren't going to get any recruits. We were going to take care of things right there and then. And thankfully, we had the means to even things up with those dickheads, even though they outnumbered us more than two to one. You see, when we drove around at night, we always had sports equipment with us that we could press into service as weapons if need be. And on this night, we had three items that could do major damage in the right hands: a baseball bat, a hockey stick, and a golf club.

Barry went up to the next intersection, turned right, and headed back to where our clueless prey were still yukking it up. He turned off the lights as he got up to the intersection, pulled over, and parked the car. We quietly got out and grabbed our instruments of choice. I got the hockey stick, of course; Barry grabbed himself the bat, and Tommy was about to go golfing. We were going to need to be as stealthy as a stalking cat to catch these fuckers by surprise.

We peered around the corner; they were maybe thirty or forty yards away, and out in the street, right under the lights, but on the same side we were on—and fortunately for us, but not for them, that stretch of sidewalk was not well lit. Yet, even if cover of darkness afforded us a measure of surprise, there were going to be a couple seconds when they knew we were coming. We were going to have to be efficient and focused. We were lined up in single file and crouching, our shoulders flush against a fence; I was in front.

We looked at each other and hissed, "Let's go." And we started running, still in a crouch, on our toes so as not to make too much noise, each of us holding hard and fast to our weapon.

Closer . . . closer . . . and, yep, we were within ten yards when one of those dudes caught sight of me. But he hadn't picked up on the fact that I was armed—and for a moment, he didn't know I had company. So he turned and faced me with his arms extended and palms up, and he snickered and said, "Oh, what? I mean, what the fuck?" Of course, at the same time, all his buddies turned our way—and then we pounced and were in full kickoff coverage team mode.

When they saw all three of us—and they saw a hockey stick, a bat, and a golf club—they started backing up, and a few turned around and started running. But not before I caught one of those pricks in the ribs with the heel of the stickblade; he yelped a high note and grabbed a hold of his side while he staggered away. I was about to chase him and feed him some more pain, but off to my right, I saw Tommy rear back with the golf club, twisting his torso about 180 degrees and pulling the club so far back that it almost touched the ground behind him. And then he went into a swing with a whole lot of force . . . and . . . CRACK!

He caught one of them off the side of the head, and the kid kind of gasped and then crumpled. He wasn't moving. Ah, shit, that wasn't good—I hoped Tommy hadn't killed him. As soon as that guy went down, everyone scrammed—them and us. We ran back to Barry's

car and got the fuck out of there—we went to South Boston and finished off a whole lot of beers.

We were worried. For real—we didn't know if that kid was dead,
or brain damaged, or what.

❖

On Tuesday morning, I was sitting in class at CM, and I hadn't heard
anything about what happened in Dorchester. Neither had my
friends. We had to feel we were in the clear.

I hadn't learned yet that it would rarely be in the cards for me,
throughout my life, to be in the clear.

So, as I sat there in class, the principal at CM, Brother Henry,
opened the door of the classroom and called over the teacher and
said something to him. My teacher pointed to me, and then Brother
Henry motioned to me with his index finger to come see him at the
door. I wasn't sure, but I was thinking that Saturday night was about
to catch up with me. It was.

Brother Henry told me that there was a police officer waiting
down at the main office for me.

I was about to find out that the kid Tommy had walloped had
lived. He had also lost an eye in the attack. This was very serious.
The cop told me I was under arrest, and he cuffed me and said something about being charged with assault with a deadly weapon.

My dad came to bail me out at the police station. When he got
there, he wasn't so much mad as he was scared. He knew just how
serious the charge was, and that I could be doing jail time. My life
could be generally and genuinely fucked for a long time, if not forever. We drove home, and I was feeling worse than ever—for I saw
the pain I was causing my father. While he drove, he shook his head

lightly; he didn't look at me, but he said, "You know, Chris, this is just so, so bad. Your mother and I work hard, and we send you to a great school, and we try to direct you right. And you do this. Is this how we raised you? You get involved with something, and some kid loses an eye. You maimed this kid—that is what you did."

I cut him off, saying, "Dad, I wasn't the one who took his eye out."

My dad waved me off with one hand and said, "Ah, I don't want to hear it. You were there, and according to the law, you did it, and we are going to have to get you an attorney. You could have a record—a felony. You could become a convicted felon. And let me tell you: even if we can figure this thing out legally, I am not sure that Catholic Memorial is not going to boot you."

Not much bothered me, at least for a prolonged period. But this was going to be different.

This time I had really, really fucked up.

All three of us were arraigned the next day in Dorchester District Court. As I stood there in the dock, who should walk in to take the bench but Judge King. When he saw me, he stopped, blinked rapidly, and then walked over to me and asked what happened. I told him. He didn't say anything other than to ask if my mother or father was there, and I pointed to my dad sitting in the courtroom. Judge King looked over at my dad, who immediately stood up, his face full of nervousness. Judge King walked up to my father, and they talked for a few minutes, and then Judge King went over to the bench and spoke to a few people—and then he left the room.

As I found out after we were arraigned, the judge had to take himself off the case because of his connection to me and my family.

My dad was starting to call around to people he knew to see if they could recommend a good lawyer. Then I started making calls, one of which was to my co-defendant, as it were, Barry Milan. He suggested I use the lawyer he was using and gave me his name. It was a name I knew well from reading the newspaper and watching the local TV news.

The lawyer was Billy Bulger, a state senator from South Boston. Senator Bulger was forty-two years old in 1974, the year I got into that mess. He grew up poor, one of six kids in his family, in a public housing project in South Boston, or "Southie," as the neighborhood is commonly known. Billy Bulger was what is called in our parts a Triple Eagle—a title inspired by the mascot of Boston College. It meant he had graduated from Boston College High School, Boston College, and Boston College Law School.

Billy Bulger was first elected to the Massachusetts state legislature in 1961, as a state representative. He was elected state senator in 1970. Bulger was building and holding on to power. Curiously enough, his older brother was Jimmy "Whitey" Bulger, one of the most notorious and ruthless crime bosses in the northeastern US.

The people of South Boston adored Billy Bulger.

My father called Bulger. From our end, my dad handled most of the legal matters. That would be about right because he was fronting the money, even if I would have to pay him back. When my father got off the phone, he told me we would meet with Senator Bulger at the district courthouse on the morning when the case would be heard and the charge against me would be read. Truth be told, I thought this was a bit odd, because I would have thought we'd have this big meeting beforehand. But as I would find out, this wasn't necessary with Billy Bulger. He would easily handle all that needed to be handled to best represent me.

So on the morning the case was to be heard in the district court in Dorchester, my father and I met Bulger in the lobby of the courthouse, and we sat on a long wooden bench.

I had seen photos of Bulger in the newspaper, and I had caught images of him on the evening TV news, but when I met him in person, I was a bit taken aback in that here was this man who exerted all sorts of influence, and physically he was not a big guy; he was rather small—only about five-and-a-half feet tall and thin.

But you only had to talk with Billy Bulger for a few minutes to understand he had that special something that enabled him to get things done. He had a very Irish face, with small, dark eyes, a nose that came to a point, and hair closely cropped with a part and a sweep to the side; it looked like he had slathered on the Brylcreem. Bulger was sharply dressed in a dark suit with white shirt and dark tie. Yet it was when he started talking, and focused his eyes on you, that you understood he was as smart as all get-out. Billy Bulger was eloquent, and his voice had some sort of lilt or accent or something—it wasn't what regular Boston guys sounded like. I don't know if it took practice or if it was natural. It did make an impression.

Yeah, he had that juice. So many people waving to him and calling "Mr. Senator."

Senator Bulger had already settled things, and put in place what needed to be done for me. In front of the jury, he argued for me and Barry powerfully and with precision. He made it obvious that we were not Tommy Gleason, and that we had not hurt or maimed anyone. Both Barry and I were found not guilty.

Tommy Gleason would receive five years' probation.

While I was not found guilty criminally, there remained a civil suit.

For that case, my family hired a different attorney—his name was Bill York, and he was the brother of Boston College hockey coach Jerry York. We settled without going to trial. I was fined $10,000. I borrowed the money from my good friend Timmy Burke. Before the end of my first year in the NHL, I had paid him back in full.

7

BECOMING A HOCKEY PLAYER

ONCE AGAIN, I WAS ABLE to get beyond a major screw-up—a catastrophic screw-up—and continue my journey at CM and in hockey. Neither the administration nor the athletic department pushed the issue. Then again, there were some judicial precedents that made it difficult for schools to impose discipline for something that did not take place on school grounds.

And, I was not convicted of any crime.

For my senior year, CM moved Bill Hanson, the varsity assistant coach, up to head coach. Hanson was also a guidance counselor at CM. I liked playing for him. He was a strict disciplinarian—a no-BS guy. And he knew hockey. Hanson appreciated my hustle and tough play. I knew this because he frequently complimented me on it—oftentimes loudly enough for the entire team to hear.

Today I take pride that I was in on the ground floor of Bill Hanson's career as a head coach of CM hockey. He still holds that position almost forty years later. He is among the winningest prep hockey coaches in US history. He oversaw and commandeered the development of CM hockey into an out-and-out dynasty. Under his leadership and tutelage, CM has won seventeen state titles and six national championships. Several Knights have played in the NHL.

We didn't win a state title or even a Catholic League title when I was a senior. But we were competitive. I didn't make all-league, but I don't think there was much of a separation between me and those who were picked ahead of me. Coach Hanson told me he thought I could play in college, but he knew, as both coach and guidance counselor, that I could use another year preparing for the next level. Also, he reminded me that I was young for my grade, and that physically I could use a year to catch up.

Coach Hanson did some prospecting and outreach for me with prep schools. So did Judge King, who had an in with the hockey coach at Northwood School in Lake Placid, New York. He arranged for me to visit Northwood and set up an interview with the coach, Ed Good. Northwood School, which was coed, had a good academic reputation; it was also something of a factory for hockey players. It pumped out college hockey talent. In fact, two of its graduates, Jack Mulhern (class of '47) and Tom Mellor (class of '68), were members of US Olympic hockey teams.

Today, its hockey alumni roster includes thirteen former NHL players, nine members of US men's hockey squads, and two members of US women's Olympic hockey teams.

Set in the beautiful and mountainous Adirondacks, and in the village that had hosted the 1936 Winter Olympic Games and was already selected and preparing to host the 1980 Winter Olympics, Northwood also had a strong tradition in cross-country and downhill skiing.

I did well enough in my interview, and had done well enough at CM, academically and in hockey, to gain acceptance to Northwood. I also received a financial aid package that paid for almost all of my tuition and room and board. It was a no-brainer—I was on my way to Lake Placid for the following school year.

❖

I felt something of the proverbial culture shock when I got to Northwood School in late August. Really, my life had been basically urban and, save for a couple weeks during the summer—one down in Marshfield, and one up on the lake in New Hampshire—I didn't know much in the way of open space. Lake Placid and the surrounding areas were country and village.

Northwood did not have a big campus. It had only a few buildings, but they were long and had two to three stories each. For the 1975–76 school year, the total student population at Northwood was about 150, with a split of approximately 100 boys and 50 girls. Two-thirds of the students boarded; I had my own room at Northwood.

While CM was an excellent academic school, living at and being on scholarship at Northwood obligated me to conform to strict schedules and ways of doing things that improved me academically, culturally, and socially. I matured and grew up, and became smarter, during my school year there.

In hockey, I fluctuated early on between the second and third lines on a team filled with exceptional talent. Coach Good—now the headmaster at Northwood School—knew hockey and helped make the game fun. We played a competitive schedule that started in late October and ended in the first week of March. We played private and public high schools, prep schools, and midget and junior teams. When on the road, we visited rinks throughout the Adirondacks and parts of Vermont and New Hampshire as well as in Canada.

I learned quickly that I was a stride slower than players on my team and on other teams, and my passing and puck control were not as elegant and crisp. But I also understood that my hustle and willingness to use my body to carve out space and open up the game for my teammates were highly valuable. And my energy seemed to lift my teammates. As well, playing with such gifted and hardwork-ing athletes, and against such talented competition, forced me to become better and up my game.

A teammate of mine at Northwood, and a good friend, was Gerard Reardon, one of the many immensely talented players to come out of the Boston neighborhood of Charlestown. Gerard went on to play at Boston College. In early May of 1984, Gerard was found stabbed to death in Charlestown, lying on his back, next to his car.

While I was playing for Northwood, I don't recall receiving much attention from college scouts. But Judge King was pressuring Northeastern University coach Fern Flaman to take a look at me, though I didn't know it at the time. Flaman came to see me play in a game in March that we had at Boston College against their junior varsity team. He must have liked what he saw well enough, because he offered me a full-tuition athletic scholarship to Northeastern. Technically, it was not a full boat because it was only for tuition—but that didn't matter that much to me because my family lived nearby in Boston, and I could use money I had saved working at Tony's in the summer to buy a car I could use for the fifteen-to-twenty-minute commute each way between the Nilan house on Gardner Street and the Northeastern University campus.

Northeastern was an excellent school. And it seemed that play-ing for Fern Flaman would be a good fit. In his competitive days, he played the game the way I liked to play it—physically.

Flaman was a product of Dysart, Saskatchewan. You grew up there, you learned to be tough. From the late 1940s through the 1950s, he established himself as one of the most bruising defensemen in the NHL. For his first five seasons in the league, he played for the Bruins. Then he spent three years with Toronto (where he won a Stanley Cup), and then was back with Boston for seven seasons, his peak as a player. During this period, he played in five NHL All-Star Games and served as the Bruins' captain for his final five years in the league.

In 1954, Fern Flaman led the NHL in penalty minutes with 150. Gordie Howe said no one he played against hit harder than Flaman.

Yes, I thought that playing for Coach Flaman might work.

I talked the Northeastern University offer over with my parents.

I would be going to Northeastern.

I earned my postgrad certificate from Northwood School in May. I also achieved on the ice at Northwood. At the end-of-the-year team banquet, I was presented with the award for most improved player.

8

NORTHEASTERN

NORTHEASTERN UNIVERSITY is a Boston school through and through. Its campus is set amid and woven into the activity of an international city, one renowned for its higher learning, medicine, and money management. NU shares a neighborhood with other colleges, trolley tracks, businesses, commercial and residential buildings, commuter thoroughfares, Fenway Park, and world-famous hospitals and museums.

If there was one street on which most of the NU buildings shared an address, it was Huntington Avenue. In fact, with the Northeastern University sports mascot being the husky, an alias for the NU teams was the Huntington Hounds.

When I attended Northeastern, it had the largest student population of any private college or university in the country. I was a bit anxious about how I would handle the academics, the workload, and all, but soon enough I realized that, between CM and Northwood, I'd had a strong grounding and preparation for college. Classes were challenging, and I surely didn't devote the time and concentration to my studies that most other students did, but I knew I was going to get through school and earn my bachelor's degree in criminal justice. I knew this.

Northeastern University is different than most colleges and universities in that its curriculum is a "co-op"—short for "cooperative education—model, in which students alternate semesters of academic study with semesters of internships or employment in the field they want to work in after graduation. NU started its co-op program more than a hundred years ago, and it is one of the most highly regarded in the world.

I was feeling important, blessed, and lucky to be at NU. And I had still had this crazy idea that I could one day play pro—and with that mindset, college to me was mostly a means to that end. Maybe I wasn't at a premier hockey school, but NU was in Division I, and that seemed to me to mean that I had absolutely taken a step toward achieving my dream—especially when you consider that in high school I had gained very little renown in the sport. Sure, I earned most-improved honors at Northwood, but that meant little in big-time college hockey.

Of the four major college hockey programs in the Boston area—Boston College, Boston University, Harvard, and Northeastern—Northeastern had a firm lock on fourth place in terms of historic win-loss record, championships won, and overall prestige. And every February, when the four schools met at the Boston Garden for the Beanpot tournament, a sold-out affair that takes place over consecutive Monday evenings, the Huntington Hounds often would lose on both of the nights and finish fourth.

NU teams were made up of kids from Canada and New England who were good, but not good enough to be offered scholarships at BC, BU, or Harvard. Yeah, you could say we played with a chip on our shoulder and a feeling of inferiority. Actually, this feeling and attitude simultaneously fired me up and pissed me off, motivating me to play and go all-out.

Our home ice was the old, bare-bones, gloomy Boston Arena, a facility (built in 1910) that we shared with local small colleges, high schools, and men's and youth teams.

What I couldn't have appreciated back then was that Fern Flaman, whom I respected highly and for whom I enjoyed playing very much, was in the process of building Huskies hockey into a respected and winning franchise.

When I was a freshman at NU, Flaman was in only his sixth year coaching the program. He would go on to coach NU for a total of nineteen seasons and 255 victories. His successes as coach of the Huskies included winning the school's first Beanpot, in 1980, along with three more, in '84, '85, and '88; two league championships; and a Frozen Four appearance in 1982. He won multiple coach-of-the-year honors. Fern Flaman could coach.

Northeastern competed in the East Coast Athletic Conference, most commonly called the ECAC. This league had fourteen teams; along with NU, there were BC, BU, all the Ivy League schools, Clarkson University, Colgate University, Rensselaer Polytechnic Institute, St. Lawrence University, the University of New Hampshire, and the University of Vermont.

During my first season for the Huskies, I did what I had always done, and always would do—played hard and physical and went all-out. My stickhandling, skating, and passing were fairly rough for major college hockey, but already proving of value were my abilities as an aggressive and hard-hitting player. When an opponent realizes there is a guy out there who is intent on rattling his bones with a check, and is able to do it, it disrupts his game and throws off his rhythm. Coach Flaman—again, a hard-hitting player himself—saw value in the way I played the game, and he had me on the ice regularly, mostly on the second and third shifts.

My freshman year, we had what had been a typical NU season, finishing 11–16–0 overall and 9–13–0 in the ECAC. You can find the stats, but I played in twenty games, had three goals and a couple assists, and did not spend a second in the penalty box. Highlighting that first college season for me was playing in the Beanpot at the

Garden. It is a dream of every kid who plays hockey in New England to play in that iconic building. Losing to BU in the opening round, and BC in the second round, was no fun, but it didn't take away from being on that ice and in front of all those people.

I was a much, much better player in my second season at Northeastern than I had been as a freshman. You may say that that development would be a given, but the thing is, there are many players who don't improve year to year, even early in their careers, when they don't have to contend with Father Time, the opponent who always wins in the end. Throughout my late teens and until I was thirty-one or so, I progressed from year to year.

It was also during my sophomore year that I received a wake-up call culturally and an education in understanding and tolerance. All this came in the person of Wayne Turner, a black kid from Kitimat, British Columbia. Turner, a center who could skate and score, had been heavily recruited by Coach Flaman. Turner was a transfer to NU, and he arrived on the team with sophomore status.

Up to that point, I had had very little contact with black people. Surely, hockey was not a sport that provided me much opportunity to broaden my scope and perspective. So now I had a teammate, a black guy with a big Afro—well, this was unusual. I learned quickly that Wayne was a super guy, a hard worker, and a standout teammate. And did I tell you he could score? Wayne and I got along well. In fact, in the '78–79 Huskies team photo, Wayne and I are sitting next to each other in the front row.

As I mentioned earlier, it was during my days at Northeastern that I was given the nickname "Knuckles." Whenever I was out at night with my hockey teammates and someone mouthed off to us, I recognized it as an invitation to fight. I didn't tolerate people looking at me or my friends the wrong way, either; that, also, was a request to battle. I didn't try to provoke things or look for a problem (with much effort, at least). I had gotten into enough trouble—and I didn't need any more. You might wonder why I didn't take the extra step of turning the other cheek—you know, with my Catholic upbringing and all. Well, turning the other cheek wasn't going to happen—ever.

I had, however, started practicing sidestepping and walking away from trouble. I also avoided hanging around with "bad seeds" and those inclined toward troublemaking.

An example: one day I was walking down the sidewalk in my West Roxbury neighborhood and this kid I knew, who was a few years younger than me and a student at CM, where he played hockey, pulled up alongside me in a car. This kid, who also lived in West Roxbury, was smiling, and he said, "Chris, jump in." I stepped up to the driver's-side window and looked in, and I saw a screwdriver sticking out of the ignition switch. For the uninitiated, back then, and maybe for a couple decades afterward, most streetwise urban teens who practiced even a tiny bit of criminal activity knew how to steal a car by playing a bit with the ignition and substituting a screwdriver for a key. After recognizing that the kid was driving a stolen car, one he almost certainly stole himself, I said, "I don't want a ride—and don't be stupid. Park the car, ditch it, or whatever, but get out of it and get away from it."

I don't know what the kid did with the car.

When I was a sophomore, the Huskies went 10–17–1 overall, and 7–16–1 in the league. I showed more promise offensively, scoring twenty-six points on nine goals and seventeen assists. It was sometime during that winter, when the Canadiens were in town to play the Bruins, that Judge King, unbeknownst to me at the time, pitched the idea of drafting me to his buddies Dickie Moore and Doug Harvey over dinner and in phone calls. Judge King pushed the point that, with one of their final picks of the upcoming draft, the Montreal Canadiens should select me.

In early spring, after my sophomore season was over, Judge King and I had pizza a few times. One of those times, the judge told me he thought there might be a chance I would be drafted by an NHL team. He also told me he had talked with the Canadiens about me and the club seemed interested.

That was all I needed to hear. I started promoting among my friends and family the notion of me being drafted. I started to anticipate the 1978 NHL draft.

9

DRAFT DAY

IT WAS THE SUMMER between my sophomore and junior years at Northeastern University. I was working about thirty hours a week at Tony's. I felt good about what was in front of me. I had successfully finished my second year of school, and had taken the full course load every semester, and had passed all my classes. Yet, of course, while I loved hockey, I had no great affection for schoolwork. I trained hard that summer.

After all, there was Northeastern University hockey—and my thoughts of going to the NHL. Judge King had put these ideas into my head.

Now, anyone who had heard him say this must have thought he was talking pure nonsense. But I was naive and hopeful enough to think he knew what he was talking about. Still, even I had to wonder how it was going to happen. I had had a solid career thus far at Northeastern, but there were many more talented wings in Division I hockey in the Northeast, and many of them didn't have their names bandied about as potential NHL draft picks.

So, in the spring of 1978, after hockey season, I started telling people I was going to get drafted. Well, that got a chuckle—nowhere more than in my parents' home in West Roxbury. In response to my claim that I was going to be an NHL draft selection, my father laughed and said the only way I was ever going to be drafted was if there was a war and I got called up by the military. My uncle had a different reaction. He said if I wanted to get drafted, I should open the back door of the house and stand there, and then a draft would come over me.

I still believed that it was going to happen.

But, then again, it wasn't like I was investing a hell of a lot of emotion in the event. I was aware that June 15 was draft day. And I knew the draft was being run out of Montreal.

Actually, and here's a little history, the draft that year was officially called the NHL Amateur Draft—as it had been known since the NHL held its first draft, in 1963. Since then, the only players who could be selected in that draft were amateurs under the age of twenty. In 1979, the name of the draft was changed to the NHL Entry Draft, because the NHL needed a process to draft not only amateurs, but also professionals from the World Hockey Association, which had recently become defunct.

Many in the US, including the area where I'm from, don't understand that the NHL draft is just as big a deal in Canada as the NBA and NFL drafts are in the United States. But even in Canada, it wasn't being televised yet. During the day, I didn't know what stage the draft was at. All I knew was that it had been going on for a few hours, and no call had come. I didn't know the particulars—that the draft had gone through the first, second, third, and fourth rounds, and sixty-nine players had been drafted, and that I wasn't much of a thought to anyone. And neither was I prominent on anyone's radar screen as the draft got through its fifth, sixth, seventh, eighth, and ninth rounds, which brought the number of drafted players up to 154. Indeed, at this point, I was still a ways down on the depth chart.

I just knew that a lot of players had to have been drafted at this point, and that I hadn't been one of them. Maybe my father and uncle were right. This wasn't going to happen.

Maybe I would get drafted next year. Sometime that day, the fourteenth round concluded and another fifty-eight players had been selected—bringing the total to 212—and I was not among them.

Anyway, late in the evening, around ten-thirty or so, I got in my car, the Mercury Montego I had bought with my earnings from Tony's, and I drove it over to one of my favorite bars, the Cask 'n Flagon, located next to the Northeastern campus (there is another Cask 'n Flagon located alongside Fenway Park). Ah, it was fun, anticipating the big event. And, as they say, maybe next year.

I sidled up to the bar, and I got myself a beer. It had to be about 11:15 or 11:20, and a guy walked up to me and extended his hand and he said, "Chris Nilan, right?"

I looked at him and shook his hand, and I said, "Yes, that's me."

And he said, "Congratulations, you must be excited."

I actually wasn't excited about much. So I asked, "Excited about what?"

He smiled and said, "You gotta be kidding me; you haven't heard?"

"No, I haven't heard anything."

He was laughing now, and he said, "You just got drafted by the Montreal Canadiens. Didn't you see, didn't you hear it, up there?" and he pointed to one of the TVs above the bar showing the local newscast. "It was just on the news."

I jumped off the bar stool and gave this guy a hug, and he continued laughing. Several people around us had heard what he said, and had seen my reaction, and they were clapping and saying congratulations and giving me a pat on the back; some of them commented that they were surprised I didn't know about it, and that they knew I had been drafted before I knew I had been drafted. I don't think it was more than a minute after I found out that I was an NHL draft pick that I was out of the bar and running down the street to get to my car. It was parked by the side of the road. Well, I wasn't thinking right, or normally, and I pulled away from the curb—and as I did so, I started to do this wide turn in the middle of the street, because my car had been parked pointing one way, and to get home the fastest, I needed to drive in the opposite direction. But as I started to make the turn, I hadn't accounted for a raised section of trolley tracks that ran along the street. I drove the car right over that little stretch of track, and the car's exhaust system got hooked on it—and of course, I was flooring the car, so a whole mess of metal got ripped off the vehicle.

It made one hell of a racket, the tearing and clunking—and people on the sidewalk stopped with their eyes wide and mouths open. I pumped the gas a bit, but not much was happening—the car was kind of jumping and heaving forward slowly. Ah, fuck. Ah, shit.

I knew the car wasn't going to be taking me anywhere—so I pressed the gas and was able to drive it another forty yards or so and park it in another space on the other side of the street. I got out and ran back to where part of the undercarriage of my car was ensnared on a bit of trolley track, and I pulled the metal— some pipes and wires and whatever—loose, and I went back to my car, threw them in the backseat, locked the car, and hailed myself a cab.

On the way to West Roxbury, I was regaling the cab driver with stories of the NHL draftee in the back seat. He was very congratulatory and, I think, impressed—maybe.

When I got home, I ran into the house and my mom and dad were all smiles. News outlets had been calling the house. My mother told me she thought it was a joke when she took the first call, and then a couple more calls had come in and she said she figured at that point that it might be real. My dad was happy, for sure—and he kept chuckling and shaking his head.

I was flying high—I didn't even get much discouraged when I found out I was the 231st pick of the total 234 players selected in the draft. I mean, really, it was only me, Judge King, and some people working for the Montreal Canadiens who ever thought I would be a NHL pick at all.

My celebrity was both modest and short-lived. Heck, I didn't even receive a phone call from the Canadiens congratulating me on being drafted. After a day or two of talking with reporters from the local media, no one seemed interested in doing interviews with me any more.

A few days after the draft, I received a letter—sent regular post—from Montreal Canadiens general manager, Irving Grundman. In the letter, Mr. Grundman offered his congratulations, and said I had an invitation to training camp to try out for the Canadiens.

No signing bonus. No salary guarantee. No guaranteed anything.

Then again, it didn't matter. That kid who walked down the street to the ice rink, wearing dungarees and sneakers, holding his skates in his hand, had been drafted by an NHL team. And not just a team—but the marquee hockey team on the planet.

10

KAREN

I DIDN'T WANT TO RETURN to Northeastern University for my sophomore year; I wanted to try out with the Montreal Canadiens, make the team, and begin my NHL career. But my father pushed me to continue my education at NU, so that's what I did—I stayed in school.

It was in late fall—maybe the last week of October or early November of 1978—that, at Boston Arena, something momentous happened in my life: I met the woman with whom I would fall in love, marry, and have three children. And it was through this woman that I would become connected and close to one of the most legendary, and eventually sought-after, criminals in US history.

It was a Thursday afternoon, and I was at the Arena to watch a Boston State College hockey game. Two of my good friends, twins named Ronald and Donald Harrington, were playing for Boston State. In the stands, there were probably no more than a hundred people. Looking around, I saw a young woman, sitting by herself a few rows back from the ice, watching the game. She was pretty. A pretty woman alone meant I at least had to start a conversation. So I figured I would sit not too close to her—but not too far away, either. Play it cool, you know. So I sat a few rows down from her, to her left, about twenty feet away. I looked up at her and gave her a smile, and she smiled back. I turned back toward the ice and watched the action for a minute.

Then I turned to her and said, "Do you know someone out there?"

She kept that smile, and she said a friend of hers was playing.

Ah, a friend—not a boyfriend. This was all the invitation I needed. I stood and stepped up and over the benches toward her, got up to where she was sitting, and held out my hand.

"Hi, I'm Chris."

Never losing that smile, she shook my hand and said, "I'm Karen. It is nice to meet you."

I sat next to her and we started talking. Yes, she was a pretty colleen (with the word "colleen" being code for a girl who is out-and-out Irish)—with cheekbones, a nose with a point, a light complexion with a few freckles, and beautiful strawberry-blonde hair.

I found out that Karen—Karen Stanley—had grown up in South Boston and still lived there. She worked as an aide at the State House for one of the state reps. I told her I had been working a co-op job at the State House, in the state treasurer's office, for four months, and had a couple months to go. We both said we thought it was funny that we hadn't run into each other before.

Of course, I made sure to let Karen know that I played hockey for Northeastern and that I was a draft pick of the Montreal Canadiens. She seemed impressed—or at least made a show of being impressed.

I think we talked for a half hour or thereabouts. When the game was over, I told her I was going to get together with my friends who had been playing. Before I left, I suggested it might be a good idea to meet for coffee or do lunch or something someday near the State House since we both worked there. Karen said that sounded like a plan.

I gotta tell you, that afternoon and night she was on my mind. Karen Stanley made an impression on me.

Well, the gods must have been smiling on me, on us, or something like that—or fate just had to pull us together. Because the very next morning, when I stepped out of the subway station down the street from State House, who did I run into exiting the station but Karen. For four months we had shared a point in our commute and a building in which we worked, but neither of us recalled ever seeing the other. Now here it was, the day after we met, and we were meeting again.

Karen seemed very happy to see me. I was definitely happy to see her. I said that, in running into her that morning, the decision was made—we had to do lunch. Karen agreed. We went on our first date the next day.

❖

Karen and I began to see a lot of each other. We became boyfriend and girlfriend. And soon enough, she shared with me some information on her family that, while not exactly a secret, was closely guarded.

It had to do with her mother's boyfriend, a man she had been dating for fifteen years.

Indeed, Karen's biological father had long been out of the picture, and her mother's boyfriend had served as a father to Karen and her two sisters and brother. Karen and her siblings called the man Charlie.

The man's name was James J. Bulger. His friends called him Jimmy. But to most of the world, he was known as Whitey—Whitey Bulger.

Again, Whitey Bulger was the older brother of state senator Billy Bulger, who represented me and Barry in that assault case a few years prior.

Whitey Bulger wasn't in politics, though. He wasn't a lawyer. He didn't go to any office on any day with a briefcase and a suit and tie. Whitey Bulger had a different type of work.

You see, Whitey Bulger was one of the most feared, powerful, intelligent, and ruthlessly cunning mob bosses in the United States.

❖

Here I need to give you some background on Whitey Bulger.

James Joseph "Whitey" Bulger Jr. was born on September 3, 1929. He was the oldest of three boys of James Joseph Bulger Sr. and his wife, Jenny. The family was poor and lived in a public housing project in South Boston. Jimmy Jr. got his nickname as a kid because of his light blond hair.

From his teenage years on, Whitey was in trouble with the law. His older brothers, Jackie and Billy, were good students. Whitey was as smart as both them, if not smarter, but he wasn't the school type. Whitey was the thieving and mugging and crime-ringleader type. He was arrested over and over and did time in a juvenile detention facility. When he got out of prison in 1948, he did a stint in the US Air Force. During his time in the service, he continued to get into trouble—serious trouble, including armed robbery and assault. He spent many months in the stockade, but managed to receive an honorable discharge in 1952. He returned to Massachusetts—and lawbreaking. In 1956, he was convicted of armed robbery and hijacking and sent to a federal penitentiary in Atlanta. He would spend the next five years in Atlanta as well as in the famed federal prisons at Alcatraz and Leavenworth.

On release in 1965, he went back to Boston, where he had a crime racket to help build and over which he would take control in a few years. His brother Billy, the Triple Eagle, was now a state representative and in the early stages of a career that would make him the most powerful public leader in Massachusetts. Jackie, meanwhile, had a job in the Massachusetts court system.

Billy Bulger helped Whitey land a job as a custodian. But, of course, this wasn't going to work. Whitey started bookmaking and loansharking; he did well at both. Maybe a year after returning to Boston and resuming his underworld career, Bulger met Teresa Stanley, a recently divorced twenty-six-year-old with movie-star good looks and four children, aged three months to seven years. Bulger and Stanley started dating.

Bulger upped his crime involvement, becoming a soldier in a battle between rival Irish gangs—the Killeens and the Mullens—for control over criminal activity in Boston. It was a bloody episode, and many mobsters, wiseguys, and flunkies were gunned down. Whitey was with the Killeen crew, which was heading toward defeat. Yet Whitey, ever the smart strategist, forged a relationship with Howie Winter, boss of the Winter Hill Gang, another Irish crime outfit. It was based in Somerville, a city about ten miles to the north of Boston. Soon after Whitey and Howie shook hands, Donald Killeen, numero uno in the Killeen group, was shot dead. Go figure.

There is a lot of dispute over just how the war came to an end, but what seems most probable is that Patrick Nee, a captain in the Mullen gang, talked with Winter and asked him for help in negotiating a truce. Winter in turn brought in the Patriarca crime family, an Italian group out of Rhode Island, to aid in the mediation. After a sit-down, the Killeens and Mullens joined forces, with Howie Winter in charge.

Even though Winter was the boss, Whitey was a powerful lieutenant who managed and ran just about every aspect of crime in South Boston. Whitey became both rich and feared. As he presided over the South Boston rackets, his sidekick was a ruthless, stone-cold killing machine, Stevie "The Rifleman" Flemmi.

In 1979, Howie Winter was convicted of fixing horse races and was sent back to the clink. Whitey solidified his power and reach. He was the criminal Caesar of the Boston area. Through the 1980s and into the '90s, his dominance of the area's underworld grew and grew, and so did his legendary status. What fueled and supported that status were his violent streak, his exceptional intelligence, his commitment to exercise and a healthy diet, and the fact that he didn't drink, smoke, or do drugs. He was also bookish, a big reader who had a particular interest in nonfiction—history and biographies and autobiographies of great leaders.

Whitey Bulger expanded his enterprise. Throughout the 1980s, Bulger was the president of Crime, Inc. By this time, as well, his younger brother Billy was president of the Massachusetts senate. You can't make this stuff up.

And through all of it, Whitey Bulger and Teresa Stanley were boyfriend and girlfriend. He basically became the father of Teresa's children.

11

MEETING JAMES J. "WHITEY" BULGER

THERE WERE TWO LOVES in my life as fall turned to winter in late 1978. One was hockey, and the other was Karen. I spent a lot of time with both. Karen attended games I played in the Boston area and joined my family and friends in the Chris Nilan fan club.

I had been over to Karen's house maybe three or four times, and never at a time when Whitey Bulger was there. I am thinking that this was on purpose. But the good thing is that I got along very well with Karen's mother.

Teresa Stanley was a beautiful woman, inside and out. She always treated me with kindness. When I first met Teresa, she was thirty-eight years old. Whitey never became a resident at the Stanley house on Silver Street, but he was over there almost every day and frequently had dinner there. He spent holidays and other special occasions with the family. Teresa was very open about the fact that Whitey supported her and her children. Whatever else Whitey had going on, he was good to Teresa and her kids. He spent a lot of money on, and a lot of time with, the Stanleys.

Did Teresa know how Whitey made his money? She surely knew

how he made a good amount of his money. It's funny: I do see parallels between the dynamic of Whitey Bulger and Teresa Stanley and that of Tony Soprano and his wife, Carmela. Carmela Soprano knew her husband was in the Mafia, but she tried her best to avoid looking too deeply into what he did. Carmela was also a good person, a good mother, and a doting wife—and she enjoyed the comfortable life that the ill-gotten money afforded her. Teresa, her relationship with Whitey, and the material comfort he provided reminded me of Carmela and Tony—kind of.

In a Boston Globe story on Teresa that ran a couple days after she died from lung cancer in August 2012, reporter Shelley Murphy wrote how, when the government grilled Teresa in court about what she knew about what Whitey did, she replied, "If I ever asked him a question, he would tell me to mind my own business. He would say it's none of my concern, so I never asked questions."

Of course, I remember the first time I met James J. "Whitey" Bulger. I also knew, well in advance, that he didn't like to be called Whitey; he preferred Jimmy. Whitey was the name the newspapers used.

Even as a kid, I knew about Whitey Bulger. He was a notorious gangster, from what I heard, who ran just about everything in the underworld in the Boston area. Now, as I've said, Boston is not that big a place, in terms of land area or population. It is an international city, and a world-leading center for academia, medicine, technology, and money management. But it is sort of incestuous as well; you don't have to reach far to find someone or know someone who can put you in touch with just about anybody.

So I knew a lot of people whose brother, cousin, or father either knew Whitey, had met him, or had even done work for him. That I was an Irish Catholic kid living in Boston obviously upped the chances that my society would intersect with his. Still, that I would actually get to know the man fairly well was never really on my radar screen. To tell you the truth, I really didn't ever want to meet Whitey Bulger.

He was a legend—but a legend to be feared, and someone, from what I'd heard, who could make you disappear fast, if you upset him.

Still, I had been dating Karen for a few months, and I had met her mother a few times, and we had gotten along very well. I did ask Karen questions about Whitey, but I didn't pry, because I needed to respect that relationship. But being a Boston kid from the streets almost required that I be fascinated with Whitey Bulger, so I pried just a bit. Karen had all her priorities in order, and she didn't say much about her mother's boyfriend.

I was supposed to pick Karen up one Friday night, and I called over to where she and her mom lived, in South Boston. Karen told me Jimmy was there, and it actually would be a good time to finally meet him. I gotta tell you, I was a tough guy who didn't back down from anything, and very little unnerved me. But when Karen told me I would soon be meeting James J. "Whitey" Bulger face to face, well, I got thrown for a little start. Not much, but at least a bit. I was also curious and fascinated, kind of like when you are a kid and you are about to get on a roller coaster; you know you are going to have a thrill, but you also know your stomach is going to lurch and there is going to be some anxiety involved, and not all of it pleasant.

I drove over to Silver Street, a bit nervous, nothing paralyzing. I got to Karen's house and rang the doorbell. She answered the door with a big smile, and I stepped inside. She led me down a hallway and into the living room of the house. Standing there in the middle of the room was Teresa; she was all smiles, and she walked over to me—even as I looked sideways to the couch where he was sitting—and she gave me a hug.

And then, slightly pulling on my hand, she gestured to the man sitting there and said, "Chris, I want you to meet Jimmy."

Jimmy stood up and extended his hand to me. As he firmly gripped my hand, I understood I was now up close, so very close, to Whitey Bulger. He didn't say a word, just looked at me. Let me tell you, there is a reason that Jimmy Bulger was sometimes called

"Jimmy Blue Eyes." Those eyes were riveting and engaging and penetrating, and they were looking at me—through me. Bulger had that receding hairline, and the hair was combed straight back. He wore a long-sleeved dress shirt open at the collar.

Those eyes bore into me.

Bulger was an exercise enthusiast who followed a strict diet, and I saw that he was trim and in shape. I said, "It is great to meet you, Jimmy." Bulger just nodded and sat back down.

Teresa knew there was a tad of tension in the air, and she said something like, "So, where are you kids off to?"

Karen said we were going to get something to eat and maybe walk around Quincy Market, which was located a couple miles away in the city. Quincy Market was, and remains today, a favorite hangout of locals and tourists; it is filled with shops and restaurants and a long stretch of a food court. Teresa, Karen, and I were standing, and Whitey sat there looking at me. He kept looking at me. This made me, well, a bit uncomfortable—I mean, would you like Whitey—er, Jimmy—Bulger staring at you? But I could handle it.

Karen said we had to get going, and she started ahead of me for the door, and I said good-bye to Teresa and Jimmy, repeated to Jimmy that it was nice to meet him, and turned to follow Karen. And then I heard Jimmy say, "Chris, hold on. I want to talk to you for a minute."

Oh no. A slight coursing of cold anxiety went through me. I looked back at him and then at Karen, and she kind of made this motion with her hand, like pushing at me with an open palm, indicating that I'd best talk with Jimmy. She said she would meet me out in front of the house. Teresa, still standing there, looked at me, and then at Jimmy, and then she did a pursed-lipped smile while closing her eyes and gently shaking her head, as if to say, "Here we go again."

Teresa left the room and headed downstairs to the kitchen.

So I guessed I was going to have a chat with James J. "Whitey" Bulger. Just me and him. How comforting.

"Sit . . . sit," he said, pointing to an upholstered chair across from him. I sat down. I sat down fast.

Whitey gave me this stone-cold look, and then he reached down near his hip and pulled out . . . oh no . . . a handgun. Although I didn't know it then, the gun was a Walther PPK, the type that James Bond sometimes carried. All I knew was that it was black and shiny, and I was sure it was real and fired real bullets. Jimmy had his hand on the gun, and he sat it on his thigh—it was not pointed at me. Thank God for small favors.

Jimmy leaned forward and grimaced a bit, and made a face as if to suggest that what I was about to hear was something he had to say, and which I might find difficult to take. If you think that is a lot for me to glean just from the location of a gun, a facial expression, and body movement, all I've got to say is that you probably didn't spend much time on mean urban streets in the 1970s.

I kept my mouth shut; meanwhile, my heart was pumping about as fast as it can when you are not moving. My eyes darted back and forth between the gun and Jimmy. I was in something of quandary, because I didn't want to act scared, but I wanted to show respect. I waited for Jimmy to speak. Thankfully, within a few seconds, he did.

"You know, Chris, I just want to make sure we understand things," he said in a very low and relaxed voice. I didn't say anything. Jimmy continued, "I know you love Karen, and she loves you—or am I wrong? I have that right, right? You love her?"

"Yes, of course," I replied.

Jimmy shook his head understandingly, and he said, "Well, that is all good, because she loves you. And of course, I know you would never hurt her, and you always will be good to her. Because, you know, it just wouldn't be a good thing if you weren't. It wouldn't end up good."

"I understand."

"Okay, then—but, you know, even if you are good to her, and for whatever reason she wants to leave you, then you have to let her leave. You got that?"

And, you know, sure I was nervous, but I also was a tad pissed—because he knew from what Karen and Teresa had told him that I was stand-up, and he had to know that I would do what was right, and he had to know that I knew that crossing him could be fatal.

So I looked straight at him and said, "Jimmy, again, I understand. I understand thoroughly. But you didn't have to take out gun to tell me that."

When I said that he smiled, and then he laughed lightly. Those blue eyes of his softened a bit—but only a bit.

While still sitting, he placed the gun on a side table. He then stood up and offered his hand. We shook. I hope he didn't see the sweat on my forehead, which I knew was there. I nodded and said thanks or something, and then turned around. I hadn't made it a step outside the living room before I heard Jimmy say, "Hey, Chris."

Ah, shit. What now? A machine gun?

I turned back, and he was still sitting there—and again he reached down toward his hip. This couldn't be good. But then he pulled out what looked like a decent-sized wad of cash in a shiny silver clip. He tossed it to me, and I grabbed it.

"Chris, you and Karen have a good time," he said. I thanked him and walked down the stairs, and then out the front door, where Karen was waiting for me. I filled her in on my impromptu "sit-down" with Jimmy. And I showed her the money Jimmy gave me. She found the story to be amusing.

We got in my car, and I was about to start the ignition when I realized I hadn't assessed the windfall that one of the most notorious mobsters in America had just given me. So I slid off the clip and counted out twenty-five $20 bills. I looked over at her and I know that surprise was all over my face.

Funny thing—Karen didn't seem surprised at all.

12

THE ENFORCER EMERGES

IT WAS DURING MY JUNIOR YEAR that the persona of "Knuckles," born on the streets, started to make its presence felt on the ice.

Again, while I was a hard-hitting checker with the Huskies, I didn't get in fights because I didn't want to get suspended for a game. But in my third and final season at Northeastern, I managed to get into some scrapes that were something of a portent of what lay ahead. Maybe, since I knew deep down that I wasn't going back to NU after the season was over, I thought I could let it out a bit. Like the incident up at Boston Arena when we scrimmaged the Boston Bruins.

Because Coach Flaman was a Bruins alum, he was able to score for us a great opportunity and experience—playing against our idols. It was a game scheduled for early October, before the college and NHL seasons began. As you can imagine, we were all excited, and nervous as all get-out, to go head to head with the Bruins. And I, for one, was committed to playing full bore. Let's remember, as well, that the Bruins that year, the '78–79 season, were a tough group, arguably the best fighting team in the league.

So during the scrimmage, which was supposed to be a friendly affair, a whistle blew, and as the action stopped, Bruins co-captain Mike Milbury pushed my teammate Mark Coates. I was only ten feet or so away, and I went right over and gave Milbury a hard push back. He looked at me with total surprise, and then a pissed look, and he said, "What is the matter with you?"

I shot right back, "Matter with me? You pushed my teammate after the whistle blew. That's what is the matter with me." A referee jumped in and told us to cool it.

Funny thing: as I skated away, I saw Terry O'Reilly looking at me with a bit of bewilderment. He could have had no way of knowing that he and I would soon start to build our own history of confrontation with one another.

Later in the season, I got into another fight. But the other guy started it—well, sort of.

We were playing Colgate at Boston Arena, and during one of the final shifts, Larry Gibson of Colgate stuck my teammate Jimmy Walsh in the eye with his stick. It was a nasty shot, and Jimmy was temporarily blinded. He was sent immediately to the Massachusetts Eye and Ear Infirmary, a world-leading specialty hospital located in Boston. Jimmy would make a full recovery and regain full sight. He wouldn't be playing for a couple weeks, though.

I was furious as soon as Gibson made that careless play, but the game ended before I could take a run at him on the ice. I was thinking of cracking him during the postgame handshake, but I didn't. I just refused to shake his hand.

I couldn't let the incident go. I think I was mad at myself for not slapping Gibson when I had the chance.

Well, I would have another chance the following week, when we were visiting Colgate. I told Jimmy Walsh I was going to get payback for him on Larry Gibson.

So, there we were, at Colgate, in the town of Hamilton in upstate New York—and again it was late in the game. I'm not sure exactly what set things up, but I think a penalty had been called and there was some confusion about what exactly had been called, or whatever.

So one of our captains, Dave Archambault, went over to an official—and Gibson, who was a Colgate co-captain, joined in the conference. I guess I had to be looking for a problem, because I skated up to the meeting as well. Gibson looked at me and said, "What the hell are you here for? You're not a captain. Get out of here, you dummy."

Never smart to talk to me like that. Not good.

"Dummy" had no sooner gotten out of his mouth than I hit him with an overhand punch that twisted his helmet halfway across his face and sent him crumbling in a daze to the ice. That started things. Players on the ice went at it, and players left the benches to join in. Fans started throwing paper and plastic cups at the Northeastern players. Particularly interesting is that our manager, Jim Stewart, began jawing with some guy in the stands, and the guy threw a half-filled cup of soda at Jim. It landed in front of him and sprayed him good. Jim was incensed and tried to get out of the bench area to go at the guy, but he was restrained by one of one our assistant coaches.

Soon enough, all the NU and Colgate coaches were on the ice, and the teams were separated. Officials called the game right then. More cops were brought in to guard us as we went to the locker room, and from the locker room to our bus. It was a good idea to add this security, for there were probably fifty or more students waiting for us in the parking lot. After we walked the gauntlet of shouting students, we got on the bus and headed back to Boston, with an escort of two police cars that rode with us to the Hamilton town limits.

Individually, after getting five penalty minutes as a freshman and twenty-eight as a sophomore, I managed to tally ninety-two penalty minutes as a junior. Once again, I played with the thought in the back of my mind that I wasn't going to return to Northeastern, and that motivated me to play with the hard-hitting abandon that would be necessary to survive at the next level. I also scored nine goals that year along with seventeen assists, which was five points more than my freshman and sophomore point totals combined.

I was improving in all areas of the game.

Northeastern had another so-so year. But the program was on the cusp of a decade-long run of success. The following year, NU would pull off a major upset in winning the Beanpot. But I had made the decision that my dream would not continue to unfold that fall at Northeastern University. Instead, it would be in another place, in another country, in a city called Montreal.

13

MY TEAMMATES

EVEN THOUGH I WASN'T going to play hockey anymore for Northeastern, I finished up my spring semester. After that, I began looking forward to the Montreal Canadiens training camp. With the college hockey season over and the school year coming to an end, I was all geared up about my future in the NHL. And I was all excited about meeting my future teammates.

I'll share with you how I introduced myself to some members of the Montreal Canadiens. Actually, it's a first-person account of events Serge Savard discusses in the foreword to this book.

I can recall the exact date: it was Wednesday, May 2, 1979. I remember it because it was the day after the Boston Bruins beat Montreal, 2–1, at Boston Garden in the third game of their best-of-seven Stanley Cup semifinal series. Montreal, which was gunning for its fourth Cup championship in a row, had won the first two games of the series at home before it came to Boston for games three and four. Game four was to be played the next night at the Garden.

My good bud Franny Flaherty and I had managed to sneak into Boston Garden to watch a Canadiens skate-around. Standing near the ice was Claude Ruel, the Canadiens' director of player personnel. I walked right up to him and told him who I was and that I had been drafted by his team. Ruel was nice enough; then again, while I know he had heard my name before, I don't think he had much confidence he would be hearing much of it in the future. I asked him if, since I was a draftee of the Canadiens, I could get a couple tickets to the fifth game of the series, which would be at the Forum in Montreal. He said sure, and he pointed to a guy who I found out was Howard Grundman, director of hockey administration for the Habs and the son of Irving Grundman. I talked to him and told him who I was. He smiled, shook my hand, and said it was nice to meet me. I asked about the tickets, and Grundman said of course he would get me the tickets for the game—and that they would be waiting for me at the "will call" box at the Forum. I thanked him profusely. Oh man, I felt important.

With that taken care of, Franny and I watched the legends of the game skate. We watched until the practice was over.

After the practice, Franny and I left the building. He'd driven that day, and we walked down the street to a lot to pick up his car—a big old boat of a Thunderbird, white and nice and wide and long, with a vinyl roof and opera windows. Inside, it had leather seats and all the automatic gadgets; the sort of car that Huggy Bear from the TV show *Starsky & Hutch* might drive.

It was a mild day and we figured on just driving around the streets near the Boston Garden for a little while. We had the windows down, and I asked Franny to take one more swing down Causeway Street, right alongside the Garden, and then take a drive down this wide alley that I knew led to an area where visiting players would wait for the team bus after a game or practice.

I hoped I might run into my future teammates. I mean, after all, I had just been drafted by this famed organization. I actually thought that some of these guys might know who I was. You think I was delusional? Perhaps.

So there we were, Flaherty and me, in that big boat of a car, and we turned into the alley, went down about fifty yards, and ... why ... I couldn't believe it.

Standing there, right outside the old Boston Garden, were three superstars—bona fide NHL idols: Jacques Lemaire, Guy Lafleur, and Gilles Lupien. Wow. They were just standing on the curb in casual dress. They didn't have any equipment or bags with them, of course, for that was all stowed away for the skate-around the next day, and the game that night.

I told Flaherty to stop—which he did, pulling up with the passenger side along the curb. I had the window down. Hockey royalty, three of them, were little more than an arm's length away. I knew the Canadiens were staying in the Hyatt in Cambridge, across the Charles River.

"You guys need a ride to your hotel?" I bellowed, totally excited. "We're Boston guys, but we love the Canadiens. We'll bring you to the Hyatt. Hop in."

So, there you have Jacques Lemaire, Guy Lafleur, and Gilles Lupien, not saying anything, just looking at each other, and then at us, and then back at each other. I think they found it a bit strange.

"C'mon . . . c'mon," I yelled, and gestured with my thumb to the backseat as I added, "just jump in back; we'll take you over. This is a big fucking deal for me."

The Canadiens kind of shrugged, and Jacques Lemaire said, in his French-Canadian accent, "Well, sure, that is kind. Thank you." They did jump in—and we were off. Their hotel couldn't have been more than two miles away—and from the north side of the Boston Garden (which is located alongside the commuter hub, North Station)—you can see the bridge that takes you across the Charles and over to Cambridge. I didn't waste any time talking with my comrades-to-be.

I turned around and told them right out that I was going to be playing on the same team with them the next year. I was actually yelling, "Isn't it going to be great . . . all of us playing for the Canadiens next year . . . even if it is going to be kind of freaky and weird, me playing against the Bruins . . . you know, I was just about as big a Bruins fan as anyone growing up."

Lemaire, Lafleur, and Lupien were turning their heads to look at one another, seeming a bit perplexed—and then they were looking at me. I am fairly confident that at this point they were absolutely sure they should not have gotten into Franny's car.

But Lemaire was prepared to go with the conversation. He asked, "Who are you?" And I happily blurted out, "Chris Nilan—you guys drafted me last year." Lemaire, now looking even more confused, said, "We did?" He then asked me who I played hockey for, and I told him Northeastern University, and that I was a forward.

My having played for a college team in the US didn't give them a reason to accord me an ounce of admiration. To these superstars, even Division I NCAA hockey, compared to the NHL, was sort of the second string on the junior varsity team. I mean, think about it: of the 234 players selected in the 1978 NHL draft, 171 were from Canada, forty-six were from the US, and seventeen were from European countries. A total of sixty-nine players were picked in the first four rounds of the draft, of whom sixty-one were from Canada, five from the US, two from Sweden, and one from Norway.

Now, for sure, American college and amateur hockey was on the brink of a major breakthrough as a path to the NHL—the US team's upset gold-medal win at the 1980 Olympics in Lake Placid would be a powerful catalyst driving that change—but in the spring of 1979 we college kids south of the border got very little love or respect from our neighbors to the north. And why would we?

We had a wonderful little drive, all of fifteen minutes, across the Longfellow Bridge into Cambridge. We dropped off the Canadiens, and they were very gracious. Each thanked us and shook our hands.

I am confident that Lemaire, Lafleur, and Lupien felt I had been telling an epic tall tale and they would never see or hear from me again.

❖

The Boston–Montreal series was an epic that went the full seven games. And in the seventh game, played at the Montreal Forum, Rick Middleton scored with four minutes remaining to give the Bruins a 4–3 lead. All of the Boston area was giddy. But with 2:34 on the clock, Boston got called for having too many men on the ice. For the ensuing power play, Canadiens coach Scotty Bowman put out five future Hall of Famers: Guy Lafleur, Larry Robinson, Serge Savard, Steve Shutt, and Jacques Lemaire. Eighty seconds later, Lafleur tied the score. Yvon Lambert scored in sudden-death overtime.

Montreal went on to face the New York Rangers in the Stanley Cup final. The Habs won the series, four games to one.

Oh, as for that game five in Montreal: yes, the Canadiens hooked me up with tickets. They were there at the window, just as I was told they would be. But there was catch.

I had to pay for them.

14

MY FIRST TRAINING CAMP

THAT SUMMER, I WORKED harder than ever to get in shape. I mostly skated at the Pilgrim Ice Arena in Hingham, including playing in the men's summer league in which a lot of Division I and minor-pro players played. I also put in many miles of roller-skating up and down the streets of West Roxbury, crisscrossing parking lots and sometimes going around the Sugar Bowl, a circular path at the tip of a peninsula that stretches from South Boston into the Atlantic.

I did the work, and I realized I was in the best shape of my life, but truthfully—and I realized this—I had next to no understanding of what I would be up against when I showed up in Montreal for training camp.

Wouldn't you know it, a little more than a month prior to leaving for training camp, I got into one hell of an off-ice brawl.

I was with Karen. It was late July, about nine at night, so there was a smidgen of daylight. We were in my car, and I was parallel parking on a street that ran alongside Faneuil Hall. As I was pulling out of a parking spot, some asshole almost sideswiped me. I pulled out right behind him and beeped, put my left arm out the window, and flipped him off. Well, that asshole put his car in park right there—right in the middle of the street—and got out. A guy in the passenger seat got out as well. They were decent-sized guys, and in shape—and they had lots of attitude.

So, of course, I got out of the car, and the driver just pointed at me and said, "Oh, go fuck yourself, you and your cunt wife."

Oh, no, no, no—not good. Not smart.

Karen was yelling, telling me to get back in the car. But I was committed, all in.

By the way, before I left the car, I popped the trunk.

Interestingly, it was the passenger who came right at me, not the shithead who called my girlfriend (whom he thought was my wife) the "C" word. I let him advance, while I stayed in place—next to my car trunk that was unlocked. Yep, I had a plan. He was throwing wild punches, and as he was about to collide with me, I rocked him with an overhand right and cracked his side with a curved and digging left. You could hear the air rush out of him. He was going down. As he fell, I grabbed him with my right arm, and pushed up the trunk lid with my left. And then I rolled him into the trunk, and pounded on him some more. I was also thinking that I might lock him in the trunk so that I could "educate" him further.

This prick was offering little resistance when . . . whack!! . . . I got rocked with something slamming my head, above the temple and just below the crown. Along with the blow came a flash of white light through my head—and off to my right, I saw a full bottle of beer hit the tar. So, that was what I had just been hit with—a full bottle of beer; and cold-cocking me with that bottle was the driver of the car. I was hurt and groggy, and I fell on top of the guy I had just bundled into the trunk. I found out he still had some fight, because he grabbed my right hand and bit down hard on my fingers. Fuck, that hurt.

Getting bit may have saved me—in a way—because the pain sorted of jolted me, making me a little more aware, and also causing me to disengage myself from that punk and get to standing position outside of the car. (The bite injury would require stitches to heal.) When I got to my feet, I saw the driver coming at me with a tire iron; he took a swipe, and I blocked the steel with my arm. As I defended myself from the tire iron, the guy in the car got out of the trunk, and as he did, the driver said, "Let's get the fuck out of here."

They sprinted and jumped in their car. I didn't bother to go after them; I was so dizzy. I actually stumbled, and then dropped on the street, as the assholes sped off. I was hurting.

But I managed to catch the license plate number of the getaway car.

So you have to know those two hadn't seen the last of me. Soon enough, I got my revenge on them—and then some. Really, it was beautiful.

You see, I found out where the guy who owned the car lived. He lived in the Boston area. So I did a bit of recon, and I got down some of his patterns. And I found out where he and his buddy liked to hang out and drink cocktails. And one night at closing time, those two, nicely sauced, left their favorite bar and, chuckling and unsteady— and feeling great, but not for long—they sauntered across the dimly lit parking lot toward the car they had arrived in. Before they got to the car, though, a few of my boys and I jumped out of the shadows and put on them a beating for the ages. Oh, it was good—the sound of bones cracking, whimpering, weak screams, and howls of pain. We did it just right—not killing anyone, but beating those dickheads to within an inch of their lives.

You should have seen it. Again, really, it was beautiful.

In early September, Karen dropped me off on a weekday morning at Logan Airport. I had my street and walking-around clothes packed in one suitcase, and the only equipment I had were my skates, which I held in my hands. The Canadiens had told me they would provide everything else, so skates were all I had. And, if you can imagine— this was more than twenty years prior to the September 11 attacks— I didn't even have to check the skates. I walked onto the plane with two long, sharp metal blades, and I sat with them in my lap for the entire flight to Montreal. It was a different time.

About an hour after takeoff from Boston, I got off the plane at Dorval International Airport (which had its named changed in 2004 to Montreal–Pierre Elliott Trudeau International Airport). There I was, Chris Nilan, draftee of one of the most prestigious and success-ful franchises in all of sports. Then again, I didn't have a contract. Not one reporter or camera was in sight. And no one from the Montreal Canadiens organization was there to meet me. So my first order of business was to get myself a cab to take to me to the . . . let's see . . . I checked what I had written down while on the phone with the Canadiens' front office. Okay, that was it: the Manoir Le Moyne Hotel. That was where I would be staying.

I got there and found out I had a roommate—some kid from Toronto; his name was Dominic Miele. He was a late-round draft pick as well. I met him when I got to the hotel. I didn't have much to say to him, which was the way I wanted it.

The next morning was the opening of training camp, at the cath-edral of hockey: the Montreal Forum.

I tell you, maybe I was in way over my head, and maybe way out of my league, but I was determined to make the best of the experi-ence. I wasn't going to leave anything on the ice, and I wasn't going to take any shit from anyone. And what the fuck anyway, I didn't even like the Montreal Canadiens. I was a Boston Bruins fan, and the Canadiens had made a tradition of kicking our asses.

When I arrived at the Forum, the first thing I did was report to where the equipment was being handed out. There were a few other guys standing outside the room; they were, as best I could tell, draftees like myself. I didn't recognize any of them. I might have muttered some words to them, but just like in the hotel room, I wasn't there to make friends.

After I got all my equipment together, I walked down to the main locker room, and this is where things started to get weird. For there I was, by myself—no friends, and no real teammates, yet—but among the draftees and guys I didn't know, and didn't care to know, were absolute legends and superstars. And I was in the same room as them. Bob Gainey was over there talking with Rod Langway, a Massachusetts kid. Guy Lapointe was sitting on the same long bench as I was. And there were Mark Napier, Steve Shutt, and Larry Robinson. Shit, I didn't have a contract, but I was mesmerized and entertained—and I hoped I didn't look too much in awe.

And then, just after I'd pulled on my workout jersey and was trying to get a hold of myself and get ready to skate, who should jump in front of me, still in street clothes, but Guy Lafleur! He had a big smile and was pointing at me while saying, "Oh Bawstahn, you said you'd be heah." So he remembered me from the car ride in Boston. He shook my hand, patted me on the shoulder, and walked away. Well, that was a positive.

Some of the other players, the guys I didn't know, fellow draftees, were looking at me, a tad perplexed.

I just sat there—and maybe thirty seconds later, who was standing in front of me, with half his equipment on, but Gilles Lupien. He was smiling as well—and said the same thing Lafleur had said to me: "Oh Bawstahn, you said you'd be heah." He shook my hand, and then shook his head and laughed. Lupien then yelled over to Lafleur, "Hey, Guy—this kid from Bawstahn; he said he'd be heah—and now he's heah." Lafleur and Lupien were getting a kick out of the kid from Boston showing up, just as he had promised.

Soon enough, the locker room was packed with players, all suited up and ready to go. Then who walked into the room in a sweat suit but Bernie "Boom Boom" Geoffrion, who had just been hired as the Canadiens' head coach. Geoffrion was an NHL legend as a player—a high-scoring winger, and tough. He played sixteen seasons in the NHL, fourteen of them with Montreal. He was given the nickname Boom Boom because of his rocket-fast slap shot.

I tell you, that day, when I saw Geoffrion in person for the first time—and he was forty-nine years old and about twelve years retired as a player—he still had an imposing presence. He was not tall—about five foot nine—but in shape, with a thick head of slicked-back black hair and thick eyebrows above dark and penetrating eyes—and that nose, which had been broken six times and curved this way and that. Geoffrion stood in the center of the room. Near him was Claude Ruel. I had met Ruel back in Boston at that team practice, and I had seen images of him on TV and in hockey magazines. But I gave him a closer look on this day. He was a very compact man, with a squat body upon which was perched a sort of block-like head.

Geoffrion was rallying everyone, explaining how things were going to go. Maybe none of this meant a hell of a lot to the veterans, but the draftees, including the long-shot hopefuls—and I guess I was about as long a shot as you can get—were hanging on every word and making damn sure we didn't miss a thing.

We were told it would be three days of hockey, in something of a hybrid event: a training camp for some, mixed with a tryout for others. I was one of the others. Four teams were formed out of all the players there—and for three days, with Geoffrion, Ruel, and other Montreal Canadiens coaches in the stands, along with scouts and team management, those teams would scrimmage against each other. Boston and Northeastern University seemed a long way away.

The meeting broke up. And within twenty minutes it all became real for me. Warm ups were over and the puck was dropped and I was skating on the same line as Guy Lafleur and doing everything I could to shake off the nerves and skate through the intimidation.

I was still in awe, but I skated with determination, and with a residual dislike of the Montreal Canadiens. I wanted to catch someone's eye, even if for a little bit, even for one fraction of one second.

I also realized I could get sent home at any moment. For some, that fear and unease can paralyze them or at least cause their game to drop and make them to lose their stride and lose sight of what needs to be done. But for me, fear and unease focused me tremendously and kept me alert and on my game.

Of course, as was the case throughout my entire life and career, I didn't take any shit from anyone. I didn't give a fuck who it was. I slammed Guy Lapointe into the boards, and his only response was to look at me as if to say, "What the fuck do you think you are doing?" Really, he seemed to be mildly pissed off, but more surprised. I just kept hustling and skating.

Right after I hit Lapointe, Steve Shutt came at me. He slashed me—and, you know, I slashed him right back. He was as surprised as Lapointe, but he said, "What the fuck are you doing?" And I said, "Fuck you. Go fuck yourself. You slashed me and I slashed you." He kind of shook his head and kept going. I think he figured I was a nobody (which was right), whom he would never see again after training camp (which was wrong).

I skated full-out those three days, and I was physical and didn't let anyone push me around. I guess I did well enough, because I didn't get cut.

Instead, I was told I was on my way to Halifax, where I was going to be given a tryout with the Nova Scotia Voyageurs, the Canadiens' American Hockey League affiliate.

Before flying to Nova Scotia, the team had me take a press photo wearing an actual Habs jersey. I took this as a good sign.

15

THE VEES

I WAS LOOKING FORWARD to my chance with the Voyageurs—one reason being that two guys I knew from hockey in the Boston area, both of whom I played against in college, were on the team.

One of the guys was Timmy Burke, a defenseman, who grew up in Melrose, a town just north of Boston, and who had a hell of a career at the University of New Hampshire. He was starting his third season with the Voyageurs. And then there was Rick Meagher, a kid from Ontario who'd played for Boston University, including a season when the Boston University Terriers won the NCAA championship.

So, just four days into my stay in Canada, I took a flight to Halifax, a city that I immediately felt some kinship with because, like Boston, it sat on the Atlantic Ocean and it had a thriving maritime and fishing trade. Salty sea air coursed through that town. Actually, the Boston area has a decent-sized slice of the population who are descended from the Scottish and Irish who immigrated to Nova Scotia in the 1700s.

So my first impulse was to like the city. But then again, Halifax was surely a small place, about the size of Worcester, Massachusetts, and I wasn't sure how well I would like it if I had to stay there for a long time.

The Canadiens put me up in the Citadel Inn in downtown Halifax. It was nice.

My first day of training with the Voyageurs, known locally as the "Vees," was the morning after the day I arrived. The team practiced and played its games at the Metro Centre, which was about a five-minute walk from my hotel. So that day, I just walked from the hotel to the arena. From the outside, the Metro Centre was not spectacular by any means—it was like this massive rectangle of gray cement and large, dark windows that was set lower than the surrounding area.

Well, this was the AHL, after all—no frills. When I got to the locker room, I started meeting some of the guys, and soon enough Timmy Burke came along. He knew I was on the way, and it was great to see him. Before I got on the ice that day, I also met up again with Rick Meagher.

Both Timmy and Rick would be helpful to me in my stay with the Voyageurs, but it was Timmy who really took me under his wing and helped me get the lay of the land—or the ice, as it were.

Before I took the ice for my initial skate with the team, I met the Voyageurs' coach, Bert Templeton, who I knew was widely respected and encouraged fierce and physical play. He was also a straight shooter and a straight talker, and didn't hold back with anyone, including the press.

Templeton would continue for years to urge his players to dish it out—and there was no better example of that than when he coached the Canadian team at the World Junior Hockey Championship in 1987 in Piestany, Czechoslovakia.

In that tournament, Canada played the Soviet Union in the final. At 13:53 of the second period of the game—with Canada up 4–2 and guaranteed a silver medal if it won and a gold medal if it won by four goals or more—all hell broke loose. Templeton and the Canadian players always maintained that the Soviets started it, but one thing was certain: the teams engaged in a brawl that got everyone off the benches. It was a keeper, with all the players going at it. There were gloves and sticks and helmets strewn across the rink. It went on for twenty minutes—and it might still be going on today had the rink staff not turned off the lights.

Many hockey fans and hockey-fight enthusiasts called this throw-down, which is now known as the "Punch-up in Piestany," the greatest hockey fight of all time. Among those involved in the game and the fight were future NHL stars from both teams: on the Canadian side, Theo Fleury, Brendan Shanahan, and Pierre Turgeon; and on the Soviet side, Alexander Mogilny and Sergei Fedorov.

All the players and coaches of the teams received suspensions of three years—although the player suspensions were quickly lifted. Templeton was roundly accused of not controlling his players. He never apologized, and said, "We're convinced in our own minds we did what was right."

It was no surprise to anybody that it didn't take long for Bert Templeton and me to forge a strong bond. I liked playing for him, and he liked my physical, never-back-down-and-never-stay-down approach to hockey.

There was a training camp of seven days in Halifax before we played our first exhibition game.

We practiced once a day, in the morning, for about two hours on the ice of the Metro Centre, which was an arena that wasn't finished. I mean, the ice and rink itself were fine, and there was a lower level of seats that were all orange, which you didn't notice during a game when people's asses were parked on them, but when you were practicing it got a bit garish. But on the upper level, where there should have been seats, there were none.

We also did something I had never done before: off-ice circuit training, which involved stations of weight lifting and plyometrics. That week was a confidence builder for me, for I proved to myself that I could play at that level. Timmy Burke was continually encouraging me, and this helped out a lot. I didn't fight at all in the training camp, but I sure as hell was physical, and I knew that Bert Templeton took notice of this.

At the end of camp, the Voyageurs began a series of four exhibition games, all against the New Brunswick Hawks, an AHL team based in Moncton, New Brunswick, which was a shared affiliate of the Chicago Blackhawks and Toronto Maple Leafs. We played one game on our home ice, another at their place, the Moncton Coliseum, and the other two at other venues in New Brunswick.

Now, remember, I still didn't have a contract, and I wasn't making any money. I only received a per diem and had my room paid for. I didn't really care, though, because I was living my dream.

It was in the second exhibition game, which was on the road, that I had my first "Knuckles" moment in the pros. I'm not sure at what point it was in the game, but I got into it a bit with a winger on the Hawks whose name was Alain "Bam-Bam" Bélanger. He was talented and tough, and he would go on to play a bit in the NHL. Anyway, we scuffled and I punched him the chest. We got separated, and he said some shit to me like he was going to get me back or whatever. Fuck him.

So I got back to the bench, and my teammate Dave Allison—a guy I really didn't know, but I could tell he had little respect for me because I'd come up through the college ranks—said to me, "Hey, college kid, what are you trying to do—start a brawl? You ever been in a brawl before? Wake up!"

I glared back at him and said, "Fuck you. What do you know about brawls? I've been in plenty of fucking brawls and I can take care of myself. Don't fucking worry about me."

Allison didn't know that I had fought all the time growing up in Boston—on the street, not in some hockey rink. Allison stared at me wide-eyed but didn't say anything back.

And I noticed, as I got ready to step on the ice for the next shift, that Bert Templeton was looking at me; he was smiling and he gave

My dad and me back in 1958.

Here I am in the fourth grade,
still kind of innocent.

As a senior in high school.
Check out the nice tie I was wearing.

That's me on the left with my dad, Henry, and my brother, Stephan.

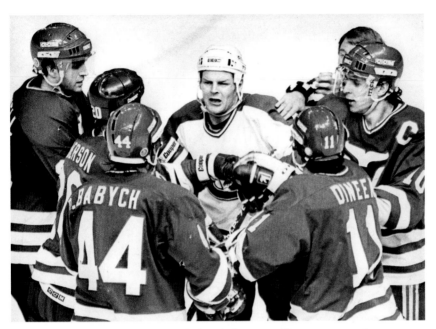

Fighting the Hartford Whalers. Where are all my teammates?

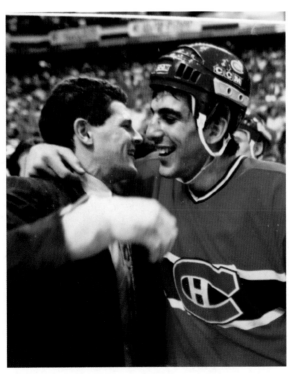

With Chris Chelios (Chelly) after winning the Stanley
Cup with the Montreal Canadiens.

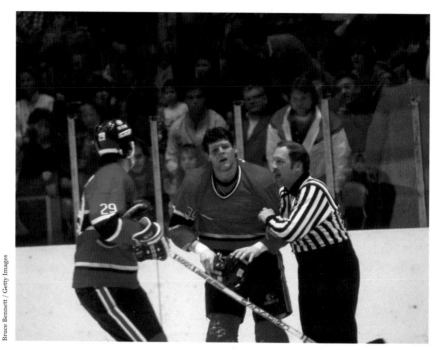

After a fight at Madison Square Garden in the mid-1980s.

Fighting Daryl Stanley of the Philadelphia Flyers during the 1987 playoffs.

Dave Semenko of the Hartford Whalers tries to get at me while Guy Carbonneau attempts to hold Semenko back, at the Hartford Civic Center in Hartford, Connecticut, in February 1987.

My Ranger teammates. Clockwise from the top left: Gresch (Ron Greschner), James Patrick, Beezer (John Vanbiesbrouck), me, Doggie Doo (Dave Shaw), and Harpo (Mark Hardy).

Little Chris still looks up to his dad (at least I hope he does!).

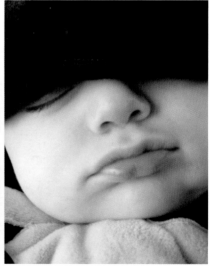

My grandson Nolan hugging his grampy.   My grandson Colin at eight months.

Holding Colin with Nolan and their nanny.

With Colin and his great-grandmother, Leslie Nilan.

Chris, Tara, and Colleen: my three beautiful children.

me a nod. I nodded back. Maybe I did have some sort of future in this pro hockey.

So the next shift, I got back on the ice, and who comes out but Bélanger. The linesman dropped the puck and we went at it right away. I gave it to him pretty good. In boxing terms, I would have won a unanimous decision. In the locker room, between periods, Allison just looked at me with an expression of disbelief and confusion.

After the four exhibition games were up, Templeton told me the Canadiens had extended my tryout in the form of the first five games of the AHL regular season. I would be paid $200 a game—and if it worked out, I could stay on the team, continue to make $200 a game, and chase my dream of playing in the NHL. Of course, I was often on the phone with Karen and with my family, keeping them up to date on what was happening.

I didn't dress for the first game of the tryout period in Halifax, but I got on the ice for the second game, also in the Metro Centre, and scored a goal and had an assist. We won and I didn't get assessed a single penalty minute. No penalty minutes in a game for me—strange.

Our next game, the third of my pro career, was going to be in Portland, Maine, against the Maine Mariners, the farm team of the Philadelphia Flyers. At the time, the Flyers were known as the Broad Street Bullies, a nickname they had earned for the physical and intimidating brand of hockey they played and because their home ice was the Philadelphia Spectrum, located at the foot of Broad Street.

The Flyers not only roughed and beat up the competition, they beat the opposition on the scoreboard as well. From 1974 through

1980, the Flyers appeared in four Stanley Cup finals, winning back-to-back Cups in '74 and '75. This game would be a test for me in that the Mariners had that bullying Flyers culture set deep within them. It was also a big game for me because it would be an opportunity for my parents and Karen to see me play, since Portland was only about an hour's drive from West Roxbury.

So the big night arrived, and Henry, Leslie, and Karen were in the stands. I saw them in warm ups and waved to them. Well, wouldn't you know it, I was on the ice for my second shift of the night, and I got slashed by Glen Cochrane, a rugged Mariner defenseman who had established himself as a junior in the Western Canada Hockey League as a brawler who could visit hurt on you fast. Cochrane was six foot two and 205 pounds. And, as I quickly found out, he not only shot left, but he threw left-handed. Cochrane would go on to play ten years in the NHL, largely as a resident enforcer for five different teams.

I had already resolved, of course, that I wasn't taking anything from anyone. I turned toward him and cracked him with an open-glove hand to the side of his helmet. That did it—it was on. We dropped the gloves and rolled up the sleeves and started trading blows. We both landed punches, but I hit him with a good right that opened up a gash under his eye. He went nuts, and so did I. So we spilled over in a clutch, and the refs separated us. We both got tossed from the game.

It was an early exit for me, but I didn't care so much because my parents and my girlfriend finally got to see me play in the pros. I was thrilled. But my dad didn't see it that way. After the game, I walked out of the locker room and into the hall, where family and friends of the players were waiting for us. I gave my parents a hug, and Karen a big hug and a kiss. Then my father told me he wasn't too happy about driving up to Portland to watch his kid play a few minutes and then get ejected. I was a bit taken aback, but I apologized and said that next time I would try to stay in the game. Not sure if I really meant it.

Apparently, I didn't—because over the next couple weeks we

played three more times in Portland, and I got tossed from two of the games. My dad read me the riot act the second time I got tossed, but he didn't really have much to say to me the third time I got thrown out of a game, because he also got ejected. Well, sort of.

Yes, the night the Nilans got thrown out. Everything was in place in the second period—at least I made it that far—and, there I was, sprinting across the ice and—kaboom—I caught Portland's Gary Morrison with his head down and leveled him. (A coaching point to all you young players: always keep your head up.) He was pissed. He got up and we went at it. I got him quickly with two hard shots and then with a third that stunned him and opened a cut above his left eye. I threw him down and just sat on him, and didn't hit him, because I could tell he was hurt.

Meanwhile, five of my teammates had paired up for fights. Fifteen seconds later, Mariners coach Bob McCammon gave his players on the bench the okay to go over the boards and join in— which, of course, they did. Templeton had no choice—he released our hounds. With all the nastiness happening all around, the refs tossed Cochrane and me, which I thought was smart. Now, as bad as things were out there, if Cochrane and I hadn't left the ice, we would have been suspended for the following game. I got off the ice first, and one of the refs held Cochrane back until I was down the aisle between the stands. Fans were dropping cups of soda and beer—and hot dogs—on me. I looked back. Cochrane stepped onto the rubber and I thought he was going to continue on his way to the Mariners' locker room. But he spun around and went back onto the ice. I said fuck that and I started back toward the ice as well. I never made it, because I got tackled by about five guys at once, all of them wearing yellow security guard jackets. I started wrestling with and fighting them. I was losing.

If you didn't think things could get any weirder, then, well, you don't know the AHL or the Nilan family. As I was getting my whooping, unbeknownst to me, my dad was running and climbing down the stands on his way to my rescue. Soon enough, he was in the fray, grabbing guys and throwing punches. His luck was that he punched an off-duty Portland cop who was moonlighting on a security gig. One of my teammates, goaltender Richard Sévigny, who was playing that night—and a good fighter in his own right—came off the ice and to our aid.

Next, there were a couple uniformed cops, on duty, armed, grabbing my father, cuffing him, and dragging his ass out of there.

This was just beautiful. Henry Nilan, who had been giving me shit for getting thrown out of a hockey game, not only got himself booted from the game, but pinched as well. As they say, you can't make this shit up.

The refs and law enforcement shuttered the game. Finis. The Voyageurs went to their locker room and the Mariners to theirs. I didn't even shower; I threw off my equipment and jumped into my street clothes, and then walked out to the hallway, where I knew my mother and Karen would be waiting. My mother was beside herself; Karen was just shaking her head.

My mom asked what we were going to do. I wasn't sure, so I went back into the locker room and asked Bert what we should do. Bert wasn't happy about any of this, but he was also a stand-up guy. He said he would hold the team bus, and he would go down to the police station with us and see if we could work something out, which, thankfully, we did. The cops let my dad go with no fine.

Henry Nilan was less than contrite about what happened—and, you know, I couldn't really squabble with him about that. After all, he was sticking up for his kid.

CHRIS NILAN

Next, it was back to Halifax for two more games. I was getting plenty of ice time and I was getting clear license to play hockey the way I thought it should be played. And what a relief—what liberation. This was the first time I had ever played at a level, and in a league, in which I could fight and throttle people and not get thrown out of the game. What was even better was that this style of hockey—one that suited me just right—seemed to meet with the approval of my coach.

I was racking up penalty minutes at an astonishing pace, spending about six minutes a game in the penalty box. I fought every tough guy out there. I also put the puck in the net, scoring three goals and picking up two assists in the first ten games. I found that when you established yourself physically on the ice, avenues opened up and pockets of space appeared—and that, of course, was attributable to the opposition not being keen on jostling and bumping you.

What I didn't know was that every game the Vees played was attended in person by scouts from the Canadiens' front office. I didn't know that my performance was being evaluated and that they were seeing evidence of the talent and ability the Canadiens needed. Or that, in phone calls to the Montreal front office, the scouts were speaking highly of me.

The morning after the tenth game I played for the Vees, as I arrived in the locker room at the Metro Centre for practice, Bert Templeton stepped out of his office and motioned to me that he wanted to see me. I walked over and into his office. The coach was sitting in a swivel chair and leaning back with a smile on his face. He didn't waste any time in telling me the Montreal Canadiens wanted to sign me to a contract.

I wondered if he was kidding. For a second or two, I thought it might be one of those gags you pull on the new kid, which I was.

I even asked Templeton if he was kidding, and he laughed and said that no, he was not. Then he asked me who my agent was.

Agent? What agent? I sheepishly told Templeton I didn't have one.

It looked like I would have to get one.

16

THE NHL

NEGOTIATING MY FIRST PRO CONTRACT was Bill Mauer, a friend of Rod Langway. I signed a two-year deal that would pay me $17,500 a year when I was in the AHL, and $65,000 a season if I was with the Canadiens in the NHL.

I had played forty-nine games for the Voyageurs. During those forty-nine games, I had scored fifteen goals, tallied ten assists, and fought every tough guy in the league, winning just about every fight.

The morning after my forty-ninth game, Bert Templeton again called me into his office. This time, he told me I was being brought up—to the varsity, to the big time, to the Montreal Canadiens. I would be wearing a Habs sweater—the next night.

Tomorrow night.

How could this be happening? Not that I was going to argue with any of it. A year before, I was an undistinguished player on a so-so Division I college hockey team, and now I was on my way to suit up and play for the Montreal Canadiens. Yes, truth is sometimes stranger than fiction.

Bert told me to get moving, that I had an afternoon flight to Atlanta. He gave me meal money, shook my hand, and said good luck.

I ran back to my apartment and called my parents, and then I called Karen and told her to cancel the plans she had made to come up to Halifax the next day to see me. I called my brothers and sisters. And then I called Fran Flaherty.

Fran had always said that if I made it to the NHL, no matter where that first game was played, he would be in the stands. I told him he didn't have to make the trip—but he wouldn't hear of it. He said he would be there.

So I got in the cab, and we were halfway to the airport when . . . oh, shit . . . I had forgotten my equipment! We had to turn around and go back. Thankfully, I had given myself plenty of time to make the flight, and I was able to go back, grab my gear, and make the flight with a half hour to spare.

I arrived late that night in Atlanta, took a cab to the hotel, and managed to get some sleep. When I got up in the morning, I made calls to Karen and my parents, telling them that everything seemed unreal. I met up with my teammates for the first time at a team luncheon at the hotel. Before we sat down, I talked with Claude Ruel, who was now the Montreal coach. At lunch, Rod Langway was on one side of me and Larry Robinson on the other. They were friendly; that put me at ease.

In warm ups that night at the Omni, I heard some guy screaming my name in the stands. I was like, "Wait, I know that voice." Sure enough, I followed where the voice was coming from, and there he was, Franny Flaherty, just like he said he would be when I played my first game in the NHL. He was wearing a big old cowboy hat and smiling, laughing, and yelling. That effort and gesture of kindness I will never forget.

So how was opening night for Chris Nilan in the NHL? As they say in Montreal, comme ci, comme ça. Yeah, so-so: not so bad, not so good.

I got in two shifts, and I was very nervous, not keyed in on the action. Thankfully, I didn't mess up. We got out of there with a 3–3 tie. I suited up but didn't play in the next two games, which were back in Montreal.

The next time I was on the ice for the Habs was in Philadelphia. That made sense. The Flyers still had a bit of that Broad Street Bullies persona, and dealing with bullies was what I was good at. This game, played on March 2, was a sort of "coming of age" event for me in the NHL.

Maybe in the back of my mind I understood that, when we traveled to Philly and met up with the Broad Street Bullies, it would be the setting and opponent that the Montreal coaching and scouting staff had in mind when they started to follow my minor-league play with more interest—and when they decided to bring me up to the big leagues. My first point and my first fight—all in the same game.

It was early in the first period. There was a face-off in our zone. As I readied myself outside the circle for the puck drop, who brushed up next to me but the Flyers' Bob "Hound Dog" Kelly, a nine-year NHL veteran, all with Philly, and the team's enforcer. Kelly sort of snickered and said, "So, why have they brought you up to fight for these guys? Is that why you are here?"

It seems that the scouting report that Hound Dog, who was about my size, had received on me was accurate.

No sooner did the puck hit the ice than Hound Dog chopped me across the waist with his stick. Here we go—welcome to prime time. We shook off our gloves. And there we were, Bob "Hound Dog" Kelly and Chris "Knuckles" Nilan, toe to toe, skate to skate, throwing bombs. I connected with a right that dazed Kelly, and I threw him down. I think my aggressiveness made my coach and teammates happy.

It was a good night. In the third period, I scored my first NHL point, assisting Pierre Mondou on the game-winning goal.

❖

Since I now had a contract, I needed a place to stay when in Montreal. I signed a lease on an apartment in a building around the corner from the Forum. Here was my commute to work: walk from my apartment down the hallway to the elevator, get in the elevator, take it three floors down to the lobby, walk across the lobby and out the front door to the sidewalk, and then around the corner to my "office."

This first season in the league was about getting my NHL legs under me. It was an exciting time—and also one in which I felt like an outsider. I mean, really, I was an aberration—a kid from America playing in the NHL when there were very few Americans in the NHL. There were twenty-eight players on the 1979–80 Habs roster; of this number, twenty-five were from Canada, and three—Rick Chartraw, Rod Langway, and me—were from the US. Yet, curiously, I was the only player on the team born in America. Chartraw was born in Venezuela while his father was employed there as an engineer; Langway was born in Taiwan when his father was in the US military and stationed on the island.

Montreal had nineteen games remaining in its regular season when I was brought up to the big time. I played in fifteen of those games, getting two assists and racking up fifty penalty minutes. Montreal was on a roll at home in the final stretch of the regular season, winning its final twenty games at the Forum.

Many of the Canadian players on the team were fluent in French, while I couldn't speak or understand a lick of it. That was a barrier.

Yet all my teammates were great to me—as were Claude Ruel

and his staff. Claude worked with me every day after practice. He was determined that I would be more than an enforcer. He gave me extra shooting drills, and as he instructed and pushed me to improve my skating, he would often yell, "Jump on your skates, Yankee boy."

And I'll say it again—it was almost beyond belief, where I had been and where I was now. I now skated with hockey royalty—Lafleur, Larouche, Shutt, Robinson, Mondou, Lambert, Napier, and Langway.

Every time I pulled on that Montreal Canadiens sweater, I had to pinch myself.

My reputation was growing around the league as someone the Canadiens had brought up to provide muscle and a jostling presence. I must say I was confident—I thought my bad-boy, Boston knuckles upbringing had sufficiently prepared me for any comer.

On April 5 we hosted Boston, winning easily 6–1. I, however, had a less successful evening, getting a tie in one fight and losing the other. But if you watch the footage of the fights, you can see I attacked with vigor and was able to skate directly to the penalty box. First on the fight card that night for me was Stan Jonathan, the rugged First Nations player from Ohsweken, Ontario. Jonathan had been in the league—and with the Bruins—for about four-and-a-half seasons. We went at it about two-thirds of the way through the first period. It was a tie. We each landed roughly the same number of punches. I was impressed, though, with how he changed hands. I put this information away for the future.

At the 3:46 mark of the second period, I was taking a face-off against Terry O'Reilly. O'Reilly, who had been with the Bruins since the 1971–72 season, when the team won the Stanley Cup, was easily one of the toughest and nastiest fighters who ever stepped onto the ice at any level. He was already an established tough-guy legend when we took that face-off—and when I jabbed him while the puck was still in the ref's hand, he took a step back and gave me, a rookie with not even a quarter of a full NHL season behind him, a look of intense anger, one fueled, obviously, by the question, "Who the fuck do you think you are?" No puck got dropped on that face-off; O'Reilly and I went at it with the intent of dropping each other. We threw down. I got O'Reilly good with the opening shot, yet he got me good with several punches after that. I had little counter for his overhand haymakers.

I learned a lesson the proverbial hard way. I resolved right then and there that I needed to be better technically as a fighter. I was operating on a whole new level now—and it wouldn't suffice just to try to overwhelm opponents with ferocity and power.

Again, though, after the fight was broken up, I was able to get right over to the box. Being able to take a punch provided me with an immense physical and emotional advantage during my fight career in hockey. Opponents wore themselves out throwing their best at me, and I was still there—which, of course, was dispiriting, to say the least.

Montreal finished the regular season in first place in the Norris Division. I was used sparingly in the play-offs, but did see shifts, which was great for my confidence and provided me with a valuable education.

Montreal swept Hartford, three games to none, in the first round of the play-offs. We lost in the quarter-final in seven games to the Minnesota North Stars.

The Canadiens did not have a first-round pick in the NHL draft that June. In the second round, with the thirty-sixth-overall pick, they selected the Swedish star Mats Naslund, who would play three more years professionally in Sweden before joining Montreal.

Six picks later, also in the second round, Montreal chose a twenty-year-old center from Sept-Îles, Quebec, by the name of Guy Carbonneau. Starting a couple seasons later, and for the better part of five consecutive seasons after that, I would play on one of Guy's wings, while Bob Gainey would play the other. This forward line remains, to this day, one of the most effective checking lines in NHL history.

❖

In the off-season, I worked construction back in Boston. I knew well that it could all go away—my good fortune, which had arrived through a strange, unusual, and I daresay almost miraculous path. I needed to stay grounded. I needed to keep working.

In August, I proposed to Karen. She said yes. Our wedding would be in Boston the following June.

17

BECOMING A HAB

IN MY SECOND TRAINING CAMP, and my first as a bona fide Montreal Canadien, I made it known to all my teammates that I understood my role, but that I wanted to be a total hockey player. And I let everyone know I would do what I had to in order to round out my game and deliver value to the Habs as more than an enforcer.

What was beyond encouraging was that my teammates and the coaches made it known over and over that they wanted me to be a total hockey player, too. Bob Gainey had no issue with me following him in practice and asking questions. He took extra time to go over how I could best position myself to score, and he would show me drills I could do to more quickly and efficiently direct a puck to where it needed to be. He focused especially on how best to handle a puck in the areas on the ice where the puck and I would most frequently intersect. And then there were the skating drills; he would skate in front of me and I would take his lead and accustom myself to generating more power with each stride.

Guy Lafleur counseled me on ways to look at the game—to "see" the game—and how to go on the attack with and without the puck. I must admit, and I think that Guy readily understood this, there was only so much he could do to educate and help me see things the way he saw them, and then react in the way he reacted. After all, even though Guy Lafleur worked hard on developing his natural gifts, he was Guy Lafleur, and Chris Nilan's natural gifts were not quite in the same league as Guy's. No matter how hard or how smart I worked and trained, I would never see the game as Guy did or be able to create the magic that he created with the puck.

Still, I surely did profit from Guy's advice and became a better player because of his instruction.

Claude Ruel had me on plenty of shifts right from the first game. Things were spelled out clearly for me, even if no one specifically told me what I had to do. I was not yet a regular in the NHL, and it was my job to check hard and relentlessly; to save pucks, which I got over to our scorers and better stickhandlers; and, when necessary, to punch and attack those who would punch and attack our offensive stars.

Fighting came easily to me; it was becoming a hockey player that was difficult.

I kept the same apartment near the Forum that I'd had the previous season, and Karen was up frequently as a guest. My mom and dad, my sisters and brothers, and my friends made several trips up to Montreal to see me play. Teresa and Jimmy came up twice to see me play.

My family and friends also came to watch me when Montreal played in Boston. But, as I have explained earlier, when I was a Bruins opponent, the Boston fans could be quite nasty to me. After a while, my parents decided to watch those Habs–Bruins games on TV, even though they were played only a couple neighborhoods away from where they lived. I totally understood. My friends continued to

attend games I played at the Garden. They just kept a low profile—
which my family was not capable of doing.

I played in fifty-seven games during the 1980–81 regular season,
with seven goals and eight assists. I also had a team-leading 262 penalty minutes—good for third place in the league behind Vancouver's
Tiger Williams (343) and Paul Holmgren (306) of the Philadelphia
Flyers.

I was getting all sorts of attitude and building belief in myself
during that season.

Here I need to explain, qualify, and specify my role as an enforcer. I was actually something of an enforcer and a provoker. Putting
pressure on the opponent involved far more than punching and
muscling and checking hard—all of which can be contained within
the action of sticking up for a teammate. You see, I liked to antagon-
ize as well. If I could piss off and irritate the guy across from or next
to me without raising my glove, well, that was fine by me. I enjoyed
getting people to lose their cool.

I also liked to be unpredictable. I wanted the opposition to think
that nothing was beyond me. This, of course, was the case—and I
didn't have to intentionally act crazily impulsive or off my rocker;
that was just the way I rolled.

Yes, I know that I had a reputation for having a screw loose.
Actually, I had a few screws loose. I had a lot of energy and pent-
up anger that needed release. When I got tossed from games, I
couldn't just go to the locker room quietly. I needed to break and
throw and knock things over on the way. Whether at the Forum or
the other arenas in the league, I was responsible for long, wide paths

of destruction: broken exit signs, thrown chairs, tables overturned, light bulbs and light fixtures broken, wastebaskets upended, windows smashed, and so on.

I had twenty-six fights that season, and I won more than I lost. And my rep continued to build. That year, I started to develop some nice one-on-one rivalries, including with Rick Lapointe of St. Louis and that snarling bulldog, Stan Jonathan.

I fought Lapointe twice in a game on February 12, winning both times. On April 5, almost a year to the day that I fought Terry O'Reilly and Jonathan in the same game, I had another doubleheader with the Bruins, both with Jonathan. I was getting smarter about fighting, and in the first go-around that day with Stan, I was able to get a hold of his arm and pin it against his body while freeing myself to impose some damage. I gave myself a narrow decision. Not so the second fight of the evening. We faced each other and went right at it. Jonathan landed more punches than I did.

During that first full season, I also landed myself my first game suspension—and initiated what would become a relationship of tight familiarity between Chris Nilan and the NHL front office. Two days after my fights with Rick Lapointe, the Washington Capitals visited us.

Five minutes into the third period of the game, the Capitals' Mark Mulvey and I got into a shouting match. One of the linesmen jumped between us and directed me to go one way and Mulvey the other. Well, to get to Mulvey, I tried to sort of skate through the ref. In doing so, I pushed against him, not using my arms or hands—but when I did so, he fell and hit the ice. He was all right, but it was not good —and I admit I was in the wrong. You never bump a ref. I was suspended for two games.

Montreal finished with the best record in the Norris Division for the regular season. We only lost once in our last twenty-seven home games. Yet when we got to the play-offs, we were without our main offensive weapon, Guy Lafleur. Guy had been injured on and off during the regular season, playing only fifty-one games. He was unavailable in the postseason. I think this threw us off our game.

I played in one of the three first-round play-off games against Edmonton. Again, we were off and not in sync, and all it took were three games out of five, an Edmonton sweep, to end our season.

Claude Ruel, a man I admired tremendously, resigned as coach following the sweep.

I was disappointed that we didn't go further. But I was fully confident that great things were ahead for Montreal—and for Chris Nilan.

18

MARRIED

WHAT A WHIRLWIND. A couple years prior, I was an unheralded American college hockey player, and now I had just completed my first full season with the Montreal Canadiens and was under contract with the Habs.

The Montreal Canadiens had signed me, Chris Nilan, to a contract.

Best yet, I was marrying Karen. I had a lot of conflict and indecision in my life. I had made plenty of mistakes. I was sure, though—actually, more certain of it than anything else in my life—that marrying Karen was the right and best thing to do. I deeply loved her. And I knew I would be a good husband and good father. And, let's face it, having a good-paying and steady job would be more than a convenience as we built that life together.

Karen and I were married on June 20, 1981, at St. Augustine's in South Boston. Officiating the wedding was a man named Father Ryan, a great guy and super priest. Karen had gotten to know Father Ryan as well, and she thought he was just wonderful, as did most anyone who met him.

Our reception was held at one of Boston's grand hotels, the Copley Plaza Hotel. It was a beautiful event. When you consider that, among the guests at the ceremony and the reception were my Montreal teammates (Bob Gainey, Yvon Lambert, Rod Langway,

Mark Napier, Doug Risebrough, Larry Robinson, and Steve Shutt), my father's Green Beret comrades, and Jimmy Bulger and some of his "friends," what you had there was one of the toughest and most badass crowds of all time. That group could have invaded and conquered a small country.

For our honeymoon, we spent two weeks in Hawaii.

It was the summer of 1981, and I was on top of the world.

19

BECOMING A PLAYER

AT THE END OF the 1981–82 season, Claude Ruel went to the front office and Montreal brought in Bob "Crease" Berry, who had resigned the previous April as coach of the Los Angeles Kings, as their new head coach. Prior to coaching L.A., Berry had a strong career as a forward for the Kings, scoring 159 goals and 195 assists over seven years. In each of the three seasons he coached the Kings, they made it to the play-offs, yet lost in the opening round each year.

Perhaps Berry's top accomplishment as coach of Los Angeles was in putting together one of the most potent and productive NHL scoring lines of all time, the Triple Crown Line of Marcel Dionne, Charlie Simmer, and Dave Taylor. Berry would have limited success coaching the Habs, but again he was able to build a potent line—one that gave opponents lots of trouble for five seasons, but not as much offensively as defensively.

Berry's number one priority in pursuit of victory was to reinforce the veteran stars—Guy Lafleur, Bon Gainey, Steve Shutt, and Larry Robinson—with younger players. Three of those younger players who contributed strongly right out of the gate in the new season were Keith Acton, a center from Whitchurch-Stouffville, Ontario, who would soon be centering a line with Lafleur and Shutt; Doug

Wickenheiser, a center from Regina, Saskatchewan; and forward Craig Laughlin, an Ontario kid.

The Habs had a solid trio of goaltenders in Rick Wamsley, Denis Herron, and Richard Sévigny.

Starting with the 1981–82 season, the Habs would be in the Adams Division. Along with Montreal, the division had the Boston Bruins, Buffalo Sabres, Quebec Nordiques, and Hartford Whalers. Among these opponents, Montreal had especially intense rivalries with the Bruins and Nordiques.

Many in the know about hockey considered that the season might be something of a rebuilding campaign. Yet through the first month of play and eleven games, we were—save for a Halloween night loss to the New York Islanders—undefeated, albeit at 6-1-4. Still, there was no doubt that we were very good.

My role remained, mostly, that of muscle and enforcer. There still was an occasional game in which I didn't get a shift. But, also, I had the opportunity to develop my total game, and there were episodes in which I demonstrated I could do more than punch, slash, pummel, and menace.

In a game in Denver on November 11, I took a big step toward rounding out my hockey player résumé when I joined in on the scoring in a Montreal rout. I had two goals that night in our 9-0 win. Of course, as would be the natural ebb and flow of my NHL career, what continued to attract more attention among the fans and in the press was not my scoring, passing, or skating, but my roughhousing and intemperate behavior.

Like my outburst on November 21 at the Montreal Forum.

That night, we had 10-3-5 record, and we faced the Pittsburgh Penguins. With the second period almost over, I came up behind Pittsburgh's Paul Baxter and gave him a light tap with my stick on the side of his leg. He responded by pitching the blade of his stick at my face. I immediately grabbed him and threw him down, and he covered, but I still slammed a couple rights to the side of his helmet before we were separated.

And let me tell you here that Paul Baxter was a virtuoso at creating a situation in which he started trouble without the refs seeing it, but when the guy he pissed off went at him, the refs would have a good line of sight on the retaliation. Yes, Baxter could be infuriating.

Anyway, we were in adjoining penalty boxes; Baxter had his helmet off—and, out of earshot of the officials, he taunted me. He said that next time he was going to "give it to me in the other eye." Did I tell you that Paul Baxter could be infuriating? So I reached into a bucket of frozen pucks that was under the bench on which I was sitting and fired one directly at Baxter, who was maybe five yards away. Bull's-eye! The edge of the puck cracked against the top of his head. Baxter's noggin snapped back, and a cut immediately formed. Pronto, there was screaming and yelling and pointing from players and coaches on the Penguins' bench. Whistles blew and the zebra stripes sprinted toward the penalty boxes.

I was thrown out of the game. And Baxter went to our training room, where our team doctor, Dr. David Mulder, would stitch him up (the gash would require ten stitches). But I wasn't done. I felt Baxter, doing what he did best—ginning up a problem and then not facing official consequences for actions—had gotten the better of me. I went to the Montreal training room, stewing and furious. I pushed open the door, and there was Baxter, lying down, with Dr. Mulder about to apply stitches. Baxter saw me and immediately sat up. I never got to him, though, because, seemingly out of nowhere, five security guards jumped on me.

I didn't put up much resistance. I realized that, even for me, what I was doing was pretty twisted. I wrestled my way toward the door, and then the security guards pushed me into the hallway. I quickly, and with a bit of embarrassment, went to the Habs' locker room.

Funny thing: the puck-throwing got me a two-game suspension. I didn't receive any other penalty for attacking Paul Baxter off the ice. So maybe I got the better of Baxter in this one.

❖

That season, I saw time in forty-nine games. I had seven goals, four assists, and again led the Habs in penalty minutes with 204. I was in thirty-four altercations on the ice; this includes twenty-seven fights and participation in six brawls. I was busy.

Our regular-season record was 46–17–17, good for first place in the Adams Division and third in the entire league. We had win streaks of eleven, six, and five games. Finishing in second place was Boston, followed by Buffalo, Quebec, and then Hartford. Our first-round play-off opponent was our nemesis, the Nordiques, which finished tenth overall, twenty-seven points behind us in the standings. Montreal and Quebec had played eight times during the regular season, with each team getting three wins, three losses, and two ties.

The last of those games was on March 27 at the Forum. Bad blood flowed in both a metaphorical and literal sense. One hundred and fifty-two penalty minutes were assessed in our 4–2 win, which was the sixteenth consecutive road loss for the Nordiques. I fought Norman Rochefort in the first period, and André Dupont in the third. There was a lot of grabbing and wrestling in both matches—and no clear winner. It all contributed to the ongoing and growing friction between our teams.

Our teams did not like each other. Not at all.

It was the battle of la belle province.

Not having Steve Shutt, who was unavailable because of injury, in the series would hurt. But beyond Steve, we were a fairly health bunch.

Montreal opened with an easy 5–1 win. Mark Napier and Mario Tremblay each had two goals to pace the victory. The next night, Quebec evened the series with a 3–2 win, even though their top scorer, Peter Stastny, was out with a kidney ailment. We outshot Quebec 35–17 in that game. The Nordiques' goaltender Daniel Bouchard had a hell of game. After losing 2–1 in game three on the road, we faced the awful possibility of losing the next game, and the series, in Quebec—and getting bounced in the first play-off round for the second consecutive year.

With everything at stake in game four, it was no surprise that something blew. It blew at 9:20 of the first period. We were up 1–0 at that time on a Doug Risebrough goal on which I assisted.

I didn't start the fun—really, you can check the film.

After the Habs' Jeff Brubaker slammed Quebec's Dave Pichette hard against the boards, Wally Weir of the Nordiques started with Brubaker. Rod Langway began to wrestle with Pichette—but Rod wasn't going to take himself out of the game for ten minutes by dropping his gloves.

I needed to jump in, which I did, against Pat Hickey. We got into a tugging and wrestling match and then fell to the ice. We jumped up and I slammed home two rights. Hickey, for whatever reason, turned his back on me and skated toward the Langway–Pichette détente. Never a good idea to turn your back on me; I never worried about being a gentleman in a fight. I went after Hickey and cracked him upside the head when he wasn't looking; it was a good shot—so good it broke my hand. A slew of Nordiques tried to come over and help Hickey out. One of them, Jean Hamel, tackled me. We were rolling on the ice when the refs pulled us apart.

Peace was not restored until fifteen minutes after the commencement of hostilities. I received a misconduct, good for ten of the 159 total minutes assessed for the brawl.

Oh yeah, after hockey resumed, Risebrough scored another goal and Pierre Mondou added two goals of his own in our 6–2 win.

I must tell you, heading back to Montreal and the deciding game, we all felt good about our chances to move on to the division final. I would play that night with the broken hand.

In game five, we were down 2–0 in the third period, but tied the game to put it into overtime. OT didn't last long. On an odd-man rush, Dale Hunter scored to end things only twenty-two seconds into the extra frame.

Once again, we were done skating in mid-April. In the 1981 and '82 play-offs, we were 2–6 and 1–4 at home.

It is difficult to explain just how painful this loss was to the Quebec Nordiques. It was very painful—very.

In the off-season, the Canadiens and Washington Capitals engineered a blockbuster trade in which we exchanged Rod Langway, Doug Jarvis, Craig Laughlin, and Brian Engblom for Ryan Walter and Rick Green. It was a trade that would work out well for both clubs; still, it was tough to see my fellow Boston-area guy, Langway, go.

20

ON FIGHTING

I GUESS THIS POINT in the book is as good as any to address the issue.

The movie *The Last Gladiators* opens with a shot of my hands—my gnarled hands and knuckles—and I make a fist of my right hand and hold the bridge of that fist in front of the camera. I smack the fist into the open palm of my left hand. I pinch the fingers of one hand with those of the other.

As my hands, my fingers, mash and roll, I say, "You know, probably 18,999 people in the stands, out of the 19,000, at one time or another, wherever they work, probably wanted to punch somebody in the mouth—whether it's their boss, somebody they work with, somebody in competition with them. They never get to do it. But they like to see somebody else do it."

They never get to do it. But they like to see somebody else do it.

I had those words, and that scene, in mind when I watched another scene—from an episode of the popular AMC drama *Mad Men*, a show that portrays the business of a Madison Avenue advertising firm, Sterling Cooper Draper Pryce, in the 1960s, and the lives of the people who work at the firm. Seriously, for all you *Mad Men* fans, was there anything better than that scene when Lane Pryce has had enough of the smarmy attitude of Pete Campbell and challenges him to take care of things like a gentleman, right there and then, in the conference room, with Don Draper, Roger Sterling, and Bert Cooper watching? (Gotta love the trash-talking between the two: as Pryce is rolling up his sleeves, he says, "As soon as I raise my hands, I warn you, it will be too late to run." Then Campbell stands up, takes off his jacket, slips the bottom half of his tie into his shirt, and says, "Fine—you want to take your teeth out, or do you want me to knock them out?") Of course, the payoff in the scene is when Lane connects with a right-left combo that breaks and bloodies Campbell's nose and sends the little toad crashing into a console and then flat on his back.

Sometimes the people in the stands "get to do it."

When I agreed to write this book, it was a given that I would have to devote one chapter just to fighting. I never wanted to be known exclusively as a fighter; I wanted to be a complete hockey player. I think I established myself as both. Maybe it will always be in the cards for me to be known first as a fighter, not as a forward who could skate, pass, score, and defend. Ah, I'm not complaining—I lasted thirteen years in the NHL.

What are my thoughts on fighting and the NHL? I'll preface my answer with a little history and background. For centuries, people all over the world have played games—set on a variety of surfaces, from grass to ice to dirt to snow—that involve participants using a stick to bat and slap all sorts of objects toward a goal. But as for modern ice hockey, it has its origins in the early 1800s in Canada. Back then, Canada was part of the British Empire, and British soldiers stationed in Canada during the cold months played a game on snow and ice, yet without skates, that resembled hockey, sort of. By the mid-1800s, the game took off, with the new version involving players on skates on ice.

Hockey's popularity grew rapidly, both in cities and on the frontier. And it was very much a wild frontier sport, not closely officiated and highly physical, which resulted in many fights.

Fighting and hockey became kin. I don't think we should separate the two. But changes should be made. Unplanned, spontaneous fighting needs to remain. It is simply part of the game, deeply embedded in it, and at its core—and it provides hockey with so much of the emotion, spirit, and energy that make it special. But I don't like planned fights—and there are a lot of these in the NHL—in which players agree to go for the purposes of entertainment or settling scores.

When I played, I never was involved in a planned fight. I mean, sure, I might have known one was coming—either one I was going to provoke, or one I was fairly certain someone would start with me. But I didn't have these fights scheduled and set in stone prior to the game. And I don't really call it a planned fight when I am pissed at someone and I say I'm going to get him—whether "getting him" means after the puck drops in a second or at some time far off in the future.

But in terms of planning a fight well in advance, just for the sake of a fight—I think hockey would be better off without it.

What were my strengths as a fighter? I think a fairly good genetic hand was dealt me, in that I was able to take a punch. Go to YouTube and check out some of my fights, and you will see that in a lot of them, whether I ended up getting the win, the loss, or the draw, I took a lot of punches. Yet I very rarely went down. I feel I was a bit like Joe Frazier, the heavyweight boxing great, who waded in and absorbed punches so he could throw and land his own.

As evidence of my ability to take punishment and remain upright and functioning, consider the throwdown I had at the Boston Garden with Jim McKenzie of the Hartford Whalers early in March 1991. I was near the end of my career, and McKenzie, at six foot four and 221 pounds, was strong and tough—and a rookie. People will remember (I sure did) that McKenzie, a lefty, fed me a lot of punches—and definitely outpointed me. But when the fight was broken up, I skated away clearheaded.

Being able to take a punch was a cornerstone of the greatness of two boxing champions from my area—from the city of Brockton, about twenty miles south of Boston.

Rocky Marciano, who retired undefeated as heavyweight champion of the world, took some shots that would have stopped so many others. I mean, if you see his first fight against Jersey Joe Walcott—the one in which Marciano won the championship—and you check out that hook that Walcott pasted Marciano with in the first round, well, that hook would have knocked out an elephant. But not Marciano. He went down, but not for long. He got up and stayed in the fight and knocked out Walcott—actually knocked him out cold—in the thirteenth round.

Marvelous Marvin Hagler moved to Brockton when he was teenager. He became the middleweight champion of the world. He lost a few fights, but, like Marciano, he was never knocked out. In the first round of that memorable brawl he had with Thomas "Hit Man" Hearns, Hearns labeled Hagler with a punch that dropped so many of Hearns's other foes for the ten count. I do think the punch dazed him, even if Hagler will never admit it. But Hagler was dazed only temporarily. In the third round, Hagler walloped Hearns with a reaching right and then a quick combination that ended the bout.

As I've explained earlier, my training ground in fighting was outside of the rink. I fought on the streets of Boston—which meant I fought on the streets and in the alleys and on playgrounds and in front- and backyards and in hallways and anywhere else in Boston and in the surrounding area. This was not disciplined fighting—it was not stylish or artistic fighting—but it was fighting. Out-and-out brawling. I was good at it.

In hockey, I knew what my role was, and no one had to tell me explicitly what to do. In fact, no coach ever told me directly to fight.

But, again, I knew what my job was. And other enforcers knew what their job was. I remember late in the 1985–86 season, the year we won the Cup, the Bruins had just brought up Jay Miller from the minors. Jay was a Boston-area kid—tough and a superb fighter. So there we were, at the Boston Garden, on the first shift we shared in the NHL. Our teammates readied to take a face-off, and Jay and I were shoulder to shoulder, in a crouch, getting ready. Ready to get our blades on the puck? Nah. I turned to Jay and said, "I know why you are here; as soon the puck drops, we are going at it." And we did.

When I got into the AHL, whatever I had learned about fighting, and whatever skills I had in this area, worked effectively enough to establish me as someone who could handle himself and visit some pain and damage on the opponent. Then again, I wasn't in the AHL that long, and I surely didn't take on every tough guy—though I took on enough of them.

But when I arrived in the NHL, I quickly found out I had a lot to learn yet. As I explained earlier, Terry O'Reilly was one of my early teachers. Yeah, I had my bell rung in that one. I got my bell rung for a few reasons—mostly because I was fighting Terry O'Reilly, but also because I was not yet technically savvy or strategic in my approach. I wasn't concerned with blocking or defending, staying balanced, or thinking a move ahead. All I knew how to do was throw punches. I left myself wide open, and I paid for it. O'Reilly caught me twice in the head, and I was definitely seeing fuzzy. But I stayed up, somehow.

When I got to the penalty box, and as I sat there and my senses returned to me, I made a resolution right there, sitting on that bench in the Boston Garden, that from then on, I was not only going to fight hard, but also smart.

Taking a long look at the NHL and at the other enforcers in the game, I understood quickly that most of them were bigger than me— taller, heavier, and with longer arms. In these circumstances, I didn't want to stay outside of them, for that would let them get more of a windup and generate more power in a punch. No, when squaring off against the bigger guy, I needed to get into a clinch and get inside his range to nullify the reach advantage he had on me. I would hold on to his jersey and pull on the sleeve inside the elbow, and this would pin down one arm. As well, if I had him tied up and knew I had taken away a good measure of his punching power, I could afford to let him get off a punch because it was a greatly weakened punch, and once it was thrown, I would throw an uppercut and then loop one over the top.

As for the issue of the fighting strap at the bottom of the jersey, which secures the jersey to your pants, and which—if it doesn't break—prevents an opponent from pulling your jersey over your head and pounding you unimpeded: for sure, I always wanted my jersey hitched tightly to my pants. But let me tell you, whether you fight with your jersey tucked in tightly or your jersey totally off, you have fairly good range of motion to throw. Again, what you don't want is for the jersey to be pulled over your head, or even pulled halfway off, because then you are in something of a straitjacket. It is said that the NHL strongly pushes the fight strap so as to protect the health of players. Ah, not really—that is kind of BS. Why the NHL wants the fight strap is so that its players don't end up punching each other in their underwear.

Anyway, as for maneuvering, if I was bigger and stronger than an opponent, I would sort of reverse strategy. I wanted to be able to throw from the outside—and I would be in no rush to clinch. I wanted room to throw bombs.

Another key advantage I had when fighting was that I worked very hard on my conditioning. Fighting is physically (and emotionally) exhausting—especially when you get into it on skates with full equipment near the end of shift. I could wear opponents down, just by continuing to press, not stopping, even if every punch I threw was not a heavily loaded one.

Of course, as my career progressed, I benefited from two elements that grew side by side, and which abetted and supported one another—I had a screw loose (okay, maybe a couple screws loose) and opponents feared me. Again, one supported the other.

21

THE LINE

IT WAS IN THE 1982–83 season that I felt I was truly becoming a Montreal Canadien. It was as if I wasn't holding on anymore; I was part of the franchise, and part of its future. And, let me tell you, I very much wanted to be part of another run of Montreal Canadiens greatness.

During the summer of 1982, for the first off-season since I'd broken into the NHL, I didn't work construction. Karen and I still spent most of the summer in the Boston area and on Cape Cod, but we also took the time and opportunity to get better acquainted with Montreal and the province of Quebec. We both had a strong affection for the city and province and for the people who lived there. And I must confess that my ego received nice boosts from being recognized and thanked for my contributions.

During Canadiens training camp in the fall of 1982, Karen and I learned she was pregnant with our first child. Now, for sure, living in an area and learning you have a baby on the way will endear you to a place.

Lafleur, Napier, and Robinson would again be our big guns during the season. I tell you, I had to remind myself I was their teammate and not a fan. Really, it could be mesmerizing watching them and the other stars play.

It was during this season that Bob Berry put Guy Carbonneau, Bob Gainey, and me on the same line. It was, first off, a checking and aggressive line designed to stymie and disrupt the offense of our opponents. We became very good at our job very fast. We three skated in sync and cooperatively; we meshed.

Carbonneau, Gainey, and Nilan would stay together as a line for five seasons. Not long after I was taken off that line, in the fall of 1987, I was traded to the New York Rangers.

Off the ice, I—make that Karen and I—continued to become more and more a part of the Canadiens family. We socialized with other players and with the players' wives and girlfriends. Not surprisingly, Carbonneau and Gainey became good friends of mine and were, along with Chris Chelios, the players I was closest with on the team.

A favorite place where the players and their families socialized after games was Ristorante Da Vinci, a superb Italian restaurant in downtown Montreal (still there today and still superb). Owner Sam Mazzaferro was a great guy—and he and the restaurant's head waiter, Aldo, took good care of all of us. I continue to have a hankering for Da Vinci's chicken parmigiana.

On December 15, we came into Vancouver in first place in the Adams Division with a record of 18–7–6. A sold-out crowd of more than 16,000 was in the stands to see a 3–2 Habs win that increased our lead to four points over second-place Boston.

The line of Carbonneau, Gainey, and Nilan had been on its game and was a reason we were playing well. Then again, there was always the very near possibility that yours truly would get himself involved in something that would make him unavailable to the line and the team.

Like what happened that very night against the Canucks.

It all started, but surely didn't finish, only thirteen seconds after the opening face-off, when Curt Fraser and I went at it. We each got a fighting major—and Curt received two minutes for roughing.

But there's more. Lots more.

Five minutes into the second period, Fraser and I fought again. Like the first fight we had that night, neither of us got a decisive victory—a lot of jockeying for position and wrestling, but no good points scored. Anyway, we were pushed apart, we got to our penalty boxes, and I yelled over to him that he could go fuck himself. He told me I could go fuck myself—and then he tossed one of his gloves at me. I snagged the glove and threw it into the stands behind me. This juvenile behavior did not escape the view of the officials, and we were promptly given misconducts—and game misconducts as well, which meant we were both done playing for the evening and we needed to go to our respective locker rooms.

Our journey to our locker rooms was where things got dicey—and totally out of hand. Fraser was walking ahead of me, maybe ten yards. I kept my mouth shut for a few seconds. Then, as he was about to turn right to enter his locker room and I was about to go left to mine, I shouted some choice language at him. He turned around and looked at me, and I charged him. I really think this surprised him. I definitely got the jump on him; I tossed Fraser to the ground and got on top of him and started walloping him. After the rapid rain of blows I delivered, and now feeling that my anger had been properly released, I said to him, "Okay, that is it; we're done. Let's just go to our locker rooms."

Fraser said he was okay with that, but when I let him up he tried to knee me in the stomach. This got me pissed, so while we stood facing each other, I cracked him with a few more good shots, he went down again, and I jumped on him. As the ridiculousness continued, Vancouver assistant trainer Gerry Dean tried to tackle me, which resulted in my teammate, Ric Nattress, who wasn't dressed for the game, tackling Dean.

Soon enough, Vancouver police were among us and they disentangled the bodies.

What sucked is that a local television crew filmed the fight under the stands. It sucked because the NHL front office would get the video.

As they say, truth is stranger than fiction.

Six days after the fight, NHL executive vice president Brian O'Neill handed down two-game suspensions for Fraser and me.

Montreal didn't maintain its lead over Boston in the Adams Division. We finished the regular season in second place with a record of 42–24–14, twelve points behind the Bruins. I led the Habs in penalty minutes for the season, with 218. I fought twenty-one times.

Our postseason was again horrendous. Another one-and-out. We were swept by the Buffalo Sabres in the best-of-five first-round series despite having home-ice advantage to start the series once again.

I did no fighting in the series. I did not do much of anything.

Our team remained, I believe, in a transitional phase. Guy Lafleur and Steve Shutt—Montreal's longtime offensive leaders, future Hall of Famers, and among the best ever, were only thirty-one and thirty years old, respectively, but it did seem that the four-to-five-year stretch of their prime was behind both of them.

I had turned twenty-five the previous February, and if anyone had told me then that, by the time I was thirty or thirty-one, I might already have played my best hockey, I would have laughed.

Soon enough, I would appreciate a different reality.

Enforcers age fast; they break down fast.

❖

Amid the brutality of my job—my dream job, by the way, and one that paid the bills—Karen gave birth to our first child, Colleen, at Royal Victoria Hospital on April 18.

A week later, I signed another contract with the Canadiens. It was for two years, plus an option year. I would have liked a longer deal, but overall, I felt that the Montreal administration treated me well.

Again, I had to remind myself: I had a future here.

22

REAWAKENING

AT THE END of the 1983–84 season, the Canadiens' spirit was reawakened. Yes, we had an unremarkable regular season, finishing fourth in the Adams Division. But Montreal Canadiens hockey achieved its unassailable renown in the Stanley Cup play-offs. Sure, we limped into the play-offs, but we had a gut check in the postseason and began to find again the competitive fire.

My best years as a player—which, fortunately, coincided with the return of the Montreal Canadiens as a force to be taken seriously and about which every team need be worried—were the three consecutive seasons that began with this one.

People cite my point totals during those years: 26 (16 goals, 10 assists) in '83–84; 37 (21 goals, 16 assists) in '84–85; and 34 (19 goals, 15 assists) in '85–86. Yes, these are solid numbers for an enforcer. Our line—again, Carbonneau, Gainey, and Nilan—checked hard and effectively and kept opponents off balance. When you do that, you not only prevent scoring and rushes, but you also open offensive avenues for yourself.

For the first two of those three seasons, I led the NHL in penalty minutes, posting 338 minutes that first year and really outdoing myself the next year with 358 minutes. Not including brawls, in which I shared the love of aggression with my teammates, I fought thirty-three times in 1983–84, when we made it to the Wales Conference final, and forty-two times the next season, when we lost in the divisional final.

When we won the Stanley Cup in 1986, it capped the season in which I had the most one-on-one fights of my career—forty-three.

No matter the season, it seemed, there weren't many consecutive games in which I wasn't involved in some newsworthy aggression.

On March 12, we were in Minnesota. There was 6:33 left in regulation time and we were crushing the North Stars 6–3. I was about to take a slap shot, and the North Stars' Willi Plett, who was, like me, a master at provoking and stirring things up, whacked me in the spine with his stick. Somehow, someway, the refs didn't see it.

But I tumbled to the ice. I was hurting. Soon, Mario Tremblay jumped over the boards to get at Plett. That started it, with players from both teams entering the fray. Amid all the friction, the most intense dance was between our guy, Kent Carlson—a six-foot, three-inch, 210-pound rookie—and their guy, Paul Holmgren, in his ninth season as an A-list enforcer in the NHL. And I gotta tell ya, Carlson tuned up the vet pretty well. Heck, I'm not dumping on Paul, with whom I had several violent scrapes, for my turn would come later in my career to be on the losing end of battles with strong and able rookies.

I got my wind back, and I got up and speared Plett with just about the same force with which he had got me.

When all the gloves had been picked up, and guys were no longer grabbing, punching, pushing, shoving, and wrestling, I received a five-minute major for spearing and Mario Tremblay got a double minor because he was the first from either team to go over the boards.

For participating in the brawl, five players were ejected: from the Canadiens, me, Carlson, and Mike McPhee; from the North Stars, Plett and Holmgren.

With a two-man advantage on the power play, Minnesota quickly scored, then added two more to tie it up. Ten seconds into overtime,

Minnesota's Tom McCarthy scored his third goal of the game, and the North Stars won 7–6.

Because I picked up my third game misconduct, I was suspended for another game. There were fourteen separate fights going on at basically the same time, give or take a break of a few seconds here and few seconds there.

❖

Near the end of the season, the Habs' front office decided a coaching change was needed, and Jacques Lemaire took over. As a player, of course, Lemaire—who played his entire twelve-year NHL career with Montreal—was one of the most accomplished athletes in the history of the league. A forward and a lefty, he was an offensive terror and retired with eight Stanley Cup rings.

After retiring as a player at the end of the 1978–79 season, he became a coach, first for a year in Switzerland and then serving as an assistant coach for two seasons at SUNY Plattsburgh, a Division II college program.

Remember back in early May 1979, when Fran Flaherty and I gave Guy Lafleur, Gilles Lupien, and Lemaire a ride to their hotel room after a play-off game at the Boston Garden? Well, when I showed up for training camp, Lafleur and Lupien were still with the Habs, but Lemaire was in Switzerland. So when Montreal made the coaching change in late March 1984, there was a luncheon at which Lemaire talked to the team as coach for the first time. Most of the players already knew Lemaire, as they were either former teammates of his or they had played against him. Anyway, he finished talking and walked around, shaking hands and saying hello to everyone. He got to me, stepped back and smiled, and then leaned forward, heartily shook my hand and said, "Oh Bawstahn, you said you'd be heah."

That's right. I wasn't talking shit.

I got along well with Lemaire. He had an intensity and a forthrightness about him that I appreciated. He liked physical play and a defensively oriented, trapping style. He was also a superb teacher of the fundamentals of the game.

I could work well in his system.

Indeed, it was Jacques who counseled me that my reputation and the way I played afforded me room to maneuver, and that I would do well to capitalize on and take advantage of that room. He worked on drills with me that helped me better control and direct the puck.

So, we lost our last six regular-season games, including the final one to Boston, which gave the Bruins first place in the Adams Division and made them our first-round opponents. In eight regular-season meetings with Boston, we had won only twice and lost six times. Many thought another first-round exit was probable.

This made our three-game sweep of the Bs—by scores of 2–1, 3–1, and 5–0—a major upset all around.

Meanwhile, the Nordiques swept Buffalo in their first-round series, setting up an Adams Division final, a Battle of Quebec, against the team we reviled and detested. This was going to be fun.

Quebec had home-ice advantage. I scored the first goal of the series, off a John Chabot assist, in game one. But a quartet of Nordiques players—Marian Stastny, Jean-François Sauvé, Louis Sleigher, and Blake Wesley—who weren't exactly potent offensively during the regular season, had six goals between them that night in a 6–2 Quebec win.

Our goalie, Steve Penney, was a standout in games two and three, and our checking and defense did what we didn't do in the first game as we won 4–1 in Quebec and 2–1 in Montreal to take a 2–1 series lead.

Quebec tied the series on our ice, outhustling and outmuscling us. We had the lead late, 3–1, but goals by André Savard and Randy Moller tied it and put the game into overtime. Bo Berglund scored the game winner in OT.

Two nights later in Quebec, Penney was brilliant and Pierre Mondou scored the only goal we would need in the second period of our 4–0 win. And, then, in a span of 2:48 in the third period, Mario Tremblay, Steve Shutt, and Matt Naslund put the game out of reach.

On Good Friday, April 20, we hosted Quebec at the Montreal Forum, with a chance to put ourselves into the Wales Conference final.

We won the Adams Division crown that night with a 5–3 victory, giving us the series, four games to two. I suspect, though, that most people just remember the fights.

Indeed, the game became known as the Good Friday Massacre.

By the way, I need to say this—there would not have been nearly as many fights that evening, and there would have been no "massacre," had referee Bruce Hood not let the game get away from him early on; then again, I feel he often lost control of games early on.

Okay, so it was the end of the second period—00:00 was on the scoreboard—Dale Hunter slammed Guy Carbonneau against the boards, punched him in the head, and pinned him on the ice. They began to fight. I came over to help Guy out. Then, quickly, a lot more guys were fighting. I think at one time during the brouhaha, which lasted about fifteen minutes, there were fourteen separate "pair-ups."

A word to the wise: when this happens, and you are tangling with one guy, you also have to be aware of someone else coming along and jumping you, suckering you. Believe me, I know: I was often that guy who came along.

A major scrum formed at one end of the ice, and among those in the scrum was Quebec's Randy Moller, whom I slammed with a right while he wasn't looking at me. This got him upset, and he broke out of the pile and we faced off. I opened him up with a cut, but truthfully, I don't think I hurt him that bad.

Far more serious was that, while a referee was between Louis Sleigher of Quebec on one side and two of our guys—Jean Hamel (yes, formerly a Nordique) and Mario Tremblay—on the other, Sleigher looped an overhand that connected hard with the side of Hamel's head and basically knocked him out. It was scary. Jean didn't move for a while.

After our trainer got over to Jean, Mario looked for trouble and found it in Peter Stastny. Mario got the win on this one, breaking Stastny's nose. Both landed a few punches, but Mario won narrowly.

And you know you have a full-on, out-and-out brawl when the goalies get into it. Yep, that happened—actually, the backup goalies, Richard Sévigny from our side and Clint Malarchuk from Quebec. Malarchuk and Sévigny wore themselves out holding on to one another.

Ten players got ejected. Here's the Montreal guilty list: moi, Mario Tremblay, Richard Sévigny, and Mark Hunter. Here's who got heaved from the Nordiques: Peter Stastny, Louis Sleigher, Randy Moller, Wally Weir, Dale Hunter, and Clint Malarchuk.

So the ice was eventually cleared, and we were in our locker rooms. Yet, here's the thing: referee Bruce Hood, whose job it was to relay the information to the coaches as to who had been tossed, didn't do this. Somehow, there was a fuck-up in the line of communication. So both teams stewed between periods, and it wasn't until the teams came out of the dressing rooms for the third period that Hood skated over to the benches to let the coaches know who had been ejected.

By the way, in the event that anyone lost sight of the score at the end of the second period, it was 2–0 in favor of Quebec.

With the intermission over, the players were back on the ice. It was only then that Bruce Hood came over to the benches to let the coaches know who had been ejected. How the heck did he let the teams leave the locker rooms to begin the third period before this information had been given to the coaches?

When Hood delivered the info, the news traveled fast, and the fighting started all over again. Mark Hunter wanted to get payback big-time on Sleigher for the bomb he dropped on Hamel. Mark was crazy incensed, a one-man wrecking ball, trying to get at Sleigher. At one point, Mark went at it briefly with his brother, Dale, who was on the Nordiques.

What was so strange was that, during the fighting, the Montreal PA announcer, Claude Mouton, just calmly read off the infractions, the players, and the penalty minutes. It took a while.

Again, ten players were thrown out of the game. The total penalty minutes assessed for the two brawls was 262.

Our fans were going berserk. When the game resumed, we seemed to draw more positive energy, or were better able to channel our energies, than did Quebec. A little more than six minutes into the final period, still down 2–0, Steve Shutt scored to pull us within a goal. That started it. Steve scored again, followed by goals from Rick Green, John Chabot, and Guy Carbonneau. Five goals in around fourteen minutes.

As the final seconds expired, the Montreal fans chanted, "Hey-hey-hey, good-bye. Hey-hey-hey, good-bye."

On to the Wales Conference final, where we faced the New York Islanders, winners of the past four Stanley Cups. Not a Montreal Canadiens–type dynasty, but still a dynasty. In fact, if the Islanders were to win the 1984 Stanley Cup, they would tie the Canadiens' record of five consecutive Stanley Cups.

We surprised the Islanders in game one at the Forum, controlling just about every aspect of the game, checking hard and constantly, keeping the explosive likes of Mike Bossy, Bryan Trottier, and Denis Potvin from making life miserable for Steve Penney. We won 3–0. Game two was remarkable, and not just because we went up in the series 2–0 against the defending champs. Mats Naslund scored two goals in our 4–2 victory. Our fans, and the pressure of chasing history, I thought, were getting to the Islanders. This went down a minute or so after both teams poured onto the ice when the final buzzer sounded. Islanders starting goalie Billy Smith and our backup, Richard Sévigny, got into a pushing match.

In game three in Uniondale, New York, the Islanders were the Islanders once more—and would be for the rest of the series. What happened was that New York figured out our checking and found a way to counter our physical play. This put Steve Penney in the predicament of facing a lot more high-quality shots.

In the first two games, New York had forty-one shots on net and scored only twice. Over the next three games, the Islanders had seventy-one shots on net and scored eleven times, a very high success percentage. New York got in front of our net repeatedly and passed as frequently and crisply as the Soviet Red Army team during its era of world dominance.

In game three, the Islanders scored the first five goals in a 5–2 win. And believe me, the score suggests a game closer than it was.

We were competitive over the next three games, but still the Islanders were able to do offensively what they had been used to doing for several years. New York evened the series up with a 3–1 win. As he did in game two, Mike Bossy scored the game winner.

We lost game five in Montreal 3–1, and the Islanders closed us out at the Nassau Coliseum with a 4–1 win.

Sure, we were unhappy to be ousted. But we did understand we had taken a step toward respectability, especially when set against the past few play-offs and the most recent regular season.

Following our elimination, Kevin Dupont, writing in the *New York Times*, noted that, despite the loss, the Canadiens "left with hope that, after 15 play-off games, they had gained respectability for a team that once ruled the National Hockey League the way the Islanders rule it now."

At the end of the 1984 play-offs, I was honored to be selected to represent the United States in the third Canada Cup, which would take place late that summer.

The Canada Cup had its roots in the 1972 and 1974 Summit Series, which pitted teams made up of top Canadian NHL and World Hockey Association players against the Soviet national team, and which rank among the most watched and most dramatic events in Canadian history.

After the 1974 series, plans were made for an international series that would bring together more countries. One of the catalysts for the creation of this tournament, which would be called the Canada Cup, was that at that time, pro players were not allowed to play in the Olympics. In the Canada Cup, which would be played in the NHL off-season, countries would be able to put together teams comprising their best players, whether pro or amateur.

There were five Canada Cups—1976, '81, '84, '87, and '91. Regular participants in the competition were Canada, the Soviet Union, the US, Czechoslovakia, Finland, and Sweden. All the tournaments were held in North America. Canada won four, and the Soviets won the other.

I made more news off the ice as a member of the US Canada Cup team than I did on the ice. Prior to the tournament, each team played a few exhibition games against other teams that would be in the Cup competition. We had an exhibition game against Canada at the Forum. Late in the game, Rick Vaive of Team Canada and I got into a scuffle, and he slashed me before the refs stepped in. Funny thing, after we were separated, my teammate Bobby Carpenter skated in at good speed and leveled Vaive. Good for Bobby. But I still wanted another go at Vaive—yet I didn't get in another shift when he was on the ice. So the game ended and I was stewing.

The next morning, I was about to enter the Forum to go to practice. I was with Neal Broten, another Team USA member. So who should come walking out of the building and onto the sidewalk, having just finished their practice, but several members of Team Canada, including Wayne Gretzky, Scott Stevens . . . and Rick Vaive. I looked right at Vaive, and he looked back at me and said, "Who are you looking at? Just go in and practice, you cement head."

Rick Vaive—right then and there the poster boy for self-destructive behavior.

I slapped Vaive in the face, and then threw him hard on the front of a car before Larry Barnett, a good friend of Gretzky, broke it up.

I felt good about getting that out of my system.

Funny thing: as word got out that I had popped Vaive, at least a few players came up me and said they'd thought Vaive had it coming, and they were supportive of me delivering the punishment.

Well, anyway, I didn't end up playing in the '84 Canada Cup, because in the next exhibition game, I sprained my knee, which kept me out of the tournament.

23

HOSPITALS

I LOVE THE PEOPLE of Montreal. They were very good to me when I played, and they have been very good to me in my post-hockey career. Not long into my playing days in Montreal, I felt a need to give back—and I must tell you that it wasn't much of a sacrifice to do so. I feel that any time I have given, in whatever way, to the Montreal community, it has returned the favor in multiples.

The Montreal Canadiens are a class act from top to bottom—and it is understood that if you play for the Habs, then you will be involved in philanthropic work. If you don't want to do this, then you aren't going to be a Montreal Canadien for long.

An area to which I devoted a lot of time was visiting with patients at Montreal Children's Hospital. Most of my visits at hospitals were with children and adolescents. Being hospitalized is not good for anyone; for children, it is especially upsetting—and oftentimes downright scary.

Red Fisher, the Montreal Gazette sportswriter, told me he wanted to write a feature on my visits and volunteering at the hospitals—and I initially told him that I preferred that it not be played up. Then I changed my mind when I decided to start a golf tournament to raise money for Montreal Children's Hospital. I knew the publicity would help the event and the cause. Red wrote an excellent story, and this helped the golf tournament get established and take off. The tournament, which I managed and ran with event promoter Jeff Nieman for four years, raised considerable funds for the hospital.

I met with perhaps hundreds of young people at the Montreal hospitals during and after my playing days. There were a couple patients with whom I became particularly close—one of the reasons being that they both battled chronic illnesses that had them in the hospital frequently.

I met Joyce Elliott when she was seventeen. She had a particularly acute and serious form of muscular dystrophy. It would get to the point that she had to be on a respirator. Joyce did not need the respirator yet when we first met, while she was receiving treatment at Montreal Children's Hospital. She smiled a lot and was a hockey fan, and when I came into her room it was just so obvious how happy she was. Her reaction was gratifying and made me feel important. I noticed that a stuffed Garfield cat was next to her bed on a table. There was another Garfield at the foot of the bed. I found out that Joyce had a major thing for Garfield stuffed animals, which gave her comfort. I decided I was going to make sure that Joyce Elliott never wanted for Garfields. Whether I was home in Montreal or on the road, if I saw a Garfield cat, I would buy it and either bring it in person to Joyce or mail it to her.

My friendship with Joyce was one of great happiness and eventually tremendous sadness. When I was traded to the New York Rangers, I could not make my regular visits to see her. I called and wrote and was able to visit in person occasionally. But we had had a tight bond, and the new arrangement did not seem, to me, to be one she could handle. Early in the second season I was with New York, I received a letter from Joyce. It was a going-away letter. It was postmarked two days prior to when I opened it up. As I read, I found out—and it hit me terribly hard—that on the day the letter was postmarked, Joyce's respirator—at her direction and with her consent—was turned off. She was gone.

One girl's story has a happier ending. I first visited a girl she was fifteen years old and suffered from anorexia. She was so, so thin. I was no medical expert, but I couldn't imagine she was long for this world. But she had good doctors and therapists, and she was able to garner her own resolve to get better. I visited with her a few times in the hospital, and on one of those occasions, I brought her a jersey. We became pen pals. We remain in touch, though we do not communicate nearly as frequently as when I played for the Habs. What is best, though, is that she is now forty years old, and healthy.

24

GETTING CLOSER

I WOULD LIKE TO TELL YOU that the next year, 1984–85, was when the Canadiens took the next step and made it to the Stanley Cup final. That didn't happen, though.

Jacques Lemaire returned as head coach, and we had a new assistant coach, Jean Perron. As the season went on, Lemaire urged me to not fight as much, to slow it down, and to concentrate more on other parts of the game. This boosted my confidence, and it was advice I liked to hear. Still, I worried that if I fought less, my job would be less secure.

This was the year I led the league in penalty minutes with 358 and had a career-best twenty-one goals. I had sixteen assists in the season as well. I was becoming something of a double threat: someone who could beat you with his fists and beat the defense with a pass or a goal. For sure, I was still far more effective as a fighter, but in the other areas of the game, I was coming along. And, of the ninety-two games the Habs played in the regular season and play-offs combined, I appeared in eighty-nine.

Did I tell you I was getting better at getting the puck past the goalie?

Take February. On the seventh of that month, in a game at Quebec, I scored two goals, including the game winner in the third period.

Later that month, at home against the Winnipeg Jets, I scored two goals, both in the third period; the first goal tied the score, and the second was the game winner.

The first goal I scored in the period was one of my happiest and proudest moments in the NHL. It was set up when I was on a breakaway, got taken down by Randy Carlyle, and was awarded a penalty shot. So there I was, having my best year offensively, yet still known mostly as an enforcer. Now, with 18,000 people watching, all that mattered were my offensive abilities. Yeah, my heart pounded hard, and electricity and anxiety shot through me as I picked up the puck and approached the net and the Jets' goaltender, Brian Hayward. I managed to fake and get Hayward off balance, and I put the puck past him on a high backhander. The Forum rolled with a thunderous roar.

Montreal finished the '84–85 campaign in first place in the Adams Division with a record of 47–27–12.

Early in the season, in an occasion that proved even the greatest and most talented athletes have an opponent they can never beat (Father Time), Guy Lafleur, among the most brilliant, focused, and gifted athletes in hockey history, with his goal production and playing minutes way down, retired.

I was having a good year, even if my relationship with the new assistant, Jean Perron, was not a good one. I felt he was dismissive toward me. In one practice, there was a drill in which he stood facing us, about thirty feet away, and fed players the puck in no particular order. Players then shot at the net. It was not like we had a line going in which you moved up, got to the head of the line, got your pass, and then went to the back of the line. We were spread out sort out horizontally in front of him. And he just couldn't seem to find it within him to get the puck to me.

Finally, after a few minutes of not receiving one feed, I said, "Hey, over here."

His response was to ignore me. When he finally shot, I took action. I took a puck and balanced it on the blade of my stick and flipped it at Perron. The puck landed on top of his head, which resulted in a gash that needed eight stitches.

Perron got all in a tizzy, and Jacques was not happy, either. Jacques confronted me on the matter, and I told him that I just got lucky; it would take a fifty-goal scorer to line up a shot that perfectly.

I had one hell of a fight streak going in the play-offs. I had fought six times, once against Boston and five times against Quebec, and I think the argument is strong that I won every bout.

Our first opponent in the 1985 postseason was Boston. Going back forty-two years, Montreal and the Bruins had met sixteen times in the play-offs. The Habs had won all sixteen series. Nothing was going to change this year.

Boston surprised us big-time in the opener of the best-of-five series. They went up 2–0 in the first period, but we rallied to tie it up 3–3 in the third period. The Bruins' Ken Linseman fed Keith Crowder nicely at 9:27 of the third period for the game winner.

In game two, the Bruins led 3–2 at the end of the second period. They wouldn't score again. In the third period, there were goals by, in order, Chris Chelios, me—following a rebound of a Bob Gainey shot—and Guy Carbonneau, who made the final score 5–3, and the series was tied. A little info here worth sharing: when I scored that goal, which would end up being the game winner, I did a little dance on the ice and wiped out and ended up on my ass right in the middle of the sold-out Forum. The fans loved it.

When the series went to Boston, we took a two-games-to-one lead with a 4–2 win. We got all the goals we needed in the first period. Steve Rooney, a rookie, scored only 1:07 into the game, and we capitalized on two power plays in the period as well, with Mats Naslund scoring on the first and Bobby Smith lighting the lamp on the second.

I have to say this about the Bruins' Ken Linseman: he had an aptitude, like me, for goading opponents; that's why he was known as "the Rat." Linseman was also an aggressive, physical player. In game four he was penalized twice in the first period, and we scored on both power plays. But he would make amends that night.

We led 4–1 and 5–3 at different points in the second period. Then, also in the second, Boston tied it at five, with Linseman scoring the tying goal. Larry Robinson put us ahead at 18:20 of the period. Yet, with the period not yet over, Linseman scored his second goal, to go along with two assists in that twenty-minute frame, to even the score going into the third. With four points in one play-off period, Linseman tied the NHL record (shared with five other players). And the Rat wasn't done; he tallied the game winner at 13:12 of the third period.

We went back to Montreal, where there would be no such offensive explosion in game five. Only one goal was scored, but the Habs were the team to score it. With fifty-one seconds remaining in regulation, Mats Naslund took a brilliant feed from Mario Tremblay and went left in front of the Boston net, tucking the puck past Doug Keans. Yet the game came so close to going into overtime. With six seconds left, the Bruins had a face-off at our blue line, and Ken Linseman won the draw and punched it to Ray Bourque, who placed a shot on goal that Steve Penney stopped, but left a rebound that, with two seconds on the clock, the Bruins' Charlie Simmer chased and took a swing at but missed.

I got a lot of attention when, in the second period, following Boston's Keith Crowder nailing Petr Svoboda with a check that sent Petr down to the ice with an injury (later diagnosed as a separated shoulder), I went right at Crowder. I threw my stick down and challenged him—but Crowder turtled and wouldn't fight. I mean, really, Keith was a tough guy; it wasn't like him. Anyway, former Boston Bruins coach Don Cherry, who was doing color commentary for the TV broadcast of the game, went ballistic on air, basically saying that Crowder should be ashamed of himself and that his conduct represented a Bruins mindset that was foreign to him.

The Bs were eliminated. But straight ahead was our opponent for the Adams Division final: our cross-province best buddies, the Quebec Nordiques.

It would be a brutal and nasty series. Then again, it would almost have to be.

I minded my manners in the first game, a game we lost at the Forum in OT 2–1. Quebec's Brent Ashton had scored the first goal of the game at 9:38 of the first period. A little more than two minutes later, Lucien DeBlois scored on a pass from Mats Naslund to make it 1–1. Defense and goalies—the Habs' Steve Penney and Mario Gosselin of the Nordiques—were the story for the remainder of regulation time. At 12:23 of OT, Michel Goulet assisted Mark Kumpel on the deciding goal.

We knotted the series in game two, even though we were down 2–0 in that game before five minutes had expired. I helped with Quebec's first goal, in that it happened on a power play while I was in the box for slashing. Yet we rebounded, with Serge Boisvert and

Chris Chelios scoring later in the period, and we were tied at the intermission. At 10:58 of the opening period, I went after Alain Côté, and I gotta tell you, I don't think he wanted any part of me. I was able to wallop him with a series of uncontested uppercuts, he went down, and the refs stepped in.

In the second period, we were on our way, with Mike McPhee and Mats Naslund notching goals, and we entered the final stanza up 4–2.

Quebec never went quietly into that good night, and they stuck around thanks in part to me. Nineteen seconds into the third period, I fought Dale Hunter, getting him good with two shots before wrestling him to the ice. He was game, though, and tried to get in some punches before the refs stopped things. For this fight, I received an extra two minutes for roughing—two minutes in which Quebec had the man advantage and during which Michel Goulet scored his second goal to pull the Nordiques within one. When Peter Stastny scored his second goal forty-five seconds later, I wasn't feeling good.

Thankfully—and really, I was most thankful—Mats scored to give us back the lead, and Bob Gainey had an empty-netter (a goal that, as Red Fisher wrote, "made life worth living again") to seal the 6–4 Montreal win. We did lose on the night: Petr Svoboda injured his knee and would be out for the remainder of the series.

Game three, at their place, was a shootout and a rough one, with thirteen goals scored and 142 penalty minutes assessed. Dale Hunter scored his first play-off goal in this game, and it was an important one—it came at 18:36 of overtime.

Michel Goulet had a hat trick, and he delivered a nice check that freed Hunter up for the game winner.

Mats had a chance in overtime on a breakaway, but Quebec goalie Mario Gosselin was able to stay with Mats and the puck and made an excellent stop.

A major problem we had the entire evening was that we didn't check effectively, we didn't cut off passing and skating routes, and we gave the Nordiques far too much ice and room to negotiate. You can't do that against a team with their scoring power. Of course, we went into OT without Chris Chelios, who, during regulation, yet again injured a knee that had already sustained enough damage for a hundred lifetimes. Chris was finished for the season.

I chalked up two wins in the fisticuffs department that night; over Pat Price, about halfway through the second period, and the other against Dale Hunter early in the third. Hunter maintains I sucker punched him. Whatever.

After game four, Quebec coach Michel Bergeron commented that he had heard or read that the Canadiens were out to hurt the Nordiques' best players, Peter Stastny and Michel Goulet, and had gone about doing that not long after the opening face-off. Here's the truth: none of the Habs discussed such a thing before, during, or after the game. Didn't happen. Ric Nattress did level Goulet with a check only 2:17 into the contest, but it was a clean check. Goulet went down and sustained a lower-back injury; he tried to play a couple more shifts but couldn't go after that.

We played disciplined, smart hockey that night; indeed, we had to with Chelios and Svoboda in street clothes.

And I was fortunate in that something I did, which could have been disastrous for us, did not end up being so. In the second period, with the score 1–1, I was called for a slashing penalty. So Quebec had a power play. Yet I got saved. With me in the penalty box, Carbonneau got away from the Nordiques at their blue line and took a long shot that Gosselin left the net to easily clear—except that there were no Nordiques to receive the puck. Guy scrambled and got the puck and easily put it into the net. It was all the offense we needed, though Mario Tremblay added a power-play goal early in the third to make the final score 3–1.

Dale Hunter continued to hurt us. In game five, he was immense. In a 5–1 Nordiques win, he notched the game winner early in the second period and also had two assists. We were on our way back to Quebec City and facing elimination.

We survived.

It is tough to explain the satisfaction of getting a very important goal—which I did—in our 5–2 win over the Nordiques at their place, with the win knotting the series at three game apiece. This was a game that featured very little disruption because of pushing and fighting. A big reason for that is that Dale Hunter was out with a hand injury.

Mike McPhee scored our first goal just forty-five seconds after the opening face-off. Gainey to Carbonneau was our second goal, making it 2–1. Ron Flockhart scored for us early in the second period, putting us up 3–1.

Later in the second period, we led by a goal, 3–2, and I managed to get my stick on the rebound of a Larry Robinson shot and to lift a backhander past Gosselin. Pierre Mondou scored our final goal.

Yes, we were feeling good. We were going to win this thing on our own ice!

Except we didn't. Oh man, that was a tough loss. We came back from an early setback, but we didn't keep it going.

In the second period, down 2–0, Pierre Mondou scored to put us within a goal—and then Mats Naslund tied it. Momentum was with us, yet we didn't get a third goal. The game went into overtime, and at 2:22, Peter Stastny put the puck in our net to end our season and send the Nordiques into the Stanley Cup semifinal against Philadelphia.

If you don't think this was a big win for Quebec and its fans, consider that even with an appearance in the Stanley Cup final not yet secured (Quebec would lose the conference final to the Flyers 4–2), there were five thousand fans waiting when the Nordiques got off the plane upon their return from beating us.

Hockey is kind of a big thing in Quebec.

After the season, Jacques Lemaire resigned, and Jean Perron became head coach of the Montreal Canadiens.

25

LORD STANLEY

IN JULY OF 1985, Karen and I and our toddler, Colleen, moved into a home that we had built in the Montreal neighborhood of Kirkland. Montreal had become our second home—a home we loved.

Life was busy, and life was good. It was going to get even better professionally.

The upcoming season would be one in which, for the first time in seven years, Montreal won the Stanley Cup. It would be the twenty-third Stanley Cup championship for the franchise.

What was curious about the adventure was that we were less than impressive during the regular season. We finished with a record of 40–33–7, scoring 330 goals and allowing 280, which put us in second place in the Adams Division, five points behind Quebec, one point ahead of Boston, and two ahead of Hartford.

But worse, between February 1 and the end of the regular season on April 5, we played twenty-eight games, with a record of 10–16–2. In March, we had a six-game losing streak.

Then again, we had Mats Naslund, Bobby Smith, Larry Robinson, Kjell Dahlin, Guy Carbonneau, Bob Gainey, and the list goes on. During the season, the Habs alternated in goal between Patrick Roy, Doug Soetaert, and Steve Penney. When we entered the postseason, though, the job was firmly Roy's. He was all of twenty years old. Of course, in those play-offs, Patrick put forth one of the top Stanley Cup performances ever for a netminder.

We also had another rookie, a kid named Claude Lemieux, who got better and better as the season went on and who, in the play-offs, would produce like any number of Canadiens legends.

And when the Habs were on, which eventually we would be, we weren't the high-flying Canadiens of the past, but were more practitioners of gritty, grinding, digging, physical hockey. Whatever got the job done.

Mario Tremblay would retire after the season, going out the best way: on top.

I played in every game that season except for eight—the eight games for which I was rightfully suspended. I was sidelined for what I did in the third game of the season against the Boston Bruins.

We arrived in Boston having won both of our first two games.

A little more than midway through the second period, Boston's Rick Middleton and I had a light collision down in our end. I thought Middleton had high-sticked me. Whether that was the case or not, my response was wrong—very wrong. I lost it and did something inconsistent with the code of fighting in the NHL: I slammed my glove—the one in which I held the butt end of my stick—sideways against Middleton's mouth. I did a lot of damage; my spearing dislodged a few of his teeth and he went down with blood coming out of his mouth. I was immediately thrown out of the game, and Montreal was assessed a match penalty (punishment for a player intentionally injuring an opponent), which leaves your team down a man for ten minutes.

Now, here's the thing: I never intended to hit Rick Middleton with my stick, and I am confident that my stick did not connect with his mouth. But with the stick encased in the glove, it can become a denser cudgel. And while Middleton lost teeth, it resulted from impact outside of the mouth; there was no trauma to the inside of the mouth, which would be suggestive of butt-ending him.

Linesman Kevin Collins grabbed me, put himself between me and a host of Bruins who were trying to get at me (I don't blame any of them), and threw me out of the game (for this decision, I don't blame him either). There was a crescendo of boos as I approached the hallway to the locker room. As I walked down the hallway between the stands, fans pelted me with soda, beer, candy, popcorn—you name it.

In terms of what is really important—and taking the cosmic view of what I did—being shorthanded for half a period doesn't rank high (and the Bruins did take a couple minor penalties during this stretch, so the teams were at equal strength for those few minutes), but when I backhanded Middleton, Boston led 2–1. Within that ten-minute penalty, Boston scored three times on the way to a 7–2 win.

As I sat in the locker room, I knew I had fucked up. I felt terrible about what I had done. I told a reporter after the game that I felt awful and shouldn't have done what I did. My father was not at the game, but he saw what I did, and he left me a phone message in which he said that what I had done was disgusting.

I felt bad about my actions, but said publicly that I wasn't trying to hit Middleton with my stick. I said that I tried to hit him with my glove, but that the end of my stick caught him.

Four days after I was kicked out of the game, Serge Savard and I were at NHL headquarters for a disciplinary hearing. Brian O'Neill was not happy, and he let me know it. Serge argued I should receive a four-game suspension. O'Neill was making noises that ten would be more appropriate.

At the end of the hearing, when I was asked if I had anything final to say, I said that Kerry Fraser, the ref who saw what I had done, had had it in for me for a long time. When we left the meeting, Serge told me that that comment was not smart.

The next day, the NHL rendered its verdict: I was suspended without pay for eight games. It was the fourth multiple-game suspension of my career.

When I returned to play my first game at Boston Garden following the Rick Middleton incident, you know that the Bruins were ready for me and had a plan in place to get revenge. That didn't stop me, though, when the teams were getting ready for the opening face-off, from skating near Middleton and saying sorry. He seemed surprised and just nodded.

My apology did not put the brakes on the Bruins' desire for retribution, and those hopes were riding on Brian Curran, a six-foot, five-inch, 215-pound defenseman with whom I had already had some good bouts in the NHL—with more yet to come.

On the opening shift, Curran went right at me, pinning me against the boards, and landed three punches to my head before the refs intervened. As they broke up the tiff, Curran was screaming all sorts of shit at me, calling me a cheap-shot artist and punk and all sorts of stuff. Sitting in our penalty boxes, we shouted shit back and forth.

With a little less than six minutes remaining in the game, Curran and I went back at it. This fight was a good one; it lasted about fifty seconds. In this bout, you can see me trying to keep Curran's dangerous right arm against his body—which I did, for the most part, but not totally. What you see here, as well, is the value of having your jersey secured tightly in the back—or not having your jersey on at all. In the fight, I had a good advantage over Curran as I pulled at his jersey, using a fold of the material to pin his arm and get some punches in. When he was able to get his jersey totally off, he was able to throw punches easily. I call the fight a tie. He did get me in a headlock before we spilled onto the ice and the officials stopped it.

Through the years, I have apologized many times to Rick Middleton for what I did. On June 24, 2013, I had Rick on my radio show, calling in from his home in the Boston area. I apologized on the air yet one more time, and Rick graciously said it wasn't necessary, and that I had apologized about "a thousand times" to him.

❖

I had a good year all around, scoring, defending, and sticking up for my teammates. And on February 19, as we were in the final part of the season, I had more good fortune when Karen delivered our second child, Christopher Jr. Christopher, like Colleen, was born at Royal Victoria Hospital.

When people ask about the Habs' turnaround, how we suddenly started to play sustained winning hockey, I cite pep talks that Serge Savard and Ronald Corey gave us with a couple of games to go in the regular season. Savard was the holder of eight Stanley Cup championship rings, and the Canadiens team president, Corey, was a wonderful man who was good to past and present Habs. Really, these speeches were moving and poignant. Both men touched on all the important points, and got us in touch with what it meant to be a Montreal Canadien; they invested us with the emotion and import and responsibility of that legacy.

We opened our chase for the Stanley Cup against Boston in the Forum. There just was bad blood all the time in our matchups, and it continued to flow. We swept the Bruins in the best-of-five series, and what many observed in those three games—and I touched on this earlier—is that we displayed less of the high-speed artistry of the great Canadiens teams of the past, and more of, well, the hard-nosed style of the Boston Bruins of yore.

Of course, we scored when we had to, and we had that kid in net, Patrick Roy, who was performing at a level at which few goalies have played. As well, in the series, we were effective at keeping the Bruins' star defenseman, Ray Bourque, off his game, and keeping the Bruins' forwards deprived of the puck.

Game one was a bad scene, except for our 3–1 victory. We were up 3–0 late in the third period. Roy made twenty-five saves.

Oh, about the bad scene. Let's see, referee Bryan Lewis handed out 207 penalty minutes. There were so many fights—Milbury–Richer; Linseman–Svoboda; Crowder–McPhee; Sleigher–Robinson; Nilan–Linseman. There were also slashing and elbowing penalties. In the second period, with players milling about near the benches, I threw a punch at Jay Miller, who was sitting on the bench. I got ten minutes for that.

In the second game, we were tied 2–2 with 2:27 left in the third period when Claude Lemieux scored the game winner and his second power-play goal of the night.

In the closeout game at the Boston Garden, we were behind twice in our 4–3 win. What was nice was Bob Gainey scoring two goals. Bob scored goals in so many of the big games, and I don't think it was appreciated. Everyone knew about Naslund, Smith, and Robinson as scorers, but Bob was an unsung hero in that department.

Our Adams Division final series against the Hartford Whalers was the most difficult and demanding seven-game stretch of hockey I ever played.

Hartford was good; they had just swept the Quebec Nordiques in their opening series. Over the final fifteen games of the regular season, the Whalers were 10-3-2. During the regular season, we were 4-3-1 against Hartford.

Hartford spanked us in the first game, thoroughly beating us 4–1 at the Forum. We knew we could rebound, though. Two days later, the *Boston Globe* ran a story in which Francis Rosa wrote, "There was no gloom and doom around the Montreal Canadiens yesterday as they prepared for Game 2 of their best-of-seven Adams Division play-off finals tonight against the Hartford Whalers. There was no weeping and moaning about Thursday's 4–1 loss—as complete a play-off defeat as Montreal has ever suffered in the Forum."

Right on the money, that comment. We had been drubbed, but we knew we could rebound. What we couldn't do was let the Whalers do what they did in the opener—get three goals and six points from their second line.

We pulled even two nights later at the Forum with a 3–1 win. Key to the victory was staying on top of Hartford's scorers, Kevin Dineen, John Anderson, and Sylvain Turgeon. Offensively, we jumped on Hartford early, scoring on two power plays in the first period. With nine seconds remaining on a Montreal power play, Stéphane Richer put us up 1–0 at 12:33. I figured in our second goal when, with about two-and-a-half minutes left in the period, I took a slap shot at Hartford goalie Mike Liut, who cleared the puck into the corner. I raced after it, dug it out, and sent it to Guy Carbonneau, who directed it into the net. Guy scored his second goal, from Gainey, in the second period and we were up 3–0.

Hartford never gave up, though. I knew this was going to be difficult. The next two games were at their place.

I tell you, when we won game three 4–1, I thought the Whalers were done for. I thought we had them beat for the series and would wrap it up in a few days in Montreal. We dominated that third game. And it was our rookies who really showed up. Kjell Dahlin scored in the first period, and Stéphane Richer and Claude Lemieux lit the red light in the second period to give us a 3–0 lead. Our defense, and

Nolan kissing my Saint Bernard, Kona.

With my friend Shane a few weeks
before he passed away from cancer.

My beautiful daughter, Tara.

Speaking during my No More Bullies tour.

With the US Marines and the Stanley Cup in Afghanistan, 2013.

Locked and loaded in Afghanistan with Brian Burke and the Canadian troops.

Me and Burkie in Afghanistan.

Bohdi, Kona, and me at Lake Saint-Louis near Montreal.

Jaime and me with our two dogs.

In northern Quebec speaking to children from the Cree community.

At Forward Operating Base Frontenac in Afghanistan just after firing the M777 howitzer with Stu Grimson and Canada's finest.

Camel racing with Probie (Bob Probert) in Dubai.

Me and my good friend Jim McCulley salmon
fishing on the Columbia River.

Mark Wahlberg supporting the Knuckles brand.

With my good friend Tim Burke.

With my beautiful children, Chris, Tara (*front*), and Colleen.

Me and my beautiful Jaime.

the Carbonneau-Gainey-Nilan line, played well with the lead, and we were able to focus on what we did best: foiling scorers.

But Hartford wouldn't quit. They won game four at home 2–1 in overtime. Kevin Dineen ended the contest on an unassisted goal just 1:07 into OT. Starting in goal for the Whalers was Steve Weeks, replacing Mike Liut, who had been injured in game three. Key to the Hartford win was that they scored first, which didn't allow us to play the defensively oriented game that gave the Whalers trouble.

When we got back to the Forum, we scored first, and we won 5–3. Scoring first was important, especially against Hartford. We had sixteen shots on goal in the first period, and three of them made it into the net to put us ahead 3–0. The Whalers would get within one goal twice in the game. Late in the third period, the score was 4–3, and then Guy Carbonneau put the puck in with 1:19 on the clock to give us the insurance goal.

Hartford tied the series up at three games apiece with a 1–0 win at the Hartford Civic Center. So, of course, we didn't score first (or at all), and that was a problem. Mike Liut was back in net, recovered from his injury—and that was also a problem. As we had done throughout the series, we outshot the Whalers—in this game 32–17. It wasn't enough. At 7:30 of the second period, Kevin Dineen tipped in a pass from John Anderson for the only goal of the night.

We were heading north.

Both teams went all-out in the finale. Both goaltenders, Patrick Roy and Mike Liut, were excellent. We had just a little bit more when we had to find it.

We struck first on the scoreboard, which of course portended good things. Mike McPhee scored the shorthanded goal with 1:13 left in the first period after stealing the puck from Ron Francis. There would be no more scoring until late in the game—very late. All 18,000-plus fans at the Forum were on their feet and creating a deafening roar as we held on to that 1–0 lead. Three minutes were left in the third period.

Then, with 2:48 on the clock, Dave Babych delivered a fifty-foot missile of a slap shot past Roy's glove side. Stay seated.

Interestingly, after the game Claude Lemieux said that while studying Liut, he saw a weakness in his glove-side defense. Perhaps Claude remembered it; for sure, it was Liut's glove side he targeted when he ended the series in OT.

Coming out of that series, I was thinking that if I never played the Hartford Whalers again, it would be too soon.

In the next day's *Hartford Courant*, Jeff Jacobs wrote, "Mike Liut again was brilliant. And the Whalers, a team that refused to quit all season, went out on their shields."

Absolutely.

In the Wales Conference final, we faced the New York Rangers. New York had beaten the Philadelphia Flyers and then the Washington Capitals to set up their meeting with us. We had played the Rangers three times in the regular season, losing twice and getting a tie. But in this series, the Habs went up three games to nothing on the way to qualifying for the Stanley Cup final with a five-game series win.

In game one, I, along with Bob and Guy, continued to have success in thwarting our opponents' scorers. New York's main offensive weapons were Pierre Larouche, Mike Ridley, and Kelly Miller. After our 2–1 victory in the opener, Larouche admitted flat out that we three made life very difficult for him throughout the game. So far, so good.

I loved, and still love, the Montreal Canadiens fans. But they can be tough sometimes. They can be impatient. After all, they are used to success. In game two, near the end of the first period, with the score tied at one, the Habs partisans felt we were playing listless and uninspired hockey. So the chant went out, "Boring . . . boring . . . boring." Really. Well, okay, Guy Carbonneau helped change their attitude. He scored two of our four second-period goals to spearhead what would be for us a huge 6–2 win and 2–0 series lead.

In the first two games in Montreal, we had done a good job of keeping the pressure off our young goaltender. As the series moved to Madison Square Garden, the Rangers' Wilf Paiement, commenting on the sparsity of shots Roy faced in those games, said, "We'll see how good he is when he [Roy] handles thirty, thirty-five, forty shots."

Well, okay, fair enough.

Montreal won game three 4–3 off Claude Lemieux's goal 9:41 into overtime. We overcame deficits of 1–0, 2–1, and 3–2. Only 2:04 was left in the third period when Bobby Smith scored to tie the game and give us a chance in the extra session.

Roy faced a lot of shots early on and late and held the Rangers off. At the end of the first period, New York led only 1–0, even though they outshot us 16–7 in the period. In OT, Patrick turned back several shots before Claude closed it out.

Two nights later, New York imposed a physical game on us—one different from the first three we played. We lost 2–0. Rangers' goalie John Vanbiesbrouck, who was almost as brilliant as Patrick Roy in the series, got his first play-off shutout. There were forty penalties called in the game, including five majors and two misconducts. New York got the better of the more rough-and-tumble play and used it to nullify our offense.

We knew we had to play a more physical game in Montreal in game five, and we did. We led 2–1 entering the final period, in which two elements cemented the win: holding the Rangers to two shots on goal, and Bob Gainey poking a rebound past goalie Vanbiesbrouck with 10:09 to play.

For the first time in the 1980s, the Habs were in the Stanley Cup final. We were going back for a record-setting thirty-second time (breaking our own record, of course) and looking to improve on our twenty-two Stanley Cup championships, also a record.

Montreal celebrated that night—admittedly a bit too exuberantly, as there was considerable vandalism caused in the streets and neighborhood around the Forum. Then again, perhaps I am not the best one to deliver a message on discipline and control.

Yes, it had been a while. Only three players—Bob Gainey, Larry Robinson, and Mario Tremblay—remained from the last Habs team to win it all, back in 1979. And while we were very much the Montreal Canadiens, less than half of our team was born in Canada. Times change. We were out to make our own history.

As we celebrated our Wales Conference championship in the locker room, we didn't know who we would be playing in the final. The Campbell Conference final, between the St. Louis Blues and Calgary Flames, was knotted at two games each. That series, in which Calgary prevailed, went the full seven games, meaning we had a nice rest of a full week between our series-clinching win over the Rangers and the opener of the Stanley Cup final on May 16 at the Olympic Saddledome in Calgary.

An all-Canada final.

Most of the prognosticators had us as the favorite. Maybe we should have been. But Calgary was a very good team. In the second round of the play-offs, the Flames had dethroned the defending champs, the Edmonton Oilers, in five games. As well, the Flames did have the home-ice advantage.

Yet Calgary was a tired team. Their previous two series had gone the full seven games, and game one of the final would be their fifteenth in twenty-eight days. When the season concluded, Calgary had played every other night for six weeks.

Perhaps we had too much rest. Perhaps staying busy was an advantage for Calgary. We lost the opener.

We lost game one because the Flames outworked, outhustled, and outhit us. Final score: Calgary 5, Montreal 2. In his commentary in the *Ottawa Citizen*, Tom Casey suggested, rightly, that all the rest we got might not have been such a positive: "Although the Canadiens were coming off a six-day rest, it was more than just being rusty. The Flames beat Montreal in every possible way."

What was worrisome was that, for the first time in the play-offs, Patrick Roy played the way most people would anticipate a twenty-year-old rookie to play on the big stage. Actually, Calgary goalie Mike Vernon, all of twenty years old himself, might have had the better game of the two netminders that night.

Hockey's a funny sport. In game two, it seemed that conventional wisdom bore out, in that we skated a lot faster and more strongly than Calgary. We might have shaken off the rust, and fatigue might have been catching up to the Flames, and the Habs evened the series at a game each. I know I felt far more on top of my game and did a better job of defending against the multiple offensive threats of the Flames than I had in the opener.

Still, we had to go to overtime to secure our 3–2 victory. And we had to erase a 2–0 deficit in the game, created by a John Tonelli goal in the first period and Paul Reinhart's goal only a few seconds into the second period. Montreal closed the gap later in the second period, when Gaston Gingras, benefiting from Reinhart inadvertently knocking me into Mike Vernon, put the puck into the space left open with Vernon out of position. In the third period, Dave Maley scored to make it 2–2.

(The day after game two, Calgary coach Bob Johnson accused me of deliberately running into Vernon. Now, I would never do this. . .

really. I have to tell you, though, "running at goaltenders" takes skill and artistry to pull off without being called on it. Not that I would know much about that.) Both Roy and Vernon were excellent, and had Vernon not been so stalwart and cool in the Calgary net, we could have won by three or four goals in regulation time—we out-shot the Flames 34–22.

Had I been more accurate in the final ninety seconds of regulation, we would not have needed overtime. Over that minute and a half, I hit the post twice on shots.

Overtime didn't last long.

Right off the face-off, the puck got kicked to Mike McPhee, who had Calgary defenseman Al MacInnis backpedaling in front of him; he was the only man between Mike and our center, Brian Skrudland, and the Calgary goalie. I think we all thought Mike was going to shoot it, but as MacInnis lunged at him, Mike heard our center, Brian Skrudland, calling for the puck. Mike obliged him with a perfect pass that gave Brian a clear look at the open side of the net. Brian's goal, only nine seconds into OT, was the fastest overtime goal in NHL history. (Twenty-seven years later, the record still stands.) Being back on our home ice seemed to awaken the ghosts of the Flying Frenchmen. We were down 2–1 late in the first period when we turned on the jets. We scored three times in sixty-eight seconds to take a 4–2 lead into the second period en route to a 5–3 win and 2–1 series lead. With 1:35 on the first-period clock, Bobby Smith had a power-play goal—our first in twelve chances. Quickly following up with goals, both off of Chris Chelios assists, were Mats Naslund (his second goal of the game) and Bob Gainey.

Right out of the face-off following Bob's goal, Calgary's Neil Sheehy and I got into a tugging and wrestling spat; it didn't last long, but when we fell to the ice, my ankle twisted as Sheehy fell on it. I got up and skated away, but I thought something might have gotten torn in the joint. It felt messed up. Then again, very rarely were all my joints absent of pain and working fluidly.

I stayed in the game and got in all my shifts; indeed, I had another fight, this one with Tim Hunter with about a minute and half left in the second period. I was on in this one, landing several punches. Hunter didn't get many in in return. For some reason, not that I was arguing, we were both given penalties only for roughing. I thought I had done a better job than that.

In the locker room, and at home later that night, a physiological process with which I was accustomed went forward—that of adrenaline and endorphins draining away and an injury once considered relatively minor becoming almost debilitating. It got worse the next day.

I went to the hospital and had the ankle looked at; the X-rays came back negative—no fracture or break. But man, the ankle was all tight and it hurt like hell, and I wasn't able to get much of a pivot on it. It swelled to three times its normal size. I wanted so badly to be in that next game. And I put up a good front; then again, some caught me limping—like Red Fisher. In his column on the day of game four, he noted that the confidence that Jean Perron and Serge Savard relayed in discussing my ability to play that night was at odds with my limping gait. Fisher asked, if I was so ready, "why did Nilan look every inch like Chester straight out of a Gunsmoke episode yesterday?"

I wouldn't be available to play for game four; I watched from the bench. The game was heavy on defense, hard hitting, and containment, and after two periods, there was no score. As anyone who has been involved with hockey any amount of time knows, this was a situation in which one mistake could change everything. And it did.

A little more than halfway through the final stanza, Calgary's Doug Risebrough tried to clear the puck from deep in the Flames' end, but he didn't put the puck where he should have, and Claude Lemieux sprinted in, stole the puck, and ripped home the game winner at 11:10.

When the game ended, the action didn't. In fact, most of the people in the sold-out Forum stuck around for about ten minutes to watch the duration of the postgame brawl. I kind of think Claude Lemieux started it. He got jawing with Doug Risebrough right after the siren roared, and when Risebrough pointed at him, Lemieux grabbed a hold of the extended digit and bit it. Soon there were throwdowns all over the ice. How strange to be in street clothes and not be in the middle of the action. But I have to tell you, at one point some of our players thought things were over and skated for the bench, and I pointed and urged them to return to battle—which they did. What resulted from the bonus excitement was the distribution of sixty-two minutes in penalties and eight game misconducts. I didn't receive a second of penalty time for my role in the melee.

Anyway, one win to go.

Would I skate that night? Would I skate Saturday night, May 24, at the Saddledome?

I made it out for the pregame warm up. My ankle was not much better. I had a decision to make: play the tough guy and gut it out, not be at my best, and have my team suffer but be a part of history that night; or forgo history and not gut it out, but allow for our team to be stronger. It was a difficult decision. I chose not to play.

It would have been nice to win the final game at home, but we surely wanted to get this thing done with as fast as possible. We wanted to end the series in Calgary. And we did.

We scored first, on a power play in the first period; it was Gaston Gingras delivering a twenty-foot rocket from the slot at 6:53. Twenty seconds later, Steve Bozek took a nice pass from Tim Hunter and placed the puck in the net to make it 1–1. About halfway through the second period, Brian Skrudland directed the rebound of a Mike McPhee shot to put the Habs back in the lead. We took a 2–1 lead into the third period and increased it to 4–1 over a nineteen-second stretch midway through the period—Rick Green scored from the top of the slot at 10:11, and at 10:30, Bobby Smith put a wrist shot past Mike Vernon.

We held on. Bozek scored his second goal with 15:46 on the clock, and with forty-six seconds left in the game, Joe Mullen brought the Flames within one goal.

And then the scoreboard showed 00:00 and a 4–3 Montreal advantage.

I shared with countless young boys and old men the dream of skating across the ice as time expired, the point at which you become a member of a Stanley Cup championship team—a moment seen in person by tens of thousands and on TV by millions.

Throughout the final, we had just the right mix of veterans and young players, including many rookies. We had leadership exemplified best by vets Larry Robinson and Bob Gainey, and the extraordinary goaltending of Patrick Roy—again, only twenty years old—who most deservedly received the Conn Smythe Trophy as the MVP of the play-offs. It was only fitting and proper that the runner-up for the Smythe Trophy was Claude Lemieux.

26

CELEBRATION

YES, IT WAS A BIG DOWNER not skating that night, but I was confident about my contribution to the team. I knew that I had played an important role that season. In the locker room, I got caught up in the jubilation, cheering, and celebrating. I opened champagne bottles and gulped the bubbly along with beer. Soon I forgot that I hadn't played in the final game of the season.

And soon our wives, and some of the players' girlfriends, were partying with us in the locker room. It was a very happy experience to share with Karen, who had supported me steadfastly in my career. I was looking forward to seeing our kids and sharing the championship with them, even if they wouldn't know what it all meant, yet.

We partied past midnight before catching a bus to the airport. Wives and girlfriends were on the plane with us.

Our plane arrived at Dorval Airport at nine in the morning. Waiting for us were 15,000 fans, jamming the concourse and screaming, holding signs, and snapping pictures. We waved, yelled our thank-yous, and shouted that we would see everyone the next day at the victory parade. Police and security guards held the crowd back, and our entourage was directed to an exit at the back of the main terminal, where we all boarded buses that took us to another point just outside the city where cabs took the coaches, players, spouses, and significant others home.

That night at the Queen Elizabeth Hotel in Montreal, a big party was held for the team and family members of the team. My mother and father and my brother were there. So too were Teresa and Jimmy. That now-famous photo of Jimmy and me together, posing with the Stanley Cup, was taken at the party. It was just a great night all around.

Then came the parade, which started at noon the next day. It started at city hall and followed a six-mile route that snaked through Montreal and finished at the Forum. All the players were on floats; we all wore sweat suits with the Canadiens logo. I rode in an open-top convertible with Guy Carbonneau and Mario Tremblay. More than a million people lined the route. People were on the streets and in windows and on rooftops. For every inch of that ride, loud music blared from speakers attached to the floats. People handed us beer, which we happily gulped. Of course, there was a long stretch on St. Catherine Street, and when we passed the world-famous strip club Club Supersexe, the dancers were in the doorway and in front of the club, flashing their breasts—which was much appreciated.

Family members of players, coaches, and management were also in the parade. They were in trolley cars and followed the team.

When we got to the Forum, we all went inside the arena, which was packed. This celebration was not over yet; inside, there was another program scheduled. A band played, and the legendary Canadian hockey announcer Claude Mouton was the master of ceremonies. He pumped up the crowd, and he announced all the coaches and players, and each of us got on the microphone and spoke a few words. When the microphone was handed to me, I started singing, "Na-na-na-na, na-na-na-na, hey-hey-hey, good-bye."

I think that, by the time the official team and city festivities finally concluded, it had been about six hours since the start of the rolling celebration through the streets of Montreal. I was wiped, and I know my teammates were as well. But I was revived for the next day, when there were some appearances scheduled for the team and the Stanley Cup—the championship sports trophy that seems to have a life of its own.

Not all the players or coaches would be at each event; our participation was parceled out. Each event, though, had a least three or four of us. Lucien DeBlois and I did an appearance with the Cup that afternoon in downtown Joliette. Fans were able to get their photo taken with Lucien and me and the trophy. The event was well attended. I think we had in the neighborhood of four hundred photos taken in a few hours. Anyway, things were wrapping up, and soon reps from the NHL and the Canadiens, along with the Pinkerton guards who were on hand to secure the Cup, would take it to its next showing, party, reception, or whatever.

Someone said, "One last picture." That was our cue. Lucien and I had a plan in place, which we executed almost flawlessly.

Okay, before I tell what happened next, this was a time prior to the custom of allowing every player on the Stanley Cup championship squad to have his own day with the Cup during the off-season. It's a nice tradition now, but it wasn't one back then. But I, for sure, had long thought it would be cool to kidnap the Cup and have it to myself for a while.

Lucien was not at my side anymore, and the organizers of the appearance were not paying close enough attention to the Cup. I grabbed it and ran full speed down the street to where Lucien was sitting behind the wheel of his convertible, which had the top down. I only had to run about thirty meters, which was good because the trophy was heavy—about thirty-four pounds—and big and unwieldy.

As I ran, I passed smiling, laughing, and cheering Montreal Canadiens fans. I also heard some guys—no doubt those entrusted with keeping the Cup safe—behind us, yelling, "Hey, stop . . . stop . . . please."

Not a chance.

I plopped the trophy in the back seat of the convertible and jumped in the passenger seat, and we screeched out of there.

Man, we were laughing like hell. It was funny. First stop would be to see Lucien's father, who was ill and in a convalescent home in Joliette. When we got to the facility, not only did we cheer and bring a smile and tears to Lucien's father, but we brightened the day for so many at the home, residents and staff alike.

Where next? So, we were on the highway, leaving Joliette, riding in a car with the Stanley Cup in the backseat. It was a beautiful day—sunny and warm. We were passing this farm, and we saw that, out in the field, there was a big hay truck with about fifteen guys working next to it. I told Lucien to pull off the highway and drive up a bit on this dirt road that would take us near the farm workers. So he did, and we stopped at a spot in the road that was probably fifty yards from them. We got out, and Lucien took the Cup and held it up over his head—just like you've seen the players do on the ice in celebrations when the final is over—and started walking toward the workers.

For a second or two, they were all just looking at us. Then one yelled, "Holy shit! That is DeBlois and Nilan and the Stanley Cup!" These guys were smiling and laughing; they ran forward, and we told them that we had a camera with us, and that we should get some photos of them and us and the Stanley Cup. We took a bunch of shots, including us sitting in the back of the hay truck, bales of hay and the trophy, and the farm hands. I took down one of the guys' name and address, and I sent him copies of the negatives.

We weren't done. Not even close.

We drove to Lucien's place, which was not far from downtown Montreal. We relaxed with the Cup and had a few beers. Then we went to my house in Kirkwood, and I took pictures of Karen, Colleen, and Chris Jr. with the trophy. Chris was still an infant, and I sat him in the Cup and videotaped and snapped photos of him smiling and giggling with his little butt parked inside one of the most iconic sports artifacts in the world.

It was early evening when Lucien and I walked out of my house. We were on our way to pay a surprise visit to a youth hockey game down the street. When we walked in the door with the Stanley Cup, the fans in the stands—mostly parents—came running and shuffling down to meet us as we positioned the trophy just on the other side of the glass from the rink. Of course, play stopped, and the players, coaches, and refs all came over, and we had pictures taken, and video was shot, and we signed autographs. We then brought the trophy onto the ice, and we repeated all the photo and video taking and autograph signing. We were there for a good forty-five minutes.

Next stop? Well, it was about 10 p.m. when we were driving down Rue Stanley—just south of St. Catherine Street—and we ended up in front of Chez Paree, one of Montreal's world famous strip—er, gentlemen's—clubs. Why not? We brought the Stanley Cup inside, and it was a whirlwind of beautiful women, drinks, hollering and screaming fans, autograph signing—and every last person having to get his or her hands on the trophy.

Lucien and I donated $1,000—the $500 we each received each for our appearance with the trophy in Joliette—to a local youth hockey organization.

27

DEFENDING CHAMPIONS

NOW IT WAS ABOUT REPEATING. The great Mario Tremblay had retired, but we had everyone else returning. In the exhibition season, however, we sustained a big setback when Bob Gainey tore a ligament in his left knee in a game against the Nordiques in Quebec. Bob would be out for a couple months.

We were playing well out of the gate, and led the Adams Division in late November when we paid a visit to our friends the Bruins. Always good for drama—particularly the game we played at the Garden on November 20.

We came into Boston with a record of 11–5–3; Boston was at 7–9–3. For sure, at this early stage in the season, things were going a lot better for us than they were for the Bruins. We beat them that night 3–1—but few remember the score.

What they remember is the melee in the second period.

People point the finger at me, like I was the only bad guy in the mess. I say look at the video. There were a lot of people punching and wrestling. First off, I surely didn't start it—it started when Tom McCarthy checked Chris Chelios hard against the glass near our bench with 4:41 left on the clock. Then Jay Miller went at my teammate, Dave Maley. A minor scrum of players developed, and I went over to the action and grabbed a hold of Boston's Paul Boutilier. I didn't hit him but pulled him from the scrum. He grabbed me, and I told him to let go. He didn't—but the bigger mistake was that he held on to me and looked away. Don't give me this bullshit about me suckering him. I say only this: protect yourself at all times. So I hauled off on Boutilier, and I really didn't care if he was looking my way at the time. Well, a ref got his hands on me and yanked me from Boutilier, at the same time as a ref had Miller pinned on the ice while Jay was pointing at me and threatening all sorts of retribution. Screw him.

Anyway, I got shown the door, so to speak. I was told to leave the ice. By the way, there were others fighting as I made my way to the exit door along the ice. When you opened the door, there was a corridor running between the two team benches and past fans who were above and to the side of you.

So I opened the door and walked in between the benches, and who should sidle up, grinning at me from the Bruins' bench, but Ken Linseman, a.k.a. "the Rat." He started shit all the time. Did he say anything to me? No. But he had that shit-eating grin on. So I popped him with my gloved fist. Quite the donnybrook ensued. It was something. Players from both teams jammed into the corridor. It was a tumble of hockey players, and a good amount of blood flowed.

It took cops and security guards to stop the fighting.

I and three of my teammates were given game misconducts, as were four on the Boston side. The brawl resulted in 124 penalty minutes being assessed.

After Brian O'Neill and his staff collected information and reviewed the tape, I was given a three-game suspension. As well, a total of $21,000 in fines was assessed to both squads.

Some good actually came out of my actions. The Bruins installed a plexiglass partition to separate the corridor and the team benches. The partition is called "the Nilan Glass."

How's this for a rotten coincidence? The evening of December 8, the night that Bob Gainey returned to our lineup following his convalescence from a torn knee ligament and the operation to correct it, I went down with—you guessed it—a torn knee ligament. We had Calgary at home that night. In the first period, I twisted my left knee, and I knew immediately it was bad. I was brought right to the hospital, where a full examination of the knee was conducted. What I learned the next day was that the injury would have me out for a couple months but would not require surgery. I guess you take the good with the bad.

❖

I healed well and was diligent in rehab and was able to be back in uniform and playing before February ended.

As we approached our postseason quest to defend the Stanley Cup, we had nice run, winning our final nine games. We hadn't lost since March 11. Our final regular-season record was 41–29–10, with 277 goals for and 241 against, which placed us second in the Adams Division, a point behind Hartford and seven points ahead of third-place Boston.

We faced Boston yet again in the opening round; it was a best-of-seven series. And again, we took the measure of the Bruins with a sweep. With Langway gone, I held on to the unique perspective of just how pissed off the Habs made the Bruins. Boston, one of the Original Six, one of the most storied franchises in sport, had that misfortune of drawing Montreal early on in the play-offs—and so many times, Montreal went on to win it all. When I was a kid growing up in West Roxbury, the notion and concept of the Montreal Canadiens irritated the hell out of me.

After game four, future Hall of Famer Ray Bourque said, "If we meet someone else in the first round, maybe we will go further."

On Sunday, April 12, the day we closed out Boston, the Quebec Nordiques beat Hartford 4–1 to tie the series 2–2 in the other Adams Division semifinal. Hartford had led the series 2–0. We had ourselves a bit of a rest, for it was on April 16 that Quebec won its fourth straight game in the series to set up another Battle of Quebec that would begin on April 20 at the Montreal Forum.

By the way, this series would take place against the historic and highly emotional backdrop of Canada and Quebec completing the final parts of an agreement through which Quebec would sign on to the Constitution of Canada. Quebec had been the lone province to hold out against ratifying it in 1982. Quebec had long had, and continues to have today, a fiercely independent streak.

It seemed only right that we should play seven. Who would have thought, though, it would go the limit after we lost the first two games of the series, both at the Forum?

So much of that first loss was my fault. I effed up.

The score was tied 4–4 early in the third period when I picked up my second penalty of the game. I had my stick high, but I didn't think that high—but it didn't matter because the ref thought it was too high, and I got called for it. I was pissed. So when I was in the penalty box, I let loose a nice torrent of expletives at the official, Andy Van Hellemond, who was one of the best in the business. Van Hellemond promptly gave me another two minutes, plus a misconduct.

Just what my team needed in a close game.

On the resulting power play, Dale Hunter redirected a Steve Finn shot from the blue line into the net and Quebec was up and would never relinquish the lead. Energized, John Ogrodnick and Paul Gillis scored for the Nordiques to pace the 7–5 win. After Gillis's goal, Jean Perron replaced Roy with Brian Hayward. It was the first time in Patrick's twenty-six-game play-off career that he was pulled.

It was our first loss in fourteen games.

Patrick Roy did not start game two, which we lost 2–1. In the first period, I had a fight with Basil McRae, which I won. Key to the Nordiques' victory was the twenty-seven-saves performance of their twenty-three-year-old goalie, Mario Gosselin. This kid was playing like Roy did about the same time the previous year. There was no score through three periods. In the third, Michel Goulet put Quebec in front 1–0—and seventeen seconds later, McRae, no worse for the wear after his fight with me, scored the winning goal. Ryan Walter had the sole Habs goal of the night with 5:21 remaining on the clock.

So what was different in game three? What changed to enable us to win easily 7–2? We did a good job of keeping the Quebec forwards off their game. Brian Hayward foiled Nordique attempt after Nordique attempt. As well, the Habs benefited from some kids who hadn't often been in the limelight until now but who showed up when we needed it. Sergio Momesso, a twenty-one-year-old left winger and Montreal native, hadn't played yet in the series, but Jean Perron started him in the hope his physical play would help us out. In fact, it did: he scored a goal only fourteen seconds into the game, and we had a lead we would never relinquish. We were leading 2–0 when Bob Gainey scored at 6:18 of the first period.

Thirty-seven seconds into the second period, Quebec's Risto Siltanen scored on a power play. But Mats Naslund got the game winner and restored our two-goal lead at the 13:10 mark of the same period. A little more than two-and-a-half minutes later, Normand Rochefort put the Nordiques within a goal at 3–2. Mike Lalor scored his first goal of the play-offs to push us ahead 5–2. In a bruising third period—yeah, call it physical—Ryan Walter, Lalor, and Shayne Corson added goals for us.

Mats Naslund scored two goals, including the game winner in sudden-death overtime as we won 3–2 on Quebec's ice to even the series at two games each. So much for home-ice advantage—for either team. Curiously, referee Bob Myers hadn't even dropped the puck to start the game before McRae had thrown off his gloves and started hammering away at Momesso, with the intent, I suppose, of intimidating Sergio and heading off the boost that Sergio's muscular play had given us in the previous game.

Well, no matter. Eighteen seconds into the game, Naslund scored. Three minutes had not yet elapsed on the scoreboard and Mike McPhee scored a goal, and we led 2–0. Quebec's goals that tied the game and forced OT came from John Ogrodnick, with twenty seconds remaining in the first period, and Anton Stastny at 5:30 of the second period.

Mats's sudden-death goal was a beautiful example of speed and precision on a slap shot from long range. At about 5:25 of overtime, Mats picked the puck up at center ice and had a slight pause at the blue line, as he was thinking of letting go from there, but he went another stride and let loose a missile of a sixty-footer that went between the legs of Gosselin.

We were heading back to Montreal—which, very recent history might have suggested, was not such a good thing. But we got ourselves the first victory of the series by a team on its own ice. This, though, did not come without controversy. With the score tied 2–2 and 2:29 left in the game, Ryan Walter scored his second goal of the evening. It would prove to be the game winner.

As for the controversy, thirty-one seconds prior to Ryan's goal, Quebec's Alain Côté had put the puck past a toppling Hayward, and the Nordiques were celebrating a huge score. But it wasn't a goal, because a millisecond prior to the puck going in the net, referee Kerry Fraser whistled Mats Naslund and Paul Gillis of the Nordiques for pushing and shoving in front of Hayward, which resulted in Brian being illegally interfered with. Oh man, the condemnation from the Nordiques. Please, we had a goal called back earlier in the game. Shit happens.

Whatever, we were up three games to two. Back to the Colisée, the Nordiques' arena.

I scored my second goal of the play-offs in game six. But we had only one other, and Quebec had three—all in the third period—and the game ended with the series knotted 3–3. Corson put us in the lead in the first period, and I scored my goal, off a wrist shot, in the second. Our defense had been superb all night, until Michel Goulet scored at 5:22 of the final period, bringing Quebec within a goal. At 13:37, John Ogrodnick tied the game with a long slap shot from inside the face-off circle. Normand Rochefort's twenty-foot wrist shot with 4:37 left provided Quebec the final advantage that moved the series once again across the province.

We were down early, 1–0, in the seventh and deciding game, and then scored five straight goals to put us in the Wales Conference final. This was how the Canadiens should play hockey in the Montreal Forum. John Ogrodnick scored in the opening period, and Quebec took the 1–0 lead into the first intermission. We were about to heat up. In the second period, at 2:03, Ryan Walter tied the game at 1–1; he wasn't done, for about two-and-a-half minutes later, he scored again to put Montreal up 2–1.

Then came the avalanche that got the 18,000 fans at the Montreal Forum delirious. Bobby Smith, Shayne Corson, and Mike McPhee scored before the second period was over to give us the 5–1 lead. It would prove more than enough.

Next up, the Philadelphia Flyers—a team we had played three times during the regular season, losing twice and tying once.

We hadn't met the Philadelphia Flyers in a play-off series since the 1976 Stanley Cup final. Perhaps they weren't the Broad Street Bullies, but they were very good and still as physical and bruising as the situation called for—or even if it didn't call for.

Philly downed us in the opener 4–3 in OT. It was a true battle from start to finish. The Spectrum crowd was loud and incessant in its cheering. Our teams played fairly evenly matched hockey, with both sides having their chances.

At 7:15 of the third, Bobby Smith scored to give us a 3–2 lead. Philadelphia's Derrick Smith tied the game with 3:51 left in regulation. We had our chances in regulation, with Guy Carbonneau putting two nice shots on net in the final minute, but the Flyers' rookie goaltender, Ron Hextall, who would have an excellent series, stopped both.

Nine minutes and eleven seconds into OT, Ilkka Sinisalo scored his second goal of the game.

Philadelphia had drawn first blood. Well, not really first blood—that would come later.

We got the series tied up in game two in Philadelphia, getting out to a 3–0 lead by the second period on the way to a 5–2 win. Hayward was great for us, including stopping five shots on a second-period Flyers power play. At 11:38 in the first period, the Habs were on the board first with Bobby Smith scoring after Claude Lemieux fed him perfectly. Brian Skrudland, John Kordic, and Lemieux had second-period goals for us.

About halfway through the second, Daryl Stanley and I teed off. This fight was fairly equal, with us both landing, but I got the win in this one because I threw an uppercut that dazed Stanley just before we went to the ice.

I scored the first goal of game three at 4:23 of the first period when I followed a Shayne Corson shot that Hextall stopped, and I jumped on the rebound to direct it home. Fifty seconds later, Chelios put us ahead 2–0. We were applying a lot of pressure on Hextall, but he responded; indeed, on the night, we outshot the visitors 39–18. We carried that advantage into the second period. In the second frame, Philadelphia's Pelle Eklund, who had not exactly been a major offensive force to date in his NHL career, scored twice to make it 2–2. In the third period, at 8:29, Eklund got the assist on Rick Tocchet's goal that put Philly ahead 3–2. Mats Naslund sent in a rebound of a Chelios shot to tie matters at 12:35. Yet Philly left winger Brian Propp scored the game winner with 3:09 remaining.

Pelle Eklund was killing us. This kid from Sweden was killing us.

In game four on Sunday night at the Forum, a 6–3 Flyers victory, Eklund scored three goals, giving him five in two games, both won by Philadelphia.

Patrick Roy was in the net for the first time in three weeks. Perron said he replaced Hayward with Roy to halt, and hopefully reverse, the momentum that the Flyers had achieved in winning two of the first three games of the series. But with all that time off, it is difficult to get in the big-game flow right away. You can have a lot of time off and practice as well as you ever did and jump into a low-pressure game and perform at your best. Yet in the Wales Conference final, especially against such a potent offensive team as Philadelphia, the challenges are immense even for the most talented and competitive athlete.

Behind the four-point performance of Larry Robinson, we won game five 5–2, continuing our road play-off success, while Philadelphia extended its mediocre home play-off record. It was our sixth win in eight road play-off games, while the Philly loss was its fifth in ten home play-off games. Larry was playing some of the best hockey of his career. He scored a go-ahead goal in the first period and assisted on three others.

Game six in the Forum was next. Oh yeah, the famous game six between the Montreal Canadiens and the Philadelphia Flyers.

First, there was the brawl—and after the brawl there was the game. Yes, the brawl happened before any hockey was played that night. After people beat on each other, the Philadelphia Flyers beat the Montreal Canadiens 4–3 to advance to the Stanley Cup final.

I would rank this brawl, which broke out in in the warm ups, as one of the nastiest and angriest in which I've been involved. Philadelphia defenseman Ed "Boxcar" Hospodar—who played sparingly in the play-offs and had a reputation for goading people—started the mess, and as far as I'm concerned, that was what he was put on the ice to do that night.

Claude Lemieux, as was his custom, and in keeping with a superstition of his, got on the ice after warm ups to slap a puck into the opponent's goal. He did this before every game. Yet this time, Hospodar went after him. It was bad. Soon all the players—save for the goaltenders—had rushed back onto the ice, most coming from their locker rooms. Some of the players didn't have their jerseys on—and I think one guy didn't even have his skates on. Everyone was swinging. Again, it was bad.

And there were no officials on the ice because they had not finished suiting up and tying their skates yet in their dressing room. When they heard what was going down, they hurriedly completed putting on their uniforms and skates and got out to try to do whatever they could.

Dave Brown, all six feet, five inches and 225 pounds of him—and someone I knew well through trading punches during my career—came right at me, which was always a challenge—but in this circumstance, it was a bigger challenge. Brown did not have his jersey or his shoulder pads on. All he had from the waist up were his pant suspenders and his belt. I was in full equipment and uniform. I would have nothing to hold on to, but he would have all sorts of opportunity to grab my jersey and use it to pin my arms while he threw bombs. I skated backward as he came at me, thinking about how to handle the situation. Chris Chelios tried to intervene, but Dave pushed him aside and kept after me. I had no choice but to oblige Dave. It was a long fight—about five minutes. We actually fell down and then got up and kept going. We were both tired, very tired, and as we held on to each other, Dave said, "Have you had enough?" To which I said no and threw another punch.

If you watch the video and conclude that Brown got the win, I won't argue. He did get in more punches. But Dave had unfair advantages; first, he had the equipment advantage, and then there was the edge he had in that he did not play regular shifts for Philly—while I had been worn out by the schedule, he was relatively fresh.

Other main matches in the melee, which lasted for fifteen minutes, featured Larry Robinson, who was jumped from behind by the Flyers' Don Nachbaur, and John Kordic, who took on Philly's Daryl Stanley.

Eventually, things were calmed somewhat, and the ice was cleared of players and equipment. Maybe ten minutes after that, players returned to the ice and a hockey game began.

We took a 3–1 lead in the game—not the fight; I'm not sure how you'd have scored the fight. Mike McPhee and Larry Robinson had first-period goals

I think Brian Hayward played very well—but I think that others, myself included, could have done a much better job keeping the pressure off him. Flyer Rick Tocchet scored the winning goal with 7:11 remaining in the game.

The day after our season ended, the NHL brass fined each player who took part in the fight $500; some players who returned to the ice after leaving it were fined an additional $500. Ed Hospodar was suspended for the remainder of the season.

In a thrilling Stanley Cup final, the Edmonton Oilers defeated the Flyers in seven games. It was the fourth Edmonton Stanley Cup championship of the 1980s.

There was another Canada Cup in 1987, and again I was selected for the US team. This time, I managed to not get hurt in the pre–Canada Cup exhibition games, and I had a solid tournament.

In our opening game, we beat Finland 4–1 at the Hartford Civic Center. We followed that game with another win, a 5–2 decision over Sweden (which had beaten the Soviet Union 5–3 in its previous game) at the Copps Coliseum in Hamilton. I scored a goal in that game.

After the win over Sweden, the US moved into first place in the tournament. We didn't stay there, losing our next three games to, in order, Canada, the Soviet Union, and Czechoslovakia and failing to make the medal round. I did score another goal in the Canada Cup; it was our lone goal in the 3–1 loss to the Czechs.

28

LEAVING MONTREAL

I DIDN'T MAKE IT through the 1987–88 season with Montreal. I loved the team, the franchise, the city, and everyone who supported the Habs, and I wanted to play my entire career there—but it didn't happen.

What it eventually came down to was that Jean Perron and I didn't get along. But the real problem was that I didn't respect him. I can disagree with you, and I can think you are a real prick, but if you are also a stand-up person, someone I respect, then we are going to be all right. I didn't respect Perron because of how he treated me near the end of my time with Montreal.

No, I didn't respect him.

I don't know if it was because Perron never played the game at a high level or what, but I assert that most of the players didn't have a heck of a lot of respect for him, either. And when it started to become apparent, early in the season, that he was planning (and putting into motion) a future for the Canadiens in which I wouldn't play a major role—or any role at all—well, it pissed me off.

He wanted to give some of the younger players a chance, which I understood. But in early October, when he took me off the checking line on which I had been so effective, on which I had played the best hockey of my career, and on which I had delivered the most value for the Canadiens, it took my unhappiness to a new level.

Oh sure, I was still getting my playing time, but it was more of a fill-in role. And it was more in the capacity of a designated fighter. I had no problem with fighting, but I sure as hell was not going to be, especially at this point in my career, merely a thug doing spot duty.

And that was what it was coming to.

Did I continue to fight? Of course. But I would have to admit that the way I was being used did not incline me to go at it with the ferocity and intensity I did in the past. I thought I wasn't being respected. I thought I was being used.

For all intents and purposes, the end came for me after a night game in Hartford late in January. We hadn't played well. We stayed overnight in Hartford and were going to take a flight in the morning to Buffalo for a game the following night against the Sabres. In the morning, before we left for the airport, Perron held a brief team meeting in a conference room at the hotel. In the meeting, he sort of read us all the riot act. He challenged us, suggesting we weren't giving our all. He called each person out individually, and when he got to me, he yelled, "Chris Nilan—when's the last time you had a fight?"

That did it. I was pissed. I shouted back, "Fuck you—what do you know about fighting? When have you ever had a fight?"

Perron glared at me and I glared back.

It couldn't have been clearer to me that my place on the team had changed, big time, than at the morning skate in Buffalo, when Perron had me wear a "black ace" jersey—the practice jersey worn by players who weren't on regular shifts.

Oh, I was furious and a bit anxious. I went back to the hotel, and the phone rang in my room. On the line was Jacques Laperrière, the Hall of Fame defenseman who played for the Canadiens in the 1960s and early '70s, who was now one of our assistant coaches. Jacques said Perron wanted to talk with me in person about playing time and asked me to go to his room. I said I was fine with that; in fact, I invited it.

I walked over to Perron's room and knocked on the door. He opened it, and I looked right at him and said, "Okay, you want to talk about playing time, here I am. Let's talk about playing time." But, as I was about to find out, he wouldn't be talking with me about much. "Serge is on the phone," he said. "He wants to speak with you."

Are you kidding me? Really? So Jean Perron was not going to hash it out with me.

I got on the phone, and Serge went right into it. He said—not exactly in these terms—that things weren't going well and that the incident in Hartford had sealed my fate. Serge said I was going to be traded to St. Louis.

I felt awful—absolutely awful. I loved being a Canadien. I didn't want to go anywhere.

But I didn't plead; that is not my style. I did say I didn't want to go to St. Louis, but Boston I would be all right with. Serge said he couldn't do a Boston deal, but wanted to know what I thought about playing for the New York Rangers, because he might be able to work that deal.

Well, I gotta tell you, New York was preferable to me—primarily because it was about the same distance from Boston, my hometown, and Montreal, my adopted home. Heck, in the broader scheme of things, it was like moving down the street. As well, it was a solid franchise with a good coach in Michel Bergeron—yes, the same Michel Bergeron who used to coach the Nordiques. I asked Serge to see if he could get me to the Rangers. He said to give him an hour.

About an hour later, Serge and I were on the phone; he told me that a trade to the Rangers was all set.

I respect and love Serge Savard, and I thought, naively, that he would take my side over the coach's. But he had to look at the bigger picture. I understand that now. As well, I wonder if it might have influenced his decision that the day before I was told I would be traded, Serge's best friend had died. I don't know.

I will say this: leaving Montreal in this way hurt very, very badly.

29

NEW YORK, NEW YORK

LEAVING MONTREAL WAS PAINFUL. Yet, as it has been said, I basically wrote my own going-away ticket.

I didn't know how I might handle the Big Apple. Even though fewer than two hundred miles separate Boston and New York City, about the only time I'd been to Manhattan was when I was playing for Montreal against the Rangers.

I actually grew to like New York and the metropolitan area. And I felt fortunate to be joining another Original Six organization—one with a great legacy.

New York had some A-game talent, most notably whiz kid goalie John "Beezer" Vanbiesbrouck and scoring superstar Marcel Dionne, who had been acquired from the Los Angeles Kings the previous season and who was in the final years of one of the most distinguished hockey careers of all time. Yes, I thought this could be a lot of fun and enjoyable. And it all would have been fun and enjoyable except for the injuries.

As I look back at my time with the Rangers, I see it as something of a jinxed period, physically. I was with New York about two-and-a-half seasons, and during that time I suffered one injury after another and spent so much time recovering from breaks and strains and fractures that I played very little hockey.

In that first season, after I came on board in late January, I played in twenty-two games. In season two, I played thirty-eight games, and in season three I played twenty-five.

The Rangers' front office, the coaches, my teammates, and the fans were great to me. In my short stay in New York, I played for three coaches. Michel Bergeron, as I mentioned, was the coach when the team acquired me. He was on the hot seat when the Rangers didn't make the play-offs that year. With two games left to play in the following regular season, and New York in third place in the Patrick Division with a 37–33–8 record, Rangers GM Phil Esposito—an NHL legend as a player—took over from Bergeron.

Espo was basically a placeholder until a permanent coach was selected. Indeed, he coached New York for only six games. We lost the final two games of the regular season, and then were swept in four games by the Pittsburgh Penguins in the first round of the play-offs. Soon after, the Rangers hired Roger Neilson as coach.

What I found particularly gratifying about the Rangers' management and coaches was that, in their dealings with me, or in PR statements the team released, they asserted the value of my leadership and emotion to the team; they said this value was evident even if I wasn't suited up for a game. Just having me around paid dividends, the team thought.

I lived a charmed life on the ice almost immediately with the Blueshirts. I joined the team in Philadelphia for the second game of a seven-game Rangers road trip. That night, I had an assist in our win. Then it was on to Boston, where, when I was announced, the fans booed me lustfully, and yet within seconds the chorus turned largely to cheers. I had a good game, scoring the first goal, not taking ill-considered penalties, and we won 4–2. I didn't have a single fight.

After the game, Bergeron was enthusiastic in telling the press how important I, the new kid, was to the Rangers.

Karma, though, never stayed positive for long with me. Game three was against our metro rivals, the Islanders. Late in the second period, I twisted my knee severely and left the game. I was diagnosed with a torn ligament the next day. I would be out for six to eight weeks.

I was back in uniform in early March. In fact, in a game against Philadelphia on March 15, I scored my first goal in Madison Square Garden. It was an important goal, coming with 1:39 left in the game and New York leading by a goal 2–1. But get this, and I don't know what I was thinking: after I scored, I did this little pirouette and dance routine, but not well. I fell and landed on my ass in front of more than 17,000 people. Served me right.

Over the final weeks of the season, we battled for fourth place in the Patrick Division, and the final play-off spot, with the Devils and Penguins. We didn't get that spot. My knee was sore over this stretch, but I held together.

After the season, New York signed me to a two-year contract that paid me $320,000 a year. Again, I considered this income more than fair.

That summer, before school started, Karen and I moved the family to a nice home we bought in Rye, New York, about twenty miles outside of the city and where the Rangers had their practice facility. It was the custom that, on the day of a home game, the team would have a light skate in Rye, then have lunch together, and then take a bus to Madison Square Garden. You didn't have to take the bus, but it was convenient, and most players took the bus most of the time. Sometimes I drove in myself.

So how did things go in what I hoped would be my first full season with the New York Rangers? I suffered ligament damage around my pelvic bone in Vancouver on December 10, 1988, and was told I'd be out for a minimum of two weeks.

I wondered if I was wearing down. I wondered if it were possible that all the injuries had piled up and left my body with so many weak spots that even mild physical trauma—let's say a hit of even semi-violent force—could result in a nagging injury.

And that pelvic injury became nagging, for sure. It resulted in my having to wear something of a walking cast. It also caused me to miss not two weeks of game play but closer to three months.

As I noted earlier, even when I was not competing in the game, New York coaches valued my being a part of the team. As evidence, I point to a game we had on February 19 in Philadelphia. It was a game that came during a stretch in which our power play was off and we were getting pushed and bullied around.

Michel Bergeron wanted me in the locker room and behind the bench in Philadelphia, even though I was not yet ready to play. He told me he liked the emotional boost I gave the team. And even if I would not be on the ice once the puck dropped, I was healthy enough to participate in warm ups. Indeed, Bergeron wanted me skating in warm ups that night. So as it happened, in warm ups I skated down into the Philly end of the ice, and as I passed Flyers goaltender Ron Hextall, I pointed my stick menacingly at him while at the same time directing nasty verbiage his way. He returned the gesture—both the stick-pointing and the expletives. Both teams converged at center ice. No brawl resulted, though.

I changed into a suit and tie for the game. I was behind the bench and barking as much encouragement as I could. We lost 3–1.

I returned to play for the final month of the regular season, which I finished with 177 penalty minutes in only thirty-eight games. When I was able to play, I gave the Rangers the enforcer they needed. I also checked aggressively.

It was difficult, though, being out for so long. I was not in sync with the other players and was not able to play the game I was capable of. More and more I understood the luxury of what I had had in Montreal, playing on the same line for seven seasons. Carbonneau, Gainey, and Nilan could almost play blindfolded and be where each of us needed to be and do what each of us needed to do.

New York was terrible in the homestretch, which cost Michel Bergeron his job. Over the final fifteen games of the regular season, we went 4–11–0, including losing streaks of five and six games (the latter included the final two games of the regular season, in which Esposito was our coach).

We lost four games to zilch against the Penguins in the first round. I had a so-so series, playing in every game, garnering an assist, and serving twenty-eight minutes in penalties.

I disagreed with Espo firing Bergeron, and I talked publicly about my views. In turn, Espo let it be known that he didn't like me voicing my opinion on the matter.

Roger Neilson was named coach of the Rangers for the 1989–90 season.

Neilson, a Toronto native, was a very smart hockey strategist and innovator who had coached Toronto, Buffalo, Vancouver, and Los Angeles before taking the job in New York. After four years in New York, including the '91–92 regular season, in which the team finished with the best record in the league, he went on to coach the

Florida Panthers, Philadelphia Flyers, and Ottawa Senators. Neilson is a member of the Hockey Hall of Fame in the Builder category.

I hit it off with Neilson. Out of the gates, I was playing well and New York was playing winning hockey. I used my physical play to create offensive chances for my teammates. At the end of October, the first month of the season, our record was 8–2–3.

So with things on the upswing, and so much looking good, a couple questions—very big questions—hung over me:

What would break next? And when?

On November 4, I was back in my old haunt. We were up against the Montreal Canadiens at the Forum.

In the third period, I chased a shot on our goal on which Patrick Roy had made a good save over his pad. I came in hard, caught my right arm on the post, and knew right away that it was another serious injury.

After the game, I was taken to the hospital and examined; an X-ray showed I had sustained a compound fracture. This put me in a bit of a bind, but not literally. We were to fly back to New York the next morning, and I needed a cast on my arm, but you can't fly with a cast, because the pressure of the cast, combined with the pressurized environment of a plane cabin, can cause blood flow problems and even an embolism. I could have stayed behind, had the arm set in a cast, and taken ground transport back to New York, but I didn't want to do that, so my arm was put in a sling, and our team doctor gave me a bottle of Percocet. I was hurting, and I took those pills quickly and willingly. I flew with the team in the morning.

When we arrived in New York, I went right away to an orthopedic specialist to have my arm set. I actually threw the remaining pain pills—about ten—down the drain.

I would not be back in action with the Blueshirts until the playoffs—and then only briefly.

When I was hurt, and not suited up, I often sat in the stands behind the Rangers' bench. I joked that I had the best seat in the house. Sitting up there, I was able to talk with the fans. Not playing was no fun—but building a rapport with the fans, and listening to and sharing with them my thoughts and opinions, was rewarding.

It was a curious experience—one in which I was a hybrid of player and fan and coach.

During the second half of the season, on March 5, while I was still recuperating, Karen gave birth to our third child, a daughter, Tara, at New York United Medical Center. As he did for Colleen and Chris, Father Ryan baptized Tara.

The next time I was in uniform for the Rangers was the fourth game of the play-offs, the division semifinal against the Islanders. We were up two games to one and were at Nassau Coliseum. In my second shift of the game, the Islanders' Ken Baumgartner—six foot one, 205 pounds, and early in his career as a highly capable and effective enforcer—came at me hard. I threw my arm against the middle of his stick, which broke the stick—and, as I would find out within a few hours, also broke the ulna in my forearm. My arm was in deep pain, but adrenaline kept me going. Shift after shift, Baumgartner tried to fight me, but I was basically incapable of moving the puck, never mind raising my arms to joust. I continued to skate and check, though.

In the third period, I said enough was enough. We were up 5–1 at the time. Who knows how much more damage I would do the arm if I stayed in the game. We won 6–1 and closed out the series two nights later with a 6–5 win at Madison Square Garden.

CHRIS NILAN

But my season—and, I was almost sure, my stay with the Rangers—had come to end in game five.

I was on the sidelines for the entire next series, the divisional final against the Washington Capitals, which we lost four games to one.

I wasn't ready to retire. But I thought that a better opportunity for me was outside of New York.

Ken Baumgartner was not only tough and strong, but a stand-up guy. It was the following October and the Rangers had a preseason game in Miami against the Islanders. Something went wrong in the refrigeration system at the rink where we were going to play, and the ice was not ready. Not knowing what exactly was up, players from both teams were standing, in their uniforms, outside the playing area; some were sitting in the stands. As I looked through the glass at a couple maintenance guys evaluating the ice, who should walk up to me but Baumgartner. He extended his hand and said, "Hey, Chris, I am sorry about that game last year and trying to fight you. I didn't know then that you had broken your arm. If I knew that, I wouldn't have kept after you."

I said thank you, that it was no big deal, and we were good.

I'll provide you with a little more background on the type of guy Ken Baumgartner is. While he was playing in the NHL, he spent the off-season attending Hofstra University on Long Island, where he earned his bachelor's degree in business and finance. He served as vice president of the NHL Players' Association. After he retired as a player, he was an assistant coach with the Bruins for a year, and then went on to earn an MBA from Harvard Business School.

Another off season and another off season of healing. I would have to say that things weren't working out, either for me or the Rangers.

I needed a change. I talked things over with my agent, Dan Rea, and then I spoke to Neil Smith, who was now the Rangers' GM. I told both of them I wanted out of New York, and that I hoped to return to Montreal or go to the Bruins, which would also be a return of sorts.

Smith supported trading me. Dan said he thought that getting traded to the Bruins had a lot higher probability than being traded to Montreal. Becoming a Bruin would be exciting, of course, not only because I would be in my hometown, but because the Bruins had made it to the Stanley Cup final the previous season and were returning with almost the entire nucleus of the club intact.

As Dan and Neil Smith told me, a deal that would make sense for the Rangers and Bruins would be one that would allow New York, in exchange for sending me to Boston, to acquire Greg Johnston, a gifted twenty-five-year-old forward who had never quite found a regular role with the Bs, was unhappy, and wanted out.

In mid-June, I would be taking my father, brother, my uncle Ed, and a few of our friends from Boston on a salmon fishing trip in the Bute Inlet in British Columbia. I love fishing, and I particularly like fishing for salmon. We would be gone for ten days. Just prior to leaving civilization, I called Dan Rea and asked him what was up. He told me to have a great time fishing and to give him a call when I returned from the wilderness. By that time, he would almost surely have good news. So I went fishing.

On June 30, the fishing trip over, I called Dan from a pay phone (pre–cell phone days) in a restaurant in a small town just outside of Campbell River. Dan answered and immediately told me that the Nilan-for-Johnston trade had gone through (the Rangers would also receive a ninth- or tenth-round draft pick). The Bruins offered me a two-year contract that would pay $300,000 a season. That was fine with me.

I immediately called Karen, who was at our home in Rye. She considered the trade to be good news as well. The Nilans were moving back to Boston.

30

BACK IN BOSTON

BRUINS COACH MIKE MILBURY, in a conversation with Francis Rosa of the *Boston Globe* about the Bruins bringing me on board, said, "We don't want 400 penalty minutes from him. We don't expect him to get 400 penalty minutes. We expect and want to bring his competitive spirit and willingness to play with the fire that he's always shown."

Milbury was surely being coy with those comments; I wasn't sure just how coy, though.

Perhaps now, after spending almost ten years in Montreal, becoming a favorite of the fans and winning a Stanley Cup there, I felt more at home in that city than I did where I was born and raised. Well, if not more at home, then more liked and more appreciated.

Yet coming home was also nice in many ways. I know that Karen was excited. She would be closer to her mother and siblings. And for me, too, it was nice to be close to my parents, my brother and my sisters, and my friends. Whatever our feelings, Karen and I and the kids were on the move again. We rented a home in Nahant, a small community on the coast, just north of Boston. When training camp opened in August, I felt as strong and as capable as ever. I was confident that the Bruins could once again compete for the Cup and that I would be a major part of the effort. Consider the talent: our forwards were

Cam Neely, Bobby Carpenter, Craig Janney, Dave Christian, Randy Burridge, John Carter, John Byce, Shayne Stevenson, Bob Sweeney, and Dave Poulin; our defenders were Ray Bourque, Glen Wesley, Al Pedersen, Don Sweeney, Garry Galley, and Michael Thelven.

As well, though, there were much-needed players, such as Gordie Kluzak, Lyndon Byers, and Andrew Brickley, who were still recovering from injuries and were iffy for the season.

One of the new players on the team was Vladimir "Rosie" Ruzicka, a talented forward from Czechoslovakia who had played internationally for several years prior to starting his career in the NHL with Edmonton at the relatively advanced age of twenty-six. After a year with Edmonton, the Bruins acquired him. Rosie didn't speak English well, and he and I developed something of an Abbott and Costello routine. A reporter would ask a question, and I would turn to Rosie, who would look at me with an expression of absolute earnestness, and I would "translate" the question, speaking total gibberish to him. He would speak in Czech to me, and then I would turn to the reporter and say something in English that was nonsensical and not related to anything. For example, after taking in Rosie's "response," I might say to the reporter, "Yes, I very much enjoy America. And later I will go to bed." Or, "Oh, thank you for the question, and yes, I enjoy the food. I very much enjoy the United States of America." Everyone, the media and everyone else, was in on our gag, of course, and it was sheer amusement all around.

The entire Bruins organization was welcoming to me.

The season started off great. Our first game was at home, against the Philadelphia Flyers. Prior to the opening face-off, there was a big ceremony where the Wales Conference championship flag was raised. Sure, it wasn't a Stanley Cup banner, but for the Bruins to be back, they had to take that step of making it to the final, which they had done, and it was appropriate to enjoy the achievement.

It was heartening when my name was announced for the first time as a Boston Bruin to the Garden crowd, who went wild, delivering a throaty and prolonged welcome. I felt great. And I continued to feel great when, on my inaugural shift with the Bruins, I smashed Philly's Craig Berube hard against the boards. Every single one of the Black and Gold partisans loved it. Later in the first period, I registered an assist on the first Bs goal of the season, which was scored by Dave Poulin.

In the second period, I collided with Poulin and sustained a deep bruise to my right knee. I played out the game, which we won 4–1, but after the game my knee began to swell and stiffen. I would miss games; I just didn't know how many.

I didn't dress for the next five games, a nice stretch for the Bs in which they won four games and tied one. I returned to play against L.A. on the road. We lost that game 7–1 and continued on a road trip in which we lost the next three games. Back in Boston, we hosted Vancouver in the first game of a home stand; we won 4–2 and I got ejected for fighting.

Things were going well for me individually on the ice, even if the team was shaky. Boston was playing three lines, and I was getting plenty of shifts and contributing. I definitely was still an enforcer— and it seemed that Milbury had decided it would either be me or Lyndon Byers out there on the ice. Because we were using only three lines, if I was healthy, it meant Lyndon was sitting. But, of course, with my track record, Lyndon had to be on deck. I also knew that if I became ineffective as an enforcer and intimidator, then either Lyndon or another tough guy would replace me.

Yet Coach Milbury had found another use for me—one that I embraced: that of a penalty killer. It was smart strategically and tactically. Sure, I was a fighter, but I also understood my job, and I played the role I was supposed to play. If I was told to help kill a penalty, I had the ability and the skills to effectively do that job. I always hustled and could deliver clean, hard checks to put an opponent on the boards or off his feet—or, at the very least, off balance. Having me on the ice kept opponents a bit wary, and this further messed with their play. Aggressiveness all around hampered the ability of the other team to press a man advantage. I also was adept at clearing the puck and passing. Again, I liked the role of a penalty killer.

I also liked that my parents and brother and sisters could once again see me play at the Boston Garden, and they were not subject to asshole comments sent their way. Karen sometimes sat with them; other times, she sat alone. After games, my family and I, and often friends from my childhood and teen years in Boston, would go for a late dinner.

❖

In a home loss to Buffalo early in November, I scored my first goal and had a decent scrap with the Sabres' Brad Smith.

At the end of the month, we were doing all right, at 11–6–3 and leading the Adams Division. I was having a great time on a line with Bob Sweeney and Randy Burridge. We three were all physical and always pressing. We killed penalties and hit opponents hard—and created scoring opportunities for ourselves and our teammates.

In mid-December, Milbury moved me to left wing—a position I had never played—and to a new line. There was Craig Janney in the middle, and on the other side, Cam Neely. Craig said he never felt as protected as when he played on that line. And, as I discovered and appreciated more and more, and once I adjusted to taking the puck on the backhand, I had a lot of options, including going to the short side or the weak side. But I understood that an important part of my job was "opening things up" for Craig and Cam.

Yeah, I was still opening things up. We always had a physical game when we played Hartford, our closest geographic rival and the only other NHL team in New England. We always brought out the worst and best in one another, like in Boston on December 13. We had beaten the Whalers 5-1 the night before at their place. I thought something might be up for the following evening at the Garden. It was.

A little more than halfway through the third period, with us leading 6-1, Ed Kastelic of the Whalers slammed Janney. I then popped Kastelic. Now, get this: I was on my way to my second home, the penalty box, and so was Kastelic. As Kastelic skated past our bench, Lyndon Byers jumped onto the ice to get to him. Coach Milbury went over the boards to grab a hold of Lyndon. What resulted right there was Lyndon getting a ten-game suspension.

With two minutes to go and the Bs crushing Hartford 8-2, I elbowed Bobby Holik hard, breaking his nose. Holik later said that he had heard about me. I needed to confirm the intelligence briefing he received. Welcome to the NHL, kid.

One hundred minutes of penalties were called in that game. Oh wow, I was back in Boston and having fun.

And Coach Milbury and the Bruins liked what I was doing.

We were 20-12-8, still leading the Adams, when we played our first game of 1991, on January 3 in Vancouver. The game was tied 3-3 in the first period, and I got called for a four-minute roughing penalty. Was Milbury pissed? Nope. He said it contributed to the spirit and emotion our team needed.

I picked up thirteen more minutes in penalties that game. Final score: Bs 8, Canucks 3.

Our next game was in Boston on Saturday night against the Capitals. We played like shit and lost 5-3. Milbury was not happy at all. He told us all to be back at the Garden at eight the next morning for a special game-tape session. So we all showed up the next morning and sat down in the locker room and went through about three hours of film, with Milbury berating us most of that time. Finally, he said that was enough for now, and told us to go to lunch and then come back.

Before heading out to lunch, I walked out to the arena floor, and there were some of my teammates playing basketball on the parquet floor, which had been laid out for a Celtics game that night. I joined in. Well, Don Warden went up for a shot, and I jumped to block it, and when I came down, I felt a sharp pain and something snap. Ah, shit, this wasn't good. You might tell me that, since I made my living playing hockey, it was not smart to play pickup basketball. And I would answer that you are absolutely right—it wasn't smart. Yes, I did some bad damage to my ankle. I couldn't put pressure on it.

Well, I got on the phone immediately to our team physician, Dr. Bert Zarins, a world-renowned orthopedic specialist. He saw me that afternoon at Massachusetts General Hospital. X-rays were taken, but with the swelling, it was tough to get a good look at what was going on. Bert said it looked like a deep, deep sprain and to stay off it for about a week, which also meant I was out for three games. Torn ligaments was the diagnosis.

Coach Milbury was angry about how I sustained the injury, and he let me know it.

But, then again, get this: Mike was the coach of the Wales Conference team that would play in the NHL All-Star Game on January 19, and in that role, he had the authority to name a couple players to the team who had not been voted in by the fans. Mike chose me, and that caused a good deal of controversy. Not that he or I cared.

As it would turn out, though, my ankle was not ready for action in time for the All-Star Game, and I watched the TV broadcast of the game from a chair in my living room in Nahant.

I initially figured that the ankle injury would keep me out for a week, maybe two, and that would be it. Yet three weeks later, the ankle was still sore, and it was wobbly and unstable when I walked on it.

Dr. Zarins had MRI scans done on the ankle from a variety of angles, and this time, with the swelling reduced, what was shown was that I had fractured my talus bone in a strange way. I was going to need surgery. I was operated on on February 8 and began my convalescence on crutches.

That season was an avalanche of injuries for the Bruins. Just as I was about to return, finally, for the last five games of the regular season, Cam Neely had been out for a few games with a hip injury, Randy Burridge still had a couple games to go before getting back on the ice after arthroscopic knee surgery, and Lyndon Byers was recovering from foot surgery.

But I was back for the play-offs. And we had the squad to do some serious damage in the postseason.

On the subject of damage, consider our final couple games of the regular season. Our second-to-last game was in Uniondale, New York, against the Islanders. We lost 5–3. I had two good bouts in this game, both against Dean Chynoweth, one in the first period and another in the second. I got the decision in both.

Of course, this was all mere prelude to the final game before the play-offs. We hosted our archenemies, the Hartford Whalers. It was one for the record books. You know that old joke, "I went to a fight the other night, and a hockey game broke out"? That was what went on in Boston on Sunday night, March 31, 1991, for there surely was some hockey played in between the fights— passing and shooting of the puck amid slugging for three periods. At the end of the game, the teams had a combined 210 penalty minutes. And yours truly set an

NHL record for infractions in a single game, with ten. Those penalties represented a total of forty-two minutes—more than two periods' worth of sitting in the box.

I had three fights during the game, and was 1–2. Already discussed in this book was the unanimous win that NHL rookie Jim McKenzie (ten years my junior) registered over me; that was the first fight, which started about midway through the second period, when we were up 5–0. But, as I explained, I skated away clearheaded. And I wouldn't let it go; later in the period, I skated over to the Whalers' bench, where McKenzie was standing, and I started pointing at him and talking shit. He was furious and gave it right back to me. Ah, a lot of fun.

Round two—ding, ding. My opponent was Doug Houda, who had been in the league for a few years, but was eight years younger than I was. I beat Houda on points. In the third period, I got another win—this one against another kid, Rob Brown, who was a decade younger than me, yet who already had lost a good deal of hair. I got Brown good with a series of uppercuts and also managed to rip out one of his plugs (this was a time when hair transplants equaled "doll" head). I kept the plug in my hand and gave it to our trainer, Don Warden, who taped it to a wall in the locker room. Under it, he put up a little sign that read "Rob Brown's hair."

We won the game 7–3. We were ready to go for the Cup. We were ready for our first opponent in the play-offs: the same Hartford Whalers.

We had a superb team in 1990–91; we were good enough, I thought, to win it all. We came close. But we didn't win.

Going into the play-offs, I continued to play an important role on a crunching and hard-checking line alongside Nevin Markwart and Ron Hoover. Craig Janney was iffy for the opening round, which was one of the reasons we loaded up with defensemen: Don Sweeney, Garry Galley, Glen Wesley, Ray Bourque, Jim Wiemer, Stéphane Quintal, and Bob Beers.

I was sure we were going to beat the Whalers.

We lost the first game at home to Hartford 5–2. We weren't good, squandering a number of power-play opportunities. As the seconds ticked off, there was some booing coming down from the stands.

We evened the series two nights later at the Garden with a 4–3 win. I did what I needed to do to piss off the Whalers, including spitting in the face of Hartford's Kevin Dineen. This made him go ballistic, swearing and pointing at me.

When the series moved to Hartford, it really wasn't much of a road game for us. Indeed, the Bruins stayed at a hotel in Massachusetts—in Springfield, about a half hour from Hartford. We were on and won easily 6–3. Actually, I need to come clean here. As a whole, the Bs were not superb, but our goalie, Andy Moog, was great. I got an assist on a Garry Galley goal that broke a 2–2 tie. With a few minutes left in the game, when the outcome had been settled, Jim McKenzie cheap-shotted me with a push to the back of the head. I chose not to retaliate—then.

I knew we needed to keep the momentum going and that it was going to take everything to win the series. In the locker room after the game, I popped a tape of the William Tell Overture (one of the prized tunes in my collection) into a boom box, cranked up the volume, and let the music roll.

Hartford wouldn't go away—just like it wouldn't go away five years earlier, when I was with Montreal and the Whalers took us to the full seven games.

After a 4–3 loss in Hartford, we came to Boston with the series tied at two games apiece.

Game five was a strange one, for sure. We were down 1–0 early in the third period, and with the Bruins on the power play, Ray Bourque got the puck on his stick and did what he had done a million times before: just dumped it down the ice so that he and his line could give chase. But the puck, strangely, bounced off Hartford center Paul Cyr and ricocheted past Whaler goalie Peter Sidorkiewicz; game tied. That started it. Boston scored five more times in the third. We won 6–1, with three of the goals coming on power plays.

We closed out the series with a 3–1 win Hartford, even though we were outshot 32–16. Needless to say, Andy Moog was again immense.

On to the Adams Division final. Bring on the Montreal Canadiens.

For the ninth consecutive year, the Bruins and Canadiens were meeting in the play-offs. As a Hab, I had been involved in a major part of that streak—and my side had won every series. Sure, I retained an affection for my old team, but let's be clear: I was now a Bruin. I knew and appreciated fully who paid me and buttered my bread. As a Bruin, I wanted to beat the Canadiens every bit as much as I had wanted to beat the Bruins when I was a Canadien.

Cam Neely scored both our goals in the opener at the Garden as the Bruins won 2–1. I kept my gloves on, which is always difficult for me. Montreal beat us in overtime 4–3 in game two.

In Montreal, we went ahead in the series two games to one by virtue of a 3–2 win. We were up in the series, but I thought we were lacking intensity. Our attack was soft. And let's be clear, I thought I had lacked some intensity. It was my job to spark and feed that emotion by whatever means.

After getting pounded 6–2 in game four, something needed to be reversed.

We were getting hurt by the Habs' second line of Stéphane Richer, Brian Skrudland, and Shayne Corson, so Mike Milbury put together a line to counter it: Ron Hoover, Randy Burridge, and Peter Douris. Janney and Neely and I needed to keep up our checking and keep applying pressure to my erstwhile teammate, goalie Patrick Roy.

Boston also had to get more physical. I, of course, felt I could help in this department. Seven seconds into the game, I pushed, then punched and briefly fought with, Mario Roberge. It wasn't much of a scrap, but it accomplished what I wanted to do early on.

Craig Janney had four assists, two of them setting up goals by Cam Neely. We won 4–1. If we played game six in Montreal on Saturday night the way we had played game five, we would advance to the Wales Conference final.

Damn Shayne Corson. We could keep him bottled up some, but not totally. It was his goal in overtime in game six that gave the Habs a 3–2 win and set up a seventh game in Beantown. The Bruins had never beaten the Canadiens in a postseason game seven—never.

We flew to Boston right after the game. We got in at about one in the morning, and I went home to Nahant. I spent time with Karen and the kids the next day, and wouldn't you know it, little Chris, all of five years old, was sulking about the loss. He gave me a lucky penny to have with me on Monday night. I had the penny with me when I took the ice for the finale; it was in tucked into my jockstrap.

Prior to the game, after warm ups, Harry Sinden gave us a Knute Rockne speech in the locker room. We were fired up and we went out and upended history. Andy Moog faced thirty-five shots and turned all away but one. Dave Christian scored on a thirty-foot shot in the second, and Cam Neely delivered on the game winner, a sixty-five-foot cannon blast with about two minutes gone in the third.

In the postgame handshake line, I hugged and talked with Corson for a few minutes. After our postgame session with Coach Milbury, where we did a short bit of celebrating and received preliminary marching orders for the Wales Conference final against the Pittsburgh Penguins—which began the very next night at the Garden—I went into the Montreal locker room to see some of my former teammates.

I thought my actions after the game were fine, but Milbury didn't. And he let me know as much the next afternoon during the team skate-around. As is my nature, I protested and gave my opinion. It was not a big deal. We got it behind us. But someone heard us talking and reported it to the media. Of course, it made the news. It was a distraction the team didn't need.

Pittsburgh was the best team in the NHL that year—and we surprised them early, going up two games to zip by scores of 5–3 and 6–4. Our big gun in those games was Rosie Ruzicka, who had helped during the regular season and against Hartford and Montreal in the play-offs, but whose scoring output had been modest. Yet he erupted against Pittsburgh, scoring eight points in those two games, figuring directly in every one of our goals except for three.

But we lost all the momentum after game two, and Pittsburgh woke up. We lost game three at their place 4–1. Man, it was hot—literally. It was something like eighty-five degrees just above the ice. Andy Moog was so dehydrated that he was out after the second period. Cam Neely sustained a charley horse and Dave Poulin pulled a groin muscle. Neither would be back at top form for the rest of the series.

We lost game four 4–1 even after Milbury had brought up Lyndon Byers to collaborate with me on pushing back physically against a Penguins squad that had been getting the better of us on the nasty part of hockey. Lyndon and I did act as aggressors, but our influence was negligible. Pittsburgh star Mario Lemieux got his panties in a knot because I slashed him during the game. He even said that was what I did—that that was my job. He got it right—sort of.

The wheels fell off the Bruins bus. In game five, Kevin Stevens had two goals and three assists, and Lemieux, Bryan Trottier, Paul Stanton, Larry Murphy, and Ulf Samuelsson also scored off Andy Moog, who was replaced by Reggie Lemelin after the Penguins scored their seventh goal, capping their easy 7–2 win.

I was not playing strong offensive hockey, and while I was asserting myself and sticking up for my teammates, it seemed that it had the result of throwing a cup of water on a forest fire. Pittsburgh was far more aggressive than us.

Mike Milbury did not play me in the sixth and deciding game of the series, which Pittsburgh won 5–3 on its home ice to advance to the Stanley Cup final for the first time in the team's twenty-four-year history. Pittsburgh won the Cup, beating the Minnesota North Stars four games to two. Pittsburgh would repeat as NHL champs the following season.

31

IN THE HOMESTRETCH

AFTER THE SEASON, I needed to take some good, hard looks at what was ahead. I wasn't the player I was even five years before, but I felt strongly that I could still contribute. Then again, there were very few guaranteed roster spots for the next year. Really, it seemed the only players who couldn't be touched were Cam Neely, Ray Bourque, and Andy Moog. I couldn't disagree with any of that.

What really concerned me about the 1991–92 season was that I didn't want to be relegated to spot duty—to only be a fighter and enforcer. When I was trying to make my bones in the league, I would have accepted that role, but not now.

What complicated things for me was that, at the end of the 1990–91 campaign, Mike Milbury resigned as coach and moved to the front office as assistant general manager under Harry Sinden. I respected Mike as a coach and a person, and I thought he had given me more than a fair shake.

Brought in to replace Milbury—and I really couldn't figure out this move—was Rick Bowness, who over the previous two seasons had coached the Maine Mariners, and not successfully. In 1989–90, Maine finished in fifth place in its AHL division with a record of 31–38–11; this was not good enough to qualify for the play-offs. Next year, the Mariners improved a little bit, ending up at 34–34–12, which again placed them fifth in their division and again assured they wouldn't see the postseason.

Early in training camp, it was obvious that I was on the cusp of making or not making the team. I was put on the "B" squad, which meant my position on the team was in jeopardy. As always, I gave a hard effort—and earned a position. It was obvious that what Bowness envisioned for me was precisely what I did not want: to play the enforcer, and not much else.

Among the newcomers on the team was Jimmy Vesey, a center, who was brought up from the Peoria Rivermen of the AHL. Jimmy, about eight years younger than me, was a local kid like myself; he was from the Boston neighborhood of Charlestown. As a prep, he starred for Christopher Columbus High School, a Catholic school in Boston (no longer in operation), and was drafted by the St. Louis Blues at the end of his senior year.

Jimmy didn't go right to the NHL; instead he attended Merrimack College, where he had a standout four years. After college, he played for a bit for the Blues but mostly for the Rivermen.

Jimmy and I had known each other for several years when we became teammates in Boston. We weren't close friends, but indeed we were, in many ways, cut from the same cloth; we grew up in working-class families in Boston, knew the same streets and many of the same people—in and out of hockey—played in the same rinks and arenas, and in the same leagues, and grew up cheering excitedly for the Bruins.

Now that we were on the same team, it would figure, as it happened, that we became good buddies. I understood him quickly to be a stand-up, trustworthy, and tough kid in whom I could confide. And when the terrible times came for me later, Jimmy would always be there for me, willing to do anything.

Today, it brings me tremendous happiness to watch and follow the hockey exploits of the sons of Jim and his wife, Ann. As I write this, Jim Vesey, the younger, has just finished his freshman year at Harvard University, and in his first season for the Crimson, he set a school record for goals by a freshman. The summer after he graduated from high school, the Nashville Predators selected Jim in the third round of the NHL draft. Jim played for Team USA in the 2013 World Junior Championships. Nolan Vesey graduated from Austin Prep, a Boston-area Catholic high school that is a powerhouse in hockey. Nolan had a standout high school career and will attend the University of Maine on a full athletic scholarship.

Right from the start of the season, I was doing a lot of sitting, not playing much. Animosity built up between Bowness and me. Of course, I never had much trouble expressing my feelings. On the other hand, I had lots of trouble withholding my thoughts. We were playing like shit. Fans and the media were on us. Cam Neely and Dave Poulin were out with injuries.

Lyndon Byers was not his normally feisty self, either; he was battling a bad ankle. In the middle of October, the Bruins brought in Al "Beef Stew" Stewart. Stewart was obtained in a trade from New Jersey and was on the Bs roster to add enforcer weight. But Al, while tough, really wasn't an enforcer type; for sure, he wouldn't back down, but he lost more fights than he won. And he wasn't into playing the tough guy. I think Bowness, though, thought Al could be the answer to dealing with a malcontent like me.

In late October, Boston went on a five-game road trip that had us first playing in Vancouver and then on to San Jose, St. Louis, and Minnesota, finishing in Chicago. I went on the trip, but I didn't dress for any of the games. It was commented on in the newspapers that when I did fight, which wasn't often, I didn't go at it with the gusto of times past. An inaccurate reflection.

Al Stewart was fighting; he was picking up the slack left by Lyndon and me. I could tell, though, that he didn't like the role he was playing. And something was bothering him beyond hockey. When we got back from the road trip, he told the Bruins he didn't want to play hockey anymore. He retired at the age of twenty-seven. Yes, he did play some minor-league hockey after that. But basically, his two weeks with the Bruins in the fall of 1991 was the swan song of his very short NHL career.

Our first game back in Boston was a Thursday night game against L.A. While on the road, Bowness felt he had his muscle role all figured out, but then Stewart quit and Lyndon Byers's ankle was still giving him trouble—he would not be able to go against L.A.

So, the morning of the Kings game, right after our skate, I was pedaling away on the bike in the locker room. Bowness walked up to me and said, "Chris, are you ready to go tonight?"

I looked right at Bowness and said, "Hey, Rick, you can go fuck yourself."

He was surprised. He said, "What's the matter with you? Are you going to play tonight?"

"Oh, fuck that," I said. "I deserve to be treated with respect, and you're not giving me any. And you think I should respect you? You think I'm going to go through a fucking wall for you? No fucking way."

Bowness didn't say another word but went to talk to Mike Milbury.

I didn't dress that night. We lost to L.A., 4–2, partially because we got pushed around.

Addressing the problem between Bowness and me, Boston Herald sportswriter Joe Fitzgerald, a man I admired and trusted, wrote in his column that Mike and I should settle the matter. I think the column inspired Mike to sit down with me to talk.

One morning a couple days after the Kings game, Mike and I, and Rick Bowness, met in Mike's office. We had a game that night at the Garden against Detroit.

Mike started things off, saying, "Okay, what is going on?"

"I don't want to be treated like shit," I said. "I am not Ray and I am not Cam, but I have been in the league for twelve years. I have paid the price, and don't want to be treated like shit. If you don't respect me, how am I going to respect you?"

Mike asked, "Chris, do you still want to play?"

"Yes."

Bowness was just sitting there, looking down, and at Mike, but not much at me.

Mike said, "Okay, but you can't tell the coach to fuck off."

"I understand that. And understand I need to be treated with respect."

Well, the long and short of what resulted from this conversation was that I would receive more playing time. And it was agreed that I wouldn't come back that night against Detroit, or the three games after, two of which were on the road. We concurred that my first game back would be seven days hence, at home, against the New Jersey Devils.

So, there was a resolution—at least for now—but the entire episode was not good for anyone—not for the team, not for the image of the team, and not for me. Still, I thought I was in the right. Some of my teammates supported me, some didn't. I was fine with all that. Bruins management did help me out in that they didn't demand I play. If they had, and I didn't play, then I could have been docked pay. What I had to do to continue to draw a paycheck was to continue to practice, which I did.

Talk about a "How You Like Me Now" return. Against the Devils, I scored two goals and we won 4–0. Bowness gave me major props in the press for making the most out of my opportunity.

As I left the ice that night I was sure things would continue on a high note.

What continued was the strange path and arc of my career. Late in the third period against New Jersey, after I had notched my second goal, and with us ahead by that final score of four–zip, I crashed into the Devils' goal. A jolt of pain went through my lower back, but I skated it off. My back felt all right in the locker room after the game. Yet on the ride home, and through the night, it began to spasm and ache incredibly. A trip to the doctor showed that I had bruised two bones in my vertebrae. I would be out for four games.

On December 26, in the third period of a game in Hartford against the Whalers, which we won 3–2, I slammed into our defenseman, Garry Galley, and twisted my long-suffering knee again. I didn't think it was bad.

Right after the game, we chartered a plane to Buffalo, where we would play the next night. The knee swelled and stiffened, and early the next afternoon I flew back to Boston to get it looked at. Analysis showed that there was more ligament damage.

I was back in the lineup in mid-January, but I was returned to on-and-off duty. Maybe I had lost it; maybe time had caught up to me.

Maybe it was time to call it a career. I only knew I didn't want to keep on in the NHL like this.

On Monday, February 10, a day after my thirty-fourth birthday, the Bruins put me on waivers. That same week, early on Thursday afternoon, with about a half hour to go before the waiver period expired and the Bruins already on the bus to go to the airport to catch a flight to St. Louis for a game the next night, I stopped in to talk with Mike Milbury in his office. I didn't really care if I spoke to Bowness. I was still hugely pissed at him.

Mike sat in a chair behind his desk, and I sat in a chair facing him on the other side of the desk. Mike was always up front and stand-up with me. He laid it on the line, told me how much he respected me and my effort and what I had done, not just for the Bruins, but also overall in hockey. Still, he said he was supporting the coach.

When we finished talking, there were only about fifteen minutes remaining until the clock struck zero on my hopes of another team picking him up. So that was that. My NHL career was over. I shook hands with Mike and walked to the locker room.

I was all alone in the locker room when I heard the phone ring in the adjacent trainer's room. No one was in there, so I walked over and picked up the phone. It was Milbury. He told me the Montreal Canadiens had just picked me up on waivers, and that I was booked on a flight to Montreal leaving in two hours from Logan Airport. The Habs wanted me on the flight so I would be able to play that night against San Jose.

I made a call to Karen and let her know what was up. Before I grabbed a cab to go the airport, I talked with Serge Savard, my old friend, on the phone. He said Montreal could use me, and that Habs coach Pat Burns was totally on board with the decision. And Serge also said there was no guarantee of me playing regularly, but that I should be in Montreal, and I should be wearing a Habs sweater.

On the way to Logan, I knew what this was about, this overture, this decision of the Montreal Canadiens. In so many ways, it was gesture of appreciation and goodwill. It would later be explained to me that there was not a lot of support within the Canadiens administration for signing me to a contract of even a year. But there was unanimous support for making sure I finished my career as a Montreal Canadien.

I made it to Montreal and the Forum in plenty of time to get dressed for warm ups. In the locker room, it was a warm reunion. Embraces with Guy Carbonneau, Mike McPhee, Patrick Roy, and Shayne Corson—members of the old guard still there.

When my name was announced to the sold-out crowd, there was a bit of bedlam, an avalanche and thunder burst of people going bonkers, screaming and stomping and yelling.

It was one of the happiest moments of my life.

I played my final seventeen regular-season games in the NHL for the Montreal Canadiens. Over that stretch, I kept hustling and kept checking and, as necessary, kept fighting. I tangled with old adversaries Rob Ray, Marty McSorley, Greg Smyth, Tony Twist, Ken Sabourin, and Doug Houda.

I played in seven of our eleven play-off games—my final NHL play-off games. We beat Hartford in seven in the division semifinal, and got swept by Boston in the division final. I never stopped skating and giving my all. I never backed down.

I finished my NHL career with the same energy, mindset, enthusiasm, and love for hockey I first manifested more than a quarter-century before on that big, frozen puddle at the end of my street.

CHRIS NILAN

32

NO LONGER A PLAYER

THAT SUMMER, I WAS BACK IN BOSTON, trying to figure what to do next. I was distracted, unhappy, unsure, and feeling unwanted. Would I play again in the NHL?

With the summer moving into August, and NHL training camps soon to start, my thoughts turned to the hard reality of decision making and facing the future.

It was mostly my decision, but I did talk about it with Karen. The kids were young, and even the oldest, Colleen, was only in second grade, and she didn't seem to care much either way what was going on.

But I knew deep in my heart that if Montreal didn't want to pick me up, I didn't want to play any more pro hockey. Not that there weren't feelers out there from other teams, but I really wanted to stay and play for the Canadiens. Even if I had to be just an occasional enforcer for the Habs, and nothing more, I would have taken that job. But I wouldn't do that job for any other team. I had a chance to play in Europe—in Balzano, Italy—but didn't want to go there.

Pat Burns had left the Canadiens at the end of the previous season and gone to the Toronto Maple Leafs to be their head coach. Replacing him in Montreal was Jacques Demers. Demers had been coaching in the league for a while, most recently for the past three seasons as head coach of the Detroit Red Wings. He would be making the personnel decisions, and I was not high on his depth chart. He was looking to bring in a younger, more offensively oriented player to replace me. I was not happy, but I could, and had to, live with it. Anyway, the call didn't come from Montreal, and that basically meant I had reached the end of the road as an NHL player. It was tough to take.

Then again, how could I have too many regrets? Hell, I was a kid from Boston who had a fairly undistinguished high school career, didn't exactly stand out in college, was one of the last people picked in the NHL draft, and went on to play thirteen years in the league, ten of them with one of the most prestigious and famed franchises in pro sports. What's more, for almost all those years, I was a valuable contributor to the team I was on. For sure, when I was a grade schooler and in junior high during those cold New England winters, walking down the street to the outdoor rink, carrying my skates, wearing sneakers on my feet, I dreamed of playing in the NHL, and I held fast to that dream until it came true. Somewhere down the road, I lived the dream—and then some.

(I must confess that, at least early on in the Jacques Demers era in Montreal, it seemed he had made all the right moves and right decisions, including not re-signing me. In Demers's first year with Montreal, the team won the Stanley Cup. Life was grand. Yet success was fleeting. The year after winning it all, the Canadiens lost in the first round of the play-offs, and the year after that, they didn't make the play-offs. After starting out 0–5 in his third season with Montreal, Demers was fired.)

So Karen and I resolved to make a fresh start of things. I really wasn't sure what that start was going to look like. Fortunately, Karen and I were always smart with our money when I was in the league and making a nice income. We didn't live extravagantly. We saved and had a good nest egg.

But I needed to work.

Karen started preparing for her own post-NHL career. She started taking classes at Quincy College and soon entered the college's nurse-training program.

In the interest of trying to help me find a job, Dan Rea introduced me to David D'Allessandro, who headed up marketing and public relations for the venerable John Hancock Mutual Life Insurance Company. D'Allessandro was a brand-building genius who started at the company in 1984 and was charged with sprucing up and modernizing the image of the firm. He did just that, overseeing and stewarding the famous "Real Life, Real Answers" advertising campaign that won a slew of awards, as well as the move of John Hancock into big-time sports marketing. It all worked. In 1998, D'Allessandro became president and COO of John Hancock and was named CEO in 2000. In the approximately twenty years that D'Allessandro was with John Hancock, it grew from a successful, revered, yet stodgy New England mutual insurance company into one of the best-known brands in the world and a fully diversified financial services corporation.

Indeed, it was in 2000, with D'Allessandro at the helm, that John Hancock "demutualized"—which meant that it was no longer owned by its policyholders, but by investors who owned stock. John Hancock Mutual Life Insurance was no more and John Hancock Financial Services was born.

Again, a component of David D'Allessandro's strategy and tactics for building the image and brand of John Hancock was to invest in sports marketing. John Hancock jumped into the sector full bore with sponsorships of the Boston Marathon and the Olympic Games.

When I retired from playing, a Winter Olympics had just been held the previous February in Albertville, France. But another Winter Olympics would be held in 1994 in Lillehammer, Norway. This was because, back in 1986, the International Olympic Committee voted to break from having the summer and winter games in the same year every four years, and to alternate between summer and winter games every two years. The new schedule would start with the Winter Olympics in Lillehammer.

John Hancock was ramping up its sponsorship of the 1994 Winter Olympics when I sat down to talk with David D'Allessandro. He and his marketing and PR team were launching a series of hockey clinics around the nation that promoted John Hancock and its association with the Olympics. He thought I would be just right as a front person and face for John Hancock as the hockey clinics campaign moved from city to city. I liked the idea, and I was hired to be in community relations, with my first role being the on-site spokesperson, emissary, and coach for John Hancock at its clinics.

D'Allessandro was a smart guy and he gave me a nice opportunity, but boy, did he have an almost royal air about him. Then again, maybe it was just me—the hardscrabble kid from West Roxbury.

I liked that job with John Hancock very much, at least at first. Being away from my family was not nice, but the job required no heavy lifting, and it dovetailed with what I liked to do: get on the ice and work with kids. I would board a plane and head to some city, stay in a nice hotel and eat at nice restaurants, and meet up at a nearby rink with the local John Hancock rep, who would brief me about the group that would be at the rink—usually, kids in youth hockey, along with their coaches and parents. I would get out on the ice with the kids and show then some drills, pass the puck, and do a free skate with them. It was great. Of course, I wore a John Hancock jersey, and when I spoke to everyone, I made sure to give love to John Hancock in what I said. We also handed out pucks and other giveaways, which I signed. I also autographed other items. What was best about this gig was that you could see that the kids were getting something out of it. No bullshit with these kids—they were not jaded or cynical yet, and they loved the game of hockey for the game itself.

When the clinic campaign came to a close, I was based back in Boston and still in community relations for the company. I soon found out what ex–pro jocks find out: that there is plenty of room in the budgets of even the best-run, best-managed, most efficient companies to sort of warehouse jocks and use them as needed.

Now, don't get me wrong, I was, and remain, very thankful to John Hancock and David D'Allessandro for the opportunity. But after a while it seemed like management was looking for something for me to do, and I wasn't too good at figuring it out for myself; this corporate thing was foreign to me.

I did see that much of what I did was important in being a face for John Hancock in its support of local youth organizations.

I also want to say that John Hancock is a tremendously giving corporate citizen—and it not only gives a lot, it also gives strategically and intelligently so that every dollar does the most good. That was the case when I worked for the company and is true today. Still, I did get the feeling that I was not that important to the cause.

I did some meet-and-greets at events, and I was a guest at some dinners, but it was kind of stale and uninteresting. I didn't mind working hard, but the day-in, day-out sameness of the job was boring me and making me restless.

During this period, I continued to skate and play in a couple adult leagues. I played in charity golf tournaments and participated in other benefit events. I went to Bruins games, local college hockey games, and took a few days here and there to go up to Montreal and watch my old team.

I was away from home a lot.

This was a time, as well, when I started to drink a bit more than I had in the past. Beginning in high school, I drank beer and, less frequently, hard alcohol—and this continued through college and throughout my NHL career. I drank in the off-season, but it wasn't like an everyday thing. Sometimes there was an entire week in which I wouldn't have a drop. Now, though, the drinking was becoming an "almost every day" thing. I started to look forward to it. But it was just booze—no pills or other drugs. I didn't yet understand how alcohol could be a gateway substance.

And it was in the summer of 1994 that I wandered from my marriage and started an affair with a woman I met at a charity event on the island of Nantucket. It was a relationship that lasted for fifteen years. In that I would be a married man for eleven more years, that would mean I had a steady girlfriend on the side for more than a decade.

Mary is the name of the woman, and I am not going to say much here about her personally, although later on in this book, I will discuss circumstances that involved us while we were still together romantically. This is not to avoid taking responsibility for my continued transgression and wrongdoing, but because I don't want Mary to have to deal with all the bullshit. I always loved and cared about her. It is over now, and she has gone on and so have I. But I take full responsibility for betraying my wife and kids. When I started the relationship with Mary, my marriage to Karen was not in a good place because of me, and I shouldn't have become involved with Mary while still married.

Anyway, as you can see, my life was complicated and becoming messed up.

33

MY MOTHER-IN-LAW AND HER BOYFRIEND DISAPPEAR

KAREN AND I AND THE KIDS always spent Christmas Eve at Teresa's. But the day before Christmas Eve 1994, Teresa told us that she and Jimmy were going on a trip, leaving that day, and would be gone for a while. We thought this peculiar, but, as had been our custom in our relationship with Teresa and Jimmy, we didn't ask too many questions. We started to get worried when it got to a week after Teresa and Whitey went on their trip and we hadn't heard from her. We also figured something big was up.

It all started to make sense on Monday morning, January 6, when it was announced in the news that on the previous night, the FBI had arrested Steve Flemmi outside a restaurant near Faneuil Hall. By that evening, it was on the TV and radio that, a couple weeks previous, the FBI had obtained several federal indictments and criminal complaints against Jimmy, Flemmi, and Frank Salemme. The feds had Flemmi, but Jimmy and Salemme were on the lam.

Someone had tipped them off that they were about to be arrested.

So Jimmy disappeared—and took Teresa with him.

So it came as no surprise when the FBI came calling at our home in Hingham. Agents also visited Karen's brother and sisters.

The FBI came calling when I was home. Our doorbell rang one morning, and Karen, with little Tara standing next to her, opened the front door to find a federal agent with a big-ass handgun holstered to his side. Tara let out a little yelp, and I came running from a different part of the house. I told Karen to take Tara and go the kitchen. It was bullshit, and I yelled at the agent, letting him know what a total asshole he was to show up at our house with a gun. What a dickhead. I told him I knew why he was there, but we didn't know anything, and we weren't answering any questions. I slammed the door shut.

Karen told me she didn't think her mother could be in it for the long haul with Jimmy. Karen knew, and I knew, that Teresa loved her kids and her grandchildren too much, and that she would want to return. Yet if this was the case, would Jimmy let her come home?

He would.

On Tuesday afternoon, February 7, at about four o'clock, the phone rang at our house. Karen picked it up; it was her mother on the line. Teresa was at a Chinese restaurant in Hingham, a couple miles from our home. All she said was that "she had just been dropped off." I got in my car and raced over to the restaurant. Teresa was standing outside in the cold afternoon, her normally silver-white hair dyed brown. I jumped out of the car and gave her a big hug and asked her if she was all right. She had tears in her eyes; she said yes.

I drove her back to our house. Teresa and Karen had a very emotional reunion. Teresa would stay at our house for the next few days. We knew she needed close-by support. Neither Karen nor I pried—even if we were beyond interested. All we knew was that she and Jimmy had traveled across many states, and that at the end of January she told him she couldn't continue; she said she had to come home to her family.

And what was the first thing that Jimmy Bulger did after Teresa stepped out of his car at the restaurant? Well, he drove directly to the South Boston waterfront, where, waiting for him was a woman named Catherine Grieg—the same woman he had been seeing for several years behind Teresa's back. Catherine got into Jimmy's car, and they were gone and would remain gone for sixteen years.

Frank Salemme didn't have as much luck staying out of handcuffs. He was arrested in Florida in August 1995, about eight months after he flew the coop.

A little at a time, Teresa gave us an account of life with the fugitive. Their jaunt started with an overnight stay at a hotel in New York City, followed by a trip down the East Coast to Florida. They drove to Chicago, and then Los Angeles, and then on to San Francisco. Then back across the US, to bring Teresa home. Always on the move, never in one place for more than a day. They slept in a different hotel every night.

It had to be expected that the FBI would again be in our lives, but more in Teresa's, actually. Teresa told the feds that she and Whitey had driven to Florida and had stayed down there and driven back. She told the FBI she didn't know where Jimmy was going after he dropped her off. And, knowing just how cunning and smart Jimmy was, I am sure that was the truth.

Beginning a couple years after Jimmy took off, information started to come out that supports the notion that truth is stranger than fiction. It emerged that, for close to twenty years, from the mid-1970s until he went on the lam, Whitey and Steve Flemmi were FBI informants. But the thing is, the relationship got too chummy, and some of the FBI agents were corrupted. One was an agent named Johnny Connolly, who was ten years younger than Jimmy, also grew up in

South Boston, and had sort of idolized Jimmy Bulger ever since the day when, as a young kid, Connolly was getting beaten up by some local toughs, and Jimmy came to his aid and bought him an ice cream.

In 1980, Connolly, in the midst of a standout career with the FBI, was transferred from New York City to Boston, where he became a liaison between Jimmy and the bureau. Connolly would later be indicted and convicted of leaking information to Jimmy about those who were going to rat or inform on Jimmy and his gang. These informants ended up dead.

And who do you think gave Jimmy Bulger the information that his arrest was planned?

Need you ask?

34

THE (SHORT-LIVED) INSURANCE SALESMAN

WHILE AT JOHN HANCOCK, I studied for my license to write and sell insurance. I took the test and passed. People kept telling me that I would be a good salesman, and that I got along well with people and enjoyed talking with them, and that I had an extensive network I could tap into to sell insurance.

It was a good thing I had that insurance license behind me, because within days of my passing the test, John Hancock terminated my position. At first, I don't think John Hancock wanted to finance the position much beyond the end of the Lillehammer Games, but the company decided to keep me on for a bit longer. Anyway, I launched an insurance business with my friend John Kilcommons. I don't know what I was thinking. I didn't like to sell, and truth be told, I wasn't that good at it. I was impatient and not particularly interested in paperwork and forms and taking care of all the minutiae that a good insurance professional needs to take care of.

I think just about the most value I brought to the enterprise was setting up appointments for John. He seemed to have a knack for selling insurance, and he kept after it. I didn't stay after it. I left the business about six months after co-founding it. John kept on selling and doing well as a broker of John Hancock insurance and investment products.

John was a good insurance salesman; he was also slick beyond what was good for him, and beyond what was good for his clients. John built an impressive client base, and managed some municipal pension money. He also started doing funny things with the money that was supposed to, but didn't, go into the managed pension fund. He got caught, of course. John paid a fine and did some probation and a couple hundred hours of community service.

Maybe it was a good thing I didn't have much of a start in insurance before I left the business.

I needed to get back into hockey. I needed to coach. I needed a chance.

35

COACHING

I AM NOT GOOD ABOUT ASKING for favors or trying to sell myself. I don't like to do it. But I was going out of my mind and I needed to do something in hockey—and I thought that coaching was that something. So in the summer of 1995, I made some calls to people I knew, and the timing was right when I made one to Jacques Lemaire.

As head coach, Jacques had led the New Jersey Devils to the Stanley Cup championship the previous season (a shortened season due to the league's lockout of the players) in his second year as coach. That was the eleventh Stanley Cup Jacques had been a part of either as a player, coach, or front-office executive. He knew how to win in the NHL.

And what happened not long after the Devils won the Cup is what happens to teams across all sports and at many levels when they win it all: their assistant coaches get hired away by other clubs. This happened with the Devils, where Larry Robinson, my former teammate, took the job as head coach of the Los Angeles Kings. So Jacques Lemaire needed an assistant coach, and he chose to give me a chance.

I was coming into a situation in which a team was on a roll and doing all the right things. Indeed, the New Jersey Devils were in a place they hadn't been before. The Devils franchise went back to the

1982–83 season, when it moved from Denver, and for the first ten years of its existence it had not won enough to generate strong fan support and media attention. In fact, in the early 1990s, Nashville was eager to land an NHL franchise, and the businesspeople leading that effort were looking toward New Jersey as a team that might be successfully wooed.

"Mickey Mouse" is how Wayne Gretzky described the New Jersey franchise back then.

Pivotal to the turnaround of the team—and keeping the Devils in New Jersey—was general manager Lou Lamoriello's hiring of Jacques Lemaire as coach for the 1993–94 campaign.

It also helped that Lemaire came into a team with solid talent, including top-scoring Claude Lemieux and a tandem of goalies in Martin Brodeur and Chris Terreri. With Robinson as his assistant coach and the right personnel on the ice, Lemaire instituted a defensively oriented trapping style of play that might have taken a while to put into place and get to a point that it was operating smoothly, but eventually it began to work quite well.

That first year, the Devils made New Jersey and metropolitan New York City take notice. New Jersey finished its season one goal away from the Stanley Cup final, losing to its rival across the Hudson River, the New York Rangers, in sudden-death double overtime in the Eastern Conference final.

New Jersey kept its players and coaches and momentum in place for the 1994–95 season, and it knew it could close the deal and win the franchise's first Stanley Cup. Then again, there almost was no 1994–95 NHL season because the league did what it seems to have a great knack for doing: it had a lockout that began on what should have been the first day of the season and went on for three months until the owners and players could figure things out.

At least there was a regular season—one of forty-eight games instead of the scheduled eighty-four.

The Devils' abbreviated season surely didn't start out looking like there would be any Cup hoisting at the end of it. They got off to a 12–13–5 start, but rebounded and went 10–5–3 over the final eighteen games and got into the play-offs as the fifth seed in the East.

And the team continued to play well in the postseason, beating the Bruins four games to one, doing the same to the Pittsburgh Penguins, and then winning the conference championship over the Flyers, four games to two. New Jersey met the heavily favored Detroit Red Wings in the final, employed the Lemaire trap almost flawlessly, and took Detroit off its game for the totally unanticipated sweep.

There had been a major player shake-up for the Devils just prior to the 1995–96 season beginning, when Claude Lemieux was traded to the Colorado Avalanche. The move was part of a three-way deal that sent Avalanche tough guy and enforcer Wendel "Captain Crunch" Clark to the New York Islanders and Islanders right wing Steve "Stumpy" Thomas, a consistent scorer, to the Devils.

New Jersey started out the season great, winning six of our first seven games. Yet even as we were winning, my experience as a coach was not a happy one—and this was true right off the bat.

There was a complaint among the players that they thought they had two head coaches. But it was my job to convey many of Jacques's decisions and orders—particularly those made during games—to the team. Jacques wanted a buffer, and I was the buffer. I had no issue with it, but the players did.

It didn't help that I was not long removed from the NHL myself, and some of the guys I was coaching I had tussled with—some more than once. What also was difficult was that I was in charge of the defense, and I had been a forward. Even beyond that, the team had some standout players that, I believe, didn't respect my abilities as a player as much as they did my abilities as a fighter.

Scott Stevens, for example, a defenseman in the later stages of a twenty-year career in the NHL and a big fan favorite in New Jersey, never warmed to my coaching. And when Jacques didn't want Stevens on a power play, it would often be my job to tell him. On the subject of fan favorites, when Jacques decided to bench another star defenseman, Ken Daneyko—who had been with the franchise since its beginning (and would play his entire twenty years in the NHL with New Jersey) and was known as "Mr. Devil"—it was me who gave Daneyko the news. That didn't make me popular.

After the strong start, we started playing poorly and continued to play at about a .500 pace for the remainder of the season. I think the talent was there, and the coaching strategy was correct, but there was dissension and a lack of intensity. So here were the Devils, the defending Stanley Cup champs, needing to win the last game of the regular season, at home against the last-place Ottawa Senators, to grab the last play-off spot.

Alas, that didn't happen. We lost 5–1, missing the play-offs by two points with a record of 37–33–12. A little history here: it was the first time in twenty-six years that the defending NHL champs didn't make the play-offs. Not good.

So I went back to Boston, and there would not be a second season with me coaching in New Jersey. Kind of a mutual agreement. But, truthfully, I couldn't be an assistant coach—I need to be a head coach.

That summer, I sold boats on Cape Cod for a good friend of mine, Brian McLaughlin, a mega-successful entrepreneur whose business successes included co-founding the D'Angelo sandwich chain. Brian is also a philanthropic leader, with the Genesis Fund and Easter Seals as two of his favorite causes.

Anyway, it was the summer and I was on the ocean and around boats, making some money, drinking some beer, and enjoying life. But I knew the fall was coming, and that what I really wanted to do was coach a hockey team. I wanted to coach a minor-league team. I started calling around and pitching myself, which, again, is something I don't enjoy. I did it, though, because I had to. I had to coach.

In the fall, I got in touch with Mike Mudd, a former goalie for St. Lawrence University who had gone on to play in the minors and had just become general manager of the newly formed Chesapeake Icebreakers of the East Coast Hockey League (ECHL), one of the two minor leagues, along with the AHL, that have a formal relationship with the NHL. Truth be told, the AHL has more prestige, and the play is of a bit higher caliber than in the ECHL, but it is also true that almost five hundred ECHL players have gone on to play in the NHL.

Mike needed a head coach for his expansion squad, which would begin play on the opening day of the 1997–98 season, and finding a coach for any expansion team, in any league, in any sport, at any level, can be a difficult task. He brought me down to Maryland to interview. It went well, and I was offered the job as head coach of the Icebreakers.

I talked things over with Karen and the kids. If I accepted the position, it would be the second hockey season in a row that I would be away from them. It wasn't like when I played for Montreal and Boston, situations in which my wife and kids were with me in both cities. As well, I was coming off a season that had not been fun as a coach and in which I had been away from my family and had been lonely.

Coaching isn't like playing. The camaraderie isn't there. You are not friends with the players you coach, and you don't share the bond that you do with teammates. Oh, for sure, you care as deeply for a player you coach as you do for a teammate, but it is a different kind of caring; a coach, at least a good one, is like a parent who sets the rules and makes sure the right game plan is followed, whether or not it meets with the approval of the kids.

I needed to do this, though. My family understood. I accepted the offer in October 1996, about ten months prior to the Icebreakers convening their first-ever training camp.

From the time I signed the coaching contract to the time I showed up to start coaching the team, I lived in Hingham and made many trips down to Maryland. I also studied and studied hockey and made lots of calls to former teammates and coaches. I knew you could never know enough hockey—and the best coaches always chased information on the game and studied ways to win and not to lose.

In August 1997, I moved to an apartment in Upper Marlboro, Maryland, the home of the Icebreakers and the seat of Prince George's County, which borders Washington, D.C. Upper Marlboro and the surrounding area are fairly rural—there are a lot of farms, including horse farms, throughout. Indeed, our home ice was the Show Place Arena, which had been converted from a facility that primarily hosted horse shows to one where horse shows were still held, along with hockey and basketball games, trade shows, business meetings, and concerts. Seating capacity for a hockey game was 5,500.

This was not the NHL.

The ECHL had twenty-five franchises in cities and towns in the Mid-Atlantic region, the Rust Belt, and the Deep South. Let me see, some of the teams were the Columbus Chill, Johnstown Chiefs, Knoxville Cherokees, Huntington Blizzard, Dayton Bombers, Toledo Storm, Hampton Roads Admirals, Raleigh IceCaps, Richmond Renegades, Jacksonville Lizard Kings, Charlotte Checkers, Louisville River Frogs, Tallahassee Tiger Sharks, and Wheeling Nailers.

Today, the ECHL has teams from coast to coast, but not in the mid-1990s.

We never flew and always traveled by bus. We stayed in economy hotels. Player per diems covered the basics—no high-end or gourmet eating.

I was fortunate in that Nelson Burton, who had played briefly for the Washington Capitals and logged several seasons in the AHL, offered to work unpaid as assistant coach of the Icebreakers. Nelson, a Nova Scotia native who had retired from playing the previous season, had settled in Maryland. Nelson knew hockey inside and out, and he loved coaching. Indeed, today he remains heavily involved in youth hockey in Maryland.

The 1997–98 Icebreakers had some tough and talented kids, including Derek Clancy, Ryan Brown, Billy Pierce (who was from the Boston area and had a solid career at Boston University, from which he'd graduated the previous spring), and P. J. O'Connor, a Princeton University kid. We also benefited for half the season from the goaltending of David Aebischer from Switzerland, who had been drafted the previous year by the Colorado Avalanche and had just moved to the US. Aebischer left us to play for the Wheeling Nailers before going on to have several successful seasons in the NHL.

The team voted O'Connor and Pierce to serve as co-captains. It was a good choice.

I was very nervous starting out, and soon I wondered whether I was in over my head. I had doubts about whether I could make my system work.

I had a philosophy and a strategy about team hockey—I was very defense-minded. I think when you get a team that is defensively oriented, the players play more cohesively and more responsibly. I learned a lot from Jacques Lemaire, and he had convinced me that defense and playing the trap well were fundamentally strong and smart hockey. Of course, if we had the opportunity to forecheck, we would.

The Chesapeake Icebreakers were not impressive out of the gate, going 3–12–5. What am I doing here? I thought. Still, I stayed with the plan and the program, and I kept after it. As well, we were spirited, and I saw that we were beginning to feed off of turnovers. I was confident that if we got things together and became comfortable with the system, we could win games.

Immediately after that 3–12–5 start, the Icebreakers launched a twelve-game winning streak. How did that happen? First off, the kids were getting their arms around the strategy and style of play, and they were becoming comfortable with each other. I also think, to some degree, that one specific event, a sort of on-ice and off-ice combo event, contributed to the team playing so well.

For the twenty-first game of the season, we were in Raleigh to take on the IceCaps. With about five minutes gone in the third period, and with Chesapeake trailing 4–1, one of my defensemen, Petri Gynther, a good kid from Finland who had played for the University of Denver, accidentally high-sticked Darren Colbourne of Raleigh.

Here we had two players with very different backgrounds.

Gynther was two years out of college and had spent the previous season with the Syracuse Crunch of the AHL, which was the first time he had played in a league in which fighting was part of the culture. Colbourne, six years older than Gynther, grew up in Canada, where he played junior hockey, and was in his eighth season in the minors. Colbourne knew hockey and fighting well; Gynther didn't.

Colbourne cross-checked Gynther after catching the high-stick and then started pummeling him. Gynther basically went into turtle mode, just covered up.

So referee Derek Woodworth gave both players five minutes for fighting, also assessing a two-minute misconduct against Colbourne. Colbourne got what he deserved, but my kid shouldn't have gotten a second of penalty time, as he had done nothing wrong. I was furious inside, but I wasn't out of control on the outside. I wanted to talk with Woodworth, and I motioned him over to our bench, but he wouldn't come. So I called my players on the ice over to the boards in front of our bench, and I told them all to stay there. I told P. J. O'Connor—again, one of our co-captains—to tell the ref I wanted to speak with him, whereupon P. J. skated over to the ref and relayed the message. In response, Woodworth told P. J. to tell me he was not going to talk with me, that he was giving me a bench misconduct, and that I had better put my team back on the ice.

When my kid relayed the ref's message, I didn't go ballistic, but I did tell P. J. to go back to Woodworth and tell him I said he could go fuck himself. My kid skated over to the ref and relayed that message. Naturally, Woodworth wasn't happy. He told my captain to tell me I just received a second bench misconduct, which meant I was automatically kicked out of the game and had to leave the bench. When I heard this, I was even more pissed (if that was possible). What I didn't know was that, after a coach is booted in this manner, there is a five-minute grace period in which he can talk with the team and coordinate things with his assistant coaches before leaving the playing area. Even though I thought I had to leave immediately, I stayed put. I told P. J. to tell Woodworth that I wasn't leaving.

P. J. gave Woodworth my message, in response to which Woodworth directed P. J. to tell me I had to leave the bench immediately or I would be fined. My response was to take out my billfold and scream at the ref as I pulled out dollar bills and waved them in front of him. Finally, Woodworth had had enough and announced that the game was over and the Raleigh IceCaps had won via forfeit.

When this happened, I motioned for the team to get right off the ice and head to the locker room, which it did, with me walking right along after the players. Unfortunately, the night was not yet over, for when Woodworth was in the tunnel under the stands on the way to his locker room, Nelson Burton was also in the tunnel, and he screamed a few choice words at Woodworth, which resulted in Nelson receiving a gross misconduct penalty.

As you can imagine, the episode made the ECHL front office in Princeton, New Jersey, unhappy—very unhappy. Indeed, the ECHL said nothing like this had ever happened in league history. An emergency meeting was set for the next day at the Icebreakers' offices. Attending would be me, Mike Mudd, and ECHL vice president of hockey operations, Andy Van Hellemond, someone I knew well, for he had had a long and distinguished career as a referee in the NHL and had sent me to the penalty box many, many times.

Mike Mudd was great in the meeting. He totally had my back and said he felt that Woodworth should have come over and talked with me about the penalty. Van Hellemond was stern and didn't hold back; he asserted that what I had done was very serious and couldn't be tolerated. He said I would be fined $1,000 and suspended five games. On the other hand, he said the league bylaws did not support Woodworth's decision to call the game and award Raleigh the win by forfeit. Van Hellemond declared the game unfinished, with the remainder to be played prior to our next scheduled game with the IceCaps.

I could live with that.

But here's the thing: maybe the incident lit a little fire under the players. With Nelson Burton and Mike Mudd behind the bench, they won those next five games. And lest you think it was because I wasn't coaching, we won the next seven games after my return. So after my little blowup, we won twelve straight. That was a nice run.

And the community took notice—sort of. Again, Show Place Arena held 5,500 for hockey, and we were, on a good night, putting 4,500 to 5,000 in the seats. Enthusiasm built as we continued to win. A good amount of that enthusiasm was generated by word of mouth, for we never seemed to catch on with the local press; the media never got that excited about us. As well, we sure didn't advertise and market much, only because there wasn't much of a budget for it.

In the thirty-seven games following the incident in Raleigh, the

Icebreakers went 23–9–5. We finished the season at 34–28–8 and qualified for the play-offs. It was a short postseason. We lost in the first round, three games to two, to the Hampton Roads Admirals, the team that would win the Kelly Cup, which is the ECHL's version of the Stanley Cup.

It was an up-and-down season. I thought the Icebreakers had accomplished a lot, even if we got bounced early in the play-offs. I was immensely proud and honored to find out, about a week after the ECHL play-offs and Kelly Cup final had concluded, that my fellow coaches in the league had voted me the ECHL's coach of the year.

Mike Mudd wanted me back, and I was happy to come back. Nelson Burton returned as assistant coach. Mike also brought in a player/assistant coach, Denny Felsner, a right wing who had starred at the University of Michigan and then had played on and off for the St. Louis Blues for three seasons.

I was excited when I found out that Gaston Gringas, my team-mate for my first two seasons in the NHL, who'd had a solid ten-year career in the league, had signed a contract to play for us for the first five games of the season so he could play alongside his nephew, Jeff Robinson. In a strange turn of events, before Gaston and Jeff could play a shift together, Jeff got brought up to the NHL. But, no matter— Gaston honored the contract and gave us five solid games.

The Chesapeake Icebreakers played mostly winning hockey dur-ing the 1998–99 campaign and were competitive in just about every game. We had a growing and excited fan base, and even managed to sell out Show Place Arena a few times.

Of course, my second season as coach had another "Chris Nilan moment"—this one coming early in the year, when we were on the road playing the Chill. Again, it was not my fault—really.

Let me set the stage. It was tied up 1–1 with about a minute left in the game. The Chill had the puck in our end and one of their play-ers decked my goalie, leaving the net open, while another Columbus player easily slipped the puck into the net for the go-ahead score. And there was no call. I was like, "What the fuck?" So I started screaming and going crazy—and the refs ignored me. Well, I had to do something. So I threw a stick onto the ice.

I was immediately assessed a bench misconduct. This didn't calm me down. So I threw another stick, and then another, and yet another. I ended up unloading all the reserve sticks onto the ice, with the final heave being four sticks at once. This outburst earned me another $1,000 fine and a two-game suspension. I never regretted throwing the sticks.

Later in the season, though, I did do something I regretted. It happened following a home game against the Johnstown Chiefs. In that game, in the second period, we were up 6–1. Then we fell apart, lost all our focus and intensity, and we didn't score again that night, but managed to give up six straight goals and lost 7–1. Oh, I was mad. And instead of letting my players head for the showers, I directed them to get back on the ice.

They were bitching and moaning. Well, they could keep bitching and moaning. I started them on a long series of up-and-backs. I worked them for about ten minutes. Then I yelled at them and said they were done and walked ahead of them into the locker room. And then I walked out of the building without talking to any of them.

As I said, I regretted it. I regretted it almost immediately. I felt that I had lost them. I already felt alone as a coach—and I now I felt more alone.

But I coached on and did my best to mentor my players.

The Icebreakers finished the regular season at 34–25–11 and again were in the play-offs.

We won our first round, a best-of-five series against the Columbus Chill, in which we lost the first game at their place and then won three straight, with the final game coming at Show Place Arena. We lost in the second round, another five-game-series, to the Roanoke Express, three games to two.

❖

It is part of the normal ebb and flow in the ECHL that teams are uprooted and move from city to city frequently. This is the nature of the beast in minor-league hockey. When the 1998–99 season concluded, so did the short life of the Chesapeake Icebreakers.

The team was sold to Mississippi Indoor Sports—headed by Bernie Ebbers, then the high-flying president and CEO of MCI WorldCom, and J. L. Holloway, president and CEO of Friede-Goldman International. They moved the Icebreakers to Jackson, Mississippi and renamed them the Jackson Bandits.

Ebbers had made his fortune in telecom. He grew up in Canada, was a hockey fan from way back, and continued to be a fan after he moved to Mississippi to go to Mississippi College, where he played varsity basketball.

J. L. Holloway grew up in modest circumstances in Mississippi, and he stayed in Mississippi. It was through oil that he became phenomenally rich.

There is something about amassing "fuck you" money that compels people to want to buy a sports team. A sports team is like the ultimate grown-up toy and playground.

I received a call from Bernie Ebbers. He said that he and Holloway wanted to talk with me about coaching the Bandits. I flew down to Mississippi and met with them, and they were both enthusiastic about my coming on board. I was thankful, but noncommittal. I said I would have to think about it. I did think about it, for two days or so, and decided I didn't want to do it.

Coaching ice hockey deep in Dixie seemed a bit strange to me. But really, the reason I didn't coach the Bandits was because I wanted to be a head coach in the AHL. I wanted to take the next step. So I did again what I didn't like to do and called around and sold myself. I talked to Bob Gainey and other former teammates, but nothing came of it. I think Bob thought I wasn't AHL coaching material.

Then I talked with Mike Milbury and Pat Burns, and they said there might be an opportunity for me to interview to be the head coach of the Providence Bruins, the Boston Bruins' affiliate. Pat said I would be getting a call. But I never did.

This might seem defeatist, but after talking to former teammates and reaching out for help in landing a coaching position in the AHL, I figured it wasn't in the cards for me to be a coach if none of them could do anything for me. I quit looking for a coaching job. Call it attitude. Call it giving up. Call it what you will—but as for me back then, I called it being realistic.

So there I was, back in Boston and trying to put together another plan.

With about twenty games to go in my second season as coach of the Icebreakers, my knee began to swell and ache something fierce—the old injuries conspiring against me. I went up to Boston for the day and had a scope of my knee done. I was under general anesthesic, and the doctor did some cleaning and removal of tissue. When I got discharged that same day, I was prescribed Percocet. I filled the prescription, and when it was done, I called the doctor and told him I was still in pain and needed some more. He wrote me another prescription.

It had now been three months since the operation, and the pain in my knee was gone, but not the painkillers. I was still taking them.

And the funny thing was, whatever I was getting out of those pain-killers, I needed to keep upping the dosage and frequency in order to keep me feeling good.

So I kept taking more pills.

36

PAST AND PROLOGUE

WHEN I WAS FIVE YEARS OLD, my father took me skiing on the hill at a local public golf course. I was having a great time, and I made several runs. On the final run that day, as I was getting some fairly good speed going, I lost my balance and tumbled, and my right leg got tangled. It hurt something awful.

As I yelped and cried in pain, my father came running down the hill, got a hold of me, and tried to calm me down. He had little success. He took off my skis, tossed them to the side (I think he just left the skis and poles there), gathered me up in his arms, walked me to the car, and laid me down on the backseat. We drove back to our house and called up my aunt Mary, who was a nurse. She came over, assessed my injury, and said I needed to go to the hospital. At the hospital, the X-rays showed that my leg was broken. I was given the pain medication Demerol and stayed the night. The next day, my leg was put in a cast. What I remember about that Demerol is how wonderful and peaceful it made me feel.

37

ADRIFT

IT WAS THE FALL OF 1999, and I was in the Boston area and I was lost. I didn't have hockey and I didn't have a job. I had some money saved from hockey, but not a lot. I needed to work, but I didn't know what to do.

Karen had finished her nursing studies and passed all her exams the previous year and was now working full time as a nurse at Quincy Hospital. Believe me, that was income we needed.

I'm not sure what exactly got me doing this—maybe it was boredom, or boredom combined with periods of anxiety about not knowing what came next, or all of this combined with not having hockey in my life—but I began to drink almost every day. And while I had taken a brief break from the pills, I reintroduced them into my life. Just a few, here and there, you know. That's how it starts.

I became a regular at bars in the area—not so much in Boston, but in the suburbs—bars and taverns in the outlying communities, like Dedham, Milton, and Quincy. I would show up when the evening news was on, and I would start drinking, mostly beer. I would drink a lot of beer. So I am talking about taking my first sip around six or so, and I would keep drinking for six to seven hours straight, until the bar closed.

Let's do the math a bit. Figure on at least two beers an hour, probably more like three—so during my night at the bar, I would have in the neighborhood of twelve to twenty beers or so. Sometimes I would drink with a friend, sometimes by myself. People would buy me beers and want to talk about hockey. I was no real celebrity, but in the gritty places in the Boston area where I drank, hockey is very popular, and the denizens of those bars know the players and teams and a lot about the game itself.

I didn't run into too many hassles at bars. People knew not to bother me. I mean, sure, they sometimes got irritating in asking questions and trying to be my buddy, but people weren't threatening or trying to cause trouble. This was good, because I didn't need a reason to get involved in trouble.

And of course, as was the case with alcohol, I upped the number of pills I swallowed. Percocet was my main poison. "Percs" are actually a combination of drugs—acetaminophen and the opioid oxycodone. Both are painkillers, but it is the opioid that is the really powerful substance. I had a slew of doctors throughout the area who would write prescriptions for percs for me. None of them knew I was also seeing the others for the same pain meds. I would get a bottle of thirty 5-milligram tablets and pop them here and there while I was drinking. A bottle of thirty would last me maybe two days. This was the fall of 1999, and I was doing a lot of alcohol and pills, yet I wasn't anywhere close to the craziness that was just around the corner.

Soon I started to show up at the bars earlier than the start of the nightly news. Soon I was there when the afternoon talk shows started. And in a little while, I would be at the bar around noontime, right around when the soap operas started up. I told myself that if this kept up, I would be at the bar watching *The Flintstones*.

So, what was my life? It was drinking, swallowing pills, and also occasionally playing in the various men's hockey games I could find at rinks in metropolitan Boston. I was not a good husband. I was not a good father. Karen and I were fighting. I was seeing a lot of Mary. In 2000, I upped my chemical consumption considerably. I also changed the type of chemical I ingested. My new poison was called OxyContin.

"Oxy" is a far more potent animal than is Percocet. Oxy is the oxycodone without the acetaminophen. You have yourself pure opioid—almost. I say "almost" because OxyContin is a time-release drug, and it comes with a coating that allows the drug to be parceled out bit by bit, not all at once.

In January, I was taking five to ten 80-milligram tablets of OxyContin a day and drinking at least a six-pack of beer, which I chased with some vodka. I got myself in a fog good and early, and I kept that fog going. I drove my car in a drugged-out state every day, and thankfully, I didn't kill anyone. Sometimes I didn't come home, choosing to crash at a hotel or a friend's house.

It all came at me fast, and before long I was out-and-out hopelessly addicted. I was a drug addict but didn't know it. And a curious thing happened. With my chasing of and need for more pills, I started skipping the drinking. I needed the painkillers and nothing else, and I didn't have time to drink. I needed to get the pills. I woke up and needed the pills. I went to bed and needed the pills. And I was having trouble finding enough doctors to write me prescriptions, so I had to scrounge and find street sources. On the streets, I had to pay about a buck a milligram for the drug, so an 80-milligram tablet cost $80.

I was staying fairly busy with a variety of NHL alumni appearances, all of which were paying gigs. I managed to get through the events high, and I took all the money I made and spent it on drugs.

Soon I needed to get those drugs into my system faster, so I started to grind and mash the tablets into powder and snort the opioid up my nose. How terrible was my life? Some days, I snorted 800 milligrams of painkiller. And, of course, the nature of addiction is that what you are doing never remains sufficient.

What most people know now, largely because there has been so much reported on it in the news, is that a primary reason addicts continue to up the amount of drugs they are taking is not necessarily to get more high but to maintain the same high. You see, fifteen 5-milligram tablets a day would make me feel just good, but only for so long—and then twenty 5-milligram tabs weren't doing the job. The body adjusts to the medicine and it needs more to feel the same way than it needed, let's say, the week before.

So what is it about the opioids that makes you want more, even if you don't have physical pain? It is because, at least for an addict, the opioids make you feel so good. You are relaxed and feeling pleasant and in a nice, comfy suspension. All is right with the world. If your body and mind have become accustomed to the nice feeling of the narcotic, and then it is not in your system, you can feel just terrible.

Withdrawal is sort of a combination of things—the bottom line being that, psychologically, you are no longer carefree; biologically and psychologically, you are craving the drug fiercely. That craving and that need make you nauseous and you sweat and shake. It is not pleasant. You will do anything to remove that feeling.

Down, down, down.

I would sit in my car with the window cracked and the motor running so that I had heat. And I would drift in and out of a pleasant world. It was bad. I got hotel rooms and crashed, in oblivion, for a day or two. Sometimes I would lie back on the couch at home and do nothing all day and all night. Karen told me I needed help and that the kids couldn't see me like this—I was wrecking the family.

She was right, of course, but I didn't care much. I only cared about the drugs.

Bob Gainey called; he said he heard I wasn't doing well, and he asked me to get in touch with Dan Cronin, who headed up the NHL substance abuse program. I thanked Bob for the concern but told him I was all right.

What a nice time it was for my kids, huh? Colleen was a senior at Hingham High School, and Chris was a freshman there. Tara was in middle school in Hingham. All three of my kids were old enough to know what was going on with their father. The irony was that when I was at my best, in the heyday of my hockey career, they were too young to appreciate my achievements—but now they were able to see what and who their dad was. Ugly all around.

I said this at the beginning of the book: the worst is not what you do to yourself, it is what you do to others. I still cringe and mentally recoil when I think back on what I did to my family.

Back then, though, I could finally see just how bad things had gotten. Not that I was willing to do much about it. But I did see it. And so I chose to make a half-assed attempt to reach out for help, to make a good show of it, even if I didn't really care that much about getting clean.

Even while very high and drugged out, I knew hockey, and I knew how to coach winning hockey teams. Over that winter, December 2000 through March 2001, I managed to coach the Boston Harbor Wolves, a Junior A hockey team. I made it to twice-a-week practices and all the games, which were played mostly against other Junior A teams based in southern New England. Our home ice was the Matt O'Neil Rink in Charlestown.

We had some talent, with several of the players eventually going on to play at the major college level. The season prior to the one I coached, the Harbor Wolves were out-and-out awful, posting a record of 1–38–0. The team I took over could only go up, which it did, finishing the season at 20–25–2. It might have been the best job I ever did as a coach.

❖

I could see clearly enough through the haze and fog of chemical stupor to coach effectively. So in the first or second week of March, I called Bob Gainey and told him that, yes, I was fucked up and needed some help. He gave me Dan Cronin's phone number. I called Cronin and said I was having some troubles and needed to speak with someone. We set up an appointment in Boston—it was for March 17, St. Patrick's Day. Now there is something curious about two Irishmen meeting on St. Paddy's Day in Boston to go about the process of beating intoxicants. But I'll leave that alone.

Dan and I met at the Boston Harbor Hotel, in the lobby. It was the afternoon and I had not taken anything that day. We sat and talked casually for a half hour or so. He asked me questions about drug-taking, and I lied to him, and I'm sure he knew I was lying to him. I told Cronin I was working out hard, and that I had some pain and was taking several Percocets a day. And yeah, I had a few beers occasionally. He pressed me on just how much I was doing in the way of drugs, and I continued to lie. Cronin gave me the name of a drug and addiction counselor, Dr. Diana Ikeda, who practiced out of Duxbury, an affluent town that borders the affluent town of Hingham.

By the way, the NHL agreed to pay the total tab for any rehab and help I needed. Signing off on the payment was Brian O'Neill, the guy who had disciplined me so many times.

I played along and called Dr. Ikeda the day after I met with Dan. We set up an appointment, and I showed up when and where I was supposed to. I was high when I got to her office. Dr. Ikeda specialized in talk therapy to help people through their problems—and it seemed to me the first step was that she wanted to get everything out and have the scope of my problem defined for both of us. She asked the questions the same way Dan Cronin did. She asked if I was on anything at the moment, right then and there in her office. I said no, and I could tell by the way she looked at me that she knew I was lying. I didn't change my story, though.

Dr. Ikeda asked me to talk about how I felt when I was on the pills. She also explained to me a little bit about the science and biology of addiction. She was trying to define the issue as clearly as possible. I was getting very itchy and uncomfortable because someone—someone in the same room, who knew what I was all about at that moment—was trying to get me to be honest. And being honest about this problem was a place I didn't want to go. I did agree, though, to another appointment in a few days.

Over the next few days, I did a small hill of pills, even as I knew I had to go back to see Dr. Ikeda. When I went back, I was more messed up than I had been for the first appointment. She described everything that was going on with me, in a calm and relaxed manner, and was unambiguous about the nature of my disease and what it was doing to me. This is painful to admit, but by the time I left Dr. Ikeda's office that day I was in the fetal position, crying like a baby. I understood that this thing was stronger than I could have imagined. Never had I felt more hopeless, weak, and defeated. My fight with addiction has been discussed, written about, and reported on many times, and the battle is invariably presented as a sort of parallel to my battles on the ice. A proper conclusion is often made that my fight trying to get and stay clean demands more of me than any throwdown in which I participated in the sports arena.

I went a couple more times to see Dr. Ikeda, but then I just stopped. I was on the fast track to oblivion.

Depending on where I was in the morning or early afternoon, whenever I got out of bed—whether I was home in Hingham, at Mary's, or a hotel or a buddy's house—if I had some Oxy, I would take it and get rolling. If I didn't have any, I needed to go on the hunt. I would grab myself a coffee and maybe a doughnut or bagel, but that was about it for food for most of the next twelve hours or so. I needed only the painkillers.

At this point, what the doctors were prescribing amounted to about 75 percent of what I needed. The other half was coming from street dealers. I was almost always broke.

I lost twenty pounds and I looked like the walking dead. During this period, I didn't visit my family over in West Roxbury, because I knew it would alarm them. But my brother called me and said he had been talking to someone who had told him I looked sick and out of it. Stephan asked me if I was all right and if there was anything he could do. I must have sounded very messed up on the phone.

I didn't know if I thought I was really going to try to get better, but I went back to see Dr. Ikeda. She told me straight out that I needed serious help, immediately, and that I needed to be admitted to an in-patient detox and rehab facility. Sitting there, I couldn't figure on how I could do without the drugs, but I told the doctor I was willing to try to get clean. Dr. Ikeda recommended a facility in California—Steps, located in Port Hueneme, a small beach community in southern California. She said it was one of the best, and even though anonymity could not be guaranteed, it would be smart to go to a place far away from Boston. I agreed to go and to try to heal.

That night, I talked it over with Karen and she was totally supportive. She knew I needed to do it. As for the time I would be away from the house, we were straight and upfront with Colleen and Chris about what was going on—and as for Tara, we explained that I would be going away for a while.

Two days after my appointment with Dr. Ikeda, I took a cab to

Logan Airport and got on a plane headed for Los Angeles. I was scheduled to be at Steps for three months.

I boarded the plane totally fucked up on Oxy. When I got into L.A., I managed to get my bags, and waiting for me in the arrivals area at the airport was one of the staff members of Steps. He was neatly and casually dressed and about my age. He had a big smile and was pleasant and upbeat as he shook my hand. He obviously saw I wasn't well.

It was a half-hour drive to the facility. And what a beautiful facility, all California and American Southwest and all that. It also was about a block away from the ocean. I met with a female doctor, and two counselors, a man and a woman. Everything was described and laid out for me. What my stay would largely be about was getting myself weaned off the poison and coming to grips with what I had done and how I had gotten there, and then setting in front of me a game plan to remain clean and healthy.

They explained to me how I would get better and prepare for staying healthy. I would do this by following and completing the twelve-step program. So Steps was not just the name of the treatment facility, it was also a reference to the model it used.

The twelve-step concept has been around for about eighty years, and it has proven to be highly effective in getting people clean and keeping them clean. Alcoholics Anonymous created the program, and since that time it has been adjusted, modified, and adapted in various ways.

Below I will give you a brief summary of the steps, in my words, not those in the official program booklet.

Step one is about stopping the denial and owning up that you have a problem. Step two is recognizing that this thing can be beaten, and in beating it, your life will be a lot better. Allowing people to help you and relinquishing some control in the process, is step three. Step four builds up your self-awareness and forces you to confront and take a full inventory of your life and your addiction. Steps five, six, and seven focus on getting rid of flaws in your character and reaching out to, and abiding by, professional and family help offered.

Taking steps eight through ten requires a person to make things right with those he has harmed or neglected in the past, and it also requires one to let go of flaws and mistakes made and not to dwell on them. Steps eleven and twelve are about forging, building, and embracing the personal development tools that will enable you to continue to grow and improve as a person and help others.

As I sat there, I couldn't care less about the particulars of the twelve steps—because I felt so sick. The doctor told me I would take a series of medications during my stay that would make it easier on me—physically and emotionally—to leave the opioids behind and not go through a painful withdrawal.

So allow me here to give advice to anyone suffering from addiction and wanting to beat it: the clinical path, with professionals administering medicine and evaluating you, is the way to go. Within a day, I was not feeling the withdrawal. Truthfully, I wasn't feeling much of anything. It is some precise science that is applied—treating you with chemicals that make you groggy and calm, yet don't incite in you a desire to keep taking those chemicals. The meds do their work but don't leave you hungering for them.

I had my own room at Steps. It was small, sort of the size of a college dorm room, and it had a bathroom. There was 24/7 staff on the halls and a security desk. We weren't in a lockdown, but anyone leaving who wasn't supposed to leave would be identified and could be booted from the program.

It is difficult for me to give you a detailed description of my first seven to ten days at Steps, because I was out of it almost all the time. I was treated with the anti-anxiety medications Librium and clonidine, both of which kept me relaxed, sleepy, and largely unable to feel the discomfort of withdrawal. I met with physicians and counselors, but I didn't remember much about the meetings. This part of the stay was mostly nice.

After ten days, I started a phase of fairly in-depth therapy and counseling sessions, both one on one and in groups. What became clear, fast, is that these sessions would compel me to get honest with myself and with others. I learned to understand why I took drugs and drank alcohol. I learned I was a drug addict and an alcoholic. I learned the choices I needed to make to stay sober—and I learned what I needed to avoid to stay clean.

Leading the effort in treating me was a great guy, a medical doctor, Dave Lewis. Dr. Lewis was smart and had seen and heard it all, and he had an ability to tell you what you needed to hear without being preachy and holier-than-thou. Preachy and holier-than-thou is surely not what I needed at that point in my life.

Included in the treatment were lectures and workshops, some of which were led by recovering addicts who had turned it around and were helping to free people from the injury they had endured. We also had recreation that was fun and good for the soul and body—going out on a boat on the ocean, going to a movie, just getting out and walking on the beach (yeah, I know, "walking on the beach" seems trite and old, but it felt good for many of us there).

There were a lot of tortured souls—me among them—at Steps. And as we managed to relieve our hunger for chemicals, we needed to grab for and hold on to healthy forms of comfort.

I remember the third month I was at Steps as one in which sunlight started to make its way into my head and body, bringing with it a clarity. I didn't hunger for pills. I gained back the twenty pounds I needed to make "playing weight."

I saw a lot of things more clearly—and some things for the first time.

When I left Steps, I was confident that I would not relapse.

A primary component of the therapy and learning centered around highly pragmatic issues—chief among them, establishing a game plan for what I would do when I got back to the Boston area. It was strongly emphasized that coming back to the place where I got doped- and boozed-up on a daily basis was fraught with a high degree of potential for problems—especially if I didn't have structure and a meticulously detailed strategy for staying busy with healthy and constructive pursuits.

Following the advice of the professionals at Steps, when I got off the plane in Boston, the top priority—after meeting up with my family and setting up a schedule of appointments with my doctor—was to find a job.

So the very same day I made it back to Boston, I called John Harwood, a good friend of mine who was the speaker of the Rhode Island House of Representatives and who, as a lawyer and agent, had represented several NHL players. Harwood had graduated from the University of Pennsylvania, where he had been a star baseball and hockey player. His law degree was from Boston College. He had a great pedigree. He was connected in politics, business, sports, and everywhere else.

Harwood had offered to help me find a job in the past, and I figured I had better connect with him now, so I did. Harwood said to give him a few days. Sure enough, a few days later, he got back to me and said he had set up an appointment for me with Rhode Island's secretary of state, Edward Inman III. As it turned out, Inman was a big hockey fan. He had played hockey for Coventry High School in Rhode Island in the late 1970s and had remained active with the school's booster club.

I drove down to Providence, to that big and beautiful capitol building you can see plainly from Interstate 95, and had a meeting with the secretary of state. Inman, only forty-one years old, was very excited and about meeting me. We talked about hockey and the NHL, and he asked me about some memorable games and memorable fights. He told me he wanted me to meet his executive assistant, Joe DeLorenzo, who was a hockey enthusiast. Apparently, DeLorenzo needed an assistant. That is why I was there, to interview to be the assistant to the secretary of state's assistant.

What I didn't know is that this was not the time to get a job in the Rhode Island government. There were all sorts of federal and state investigations ongoing—some not yet revealed—into elected and appointed public officials, at the state level and the municipal level in Providence, the state capital. In fact, the mayor of Providence, the flamboyant Buddy Cianci, would soon be indicted on corruption charges and would eventually do jail time. Others in city government would be carted off to the federal pen as well. Really, it was a mess down there.

What is so much fun, and what often makes politics and government such a crazy business in Massachusetts and Rhode Island (and in Boston and Providence), is that both states decided to make their biggest city their state capital. Government is messy and corrupt anyway, and having so much money and power all clumped together in one place ups the chances there is going to be trouble.

Look at some of our biggest states. New York has its capital in Albany, not New York City. California has its capital in Sacramento, not Los Angeles or San Francisco. For Texas, it's Austin, not Dallas. For Florida, it's not Miami, but Tallahassee. When you visit the state capital in Illinois, you are in Springfield, not Chicago. There is a reason why states do it that way.

Anyway, I met with Joe DeLorenzo. He was nice enough, a member of the large tribe of Italians who control so much in Rhode

Island. What I didn't know then—you see, there was a lot I didn't know then—is that DeLorenzo was peddling his government connections and his relationship with the secretary of state to try to cut various deals—and he was doing this outside of the proper governmental purview.

DeLorenzo and I talked hockey. I was content to gab with him about the sport and the glory days of the past. Now, as for what I would be doing for DeLorenzo, he said he needed someone to help out with various matters in his office. I told him I really didn't have much experience in politics or government or anything. He said that wouldn't be a problem and wanted to know when I could start.

It was a paycheck and a job, and I needed both. My salary would be, I think, $700 a week, which was fine with me—in that it was $700 more a week than I had been making.

I'm not sure what day I had my "interview" with Joe DeLorenzo—it might have been a Thursday or Friday. What I do know is that I started the job on the following Monday. So I got there at nine in the morning, Secretary Inman and DeLorenzo showed me around the office, and I met other staff members. Then the three of us went for a walk around the corridors of the capitol building, and I was introduced to that person, and that rep, and that senator, and that big shot, and then another rep . . . and so on. If the person to whom I was introduced didn't know who I was—that is, Chris Nilan of hockey fame—then he or she was quickly filled in.

I soon found out that, in this job, I didn't do much of anything. I didn't report to anyone. I didn't have any real assignments or job duties or responsibilities. I was showing up every day, and I had a desk at which I sat, and sat, and sat. Sometimes I would be given the task of walking some papers or a folder over to an office. Other times I would be sent to pick up papers or a folder at another office and bring them back to our office. Well, I started taking long coffee breaks and long lunches. No one seemed to mind that I wasn't around.

I was there for six months, and by this time I was showing up maybe once a week for half a day, and I was still getting paid. I guess, technically, it wasn't a no-show job, but it was the next closest thing to a no-show job. Funny thing is, when I was sometimes at the office, I would run into Secretary Inman or Joe DeLorenzo. They were all smiles all the time, and always asked how things were going. I told them things were going fine, and they didn't ask any more questions.

I rarely saw or talked with John Harwood.

As for the rest of my life, I remained totally clean. I didn't take one pill or imbibe a drop of alcohol. Karen and I were getting along, and I was recommitted to being a good father. I spent plenty of time with my kids. I saw them every day and was involved with their lives. Then again, I should hope I was involved in the lives of my children. After all, it wasn't like I was working particularly hard.

About a year after I started the "job" in Providence, it came to an end. It had to. Mayor Cianci was about to go on trial. Joe DeLorenzo was in hot water about some casino deal he was involved in. And Secretary Inman had a challenger for the upcoming election. Mike Ryan was the name of his opponent, and Ryan was doing a great job of painting Inman's administration as shady, corrupt, and misman-aged. Then again, it wasn't difficult. An exhibit Ryan pointed to over and over was yours truly. He said I wasn't coming to work, and yet I was getting paid. He issued a news release in which he called for my time sheets to be made available.

I had to get out of Dodge. Really, no one pressured me to resign, but I knew what had to be done. It was only right. Some people had helped me out, and by staying on it could only screw them over. I quit the job in March of 2002.

So here I was again. What next?

38

MONSIGNOR RYAN

AGAIN, I FOUND MYSELF with time on my hands. Yet, busy or not, it had always seemed in my life that a problem—of my own making or someone else's—was going to roll into my path or circulate around me.

So a month or so after I left the State House in Providence, I found myself and my name in the newspapers, a witness to one holy hell of a scandal in the Catholic Church.

You've already read about how important the Catholic Church was to my family and to families throughout Greater Boston. It was fundamental to our lives. We placed extraordinary trust in the church and all those clerics who served it. I guess, in many ways, it was infallible to us.

I still call myself a Catholic despite all the shit that has gone on with the church—and all the shit that has gone on with me. I was married in the church, and my wife and I had all three of our children baptized in the church. I don't go to church much nowadays, but I still go—if only a few times a year. I still believe in God. As an Irish Catholic kid growing up in a tough disciplinary environment, the church became embedded in my soul—and it will never be separated from me.

The church was embedded deep in the soul and culture of all the Boston area throughout the twentieth century.

In fact, for decades the Catholic church was deeply entwined in the everyday politics of the city. The Irish in Boston made their way with the three "Ps"—that is police, politics, and the priesthood. And woven throughout all of it was the church.

I love the story of how, in the final few nights of one of his campaigns—and this was probably in the mid- to late 1940s—James Michael Curley, wearing this thick raccoon coat, rode up to the front steps of St. Mary's Parish in Dorchester in the back of a long, wide town car with the top down. And the throngs were all there and all excited for a speech. So Curley got out of the car and took off the coat and laid it over the back of the car, and then he walked up to the top of the steps. Then what did he do? Well, he began to lead the crowd in the Lord's Prayer. Yeah, it was like that for a long, long time in Boston.

Of course, before he had finished with the prayer, Curley looked down and saw someone trying to make off with his raccoon coat— and this caused Curley to stop and blurt out, "Hey, someone get that son of a bitch. He's stealing my coat." In Boston, our Catholicism had an edge.

When, early in 2002, formal charges started being filed against priests and former priests in the Archdiocese of Boston for molesting children, and as all the sickening and filthy details of the accusations came out, along with the extent of the abuse that was alleged, I was surprised. You may say to yourself that that is hugely naive, especially in that I had gone to Catholic school from nursery school through high school. I regularly attended church. The church was all around me.

For sure, we thought it a bit weird that priests and brothers in the church did not get married and that they had to remain celibate. I mean, really. But we didn't dwell much on the sexual and romantic lives of priests. It was just known that celibacy was part of their calling. There was next to no suggestion that any cleric ever had a physical relationship with anyone, never mind forced himself on and molested kids. It was beyond depraved—there was no way.

And eventually I would become part of the story, a well-known jock who became aware of some of the abuse, and I was drawn in and subpoenaed to testify, and my name was featured in the newspapers and on TV news broadcasts. It was one more difficult and uncomfortable period for me, but if I had to do it over again, I would. When I discovered what had happened, I had no choice but to come forward and try to make sure justice was done and that I contributed in some way to stopping the abuse.

In March 2002, Garry, who I knew from Catholic Memorial, made public claims that Father Frederick Ryan—yes, that Father Ryan—had molested him when Garry was a student at CM and Father Ryan was a teacher there.

This was terrible—the notion that Father Ryan, the man who married Karen and me and who baptized our three children, was a diddler. It couldn't be. No way.

Right away, I knew I had to look hard at who was making this terrible accusation. Because, for sure, when Garry was a teen and into his early twenties, he had a track record of troublemaking and criminal behavior. Of course, the worst of it went down in 1984, when he and a buddy, a Northeastern University kid, got into a fight with four guys from Boston College. Garry's pal cracked one of the BC guys over the head with a tire jack and the guy ended up dying. Since Garry didn't wield that jack—and, it seems, because he and his buddy were outnumbered—he was allowed to plead guilty to assault with a dangerous weapon. Garry received a sentence of five years of community service.

I also knew that while Garry got the bad actions behind him, graduated from college, married, had kids, made a boatload of money as a salesman in the high-tech industry, and lived in a mini-mansion, difficulties had resurfaced. Yes, during the 1990s, Garry had been a high-flying salesman at the data storage company EMC; he had a few years in a row when he made between $500,000 and $1 million. But he battled booze and depression, lost his job, and then went to another company and lost that job. Maybe Garry was suing the church in search of money.

I had heard rumors for several weeks, and I finally called Garry to talk with him about it. What was being bandied about bothered me. I mean, nothing squared, because for years, Father Ryan was only about being good and stand-up to us. Talking to Garry on the phone, he said that what he alleged was all true. He came across as a guy who was in genuine pain. We met in person.

Garry told me that the molestation had occurred in 1979, after Father Ryan left CM and became a vicar and vice-chancellor with the Archdiocese of Boston. In this role, he was sort of in the cabinet of Cardinal Humberto Medeiros. Anyway, Father Ryan, now living in luxury in the chancery compound in the Boston neighborhood of Brighton, kept in touch with Garry and some of the other kids at CM.

So it was, as Garry told it, that when he was fourteen years old and a freshman at CM, he was visiting Father Ryan one night at the chancery. Garry said that that night, Father Ryan gave him booze and got him messed up, and then molested him and took photos of Garry naked. Garry said Father Ryan had held on to the photos and used them against him through the years as a sort of blackmail, an insurance policy against Garry telling anyone what happened, lest Father Ryan distribute the photos.

And get this: when Garry was telling me this—and again we were now in 2002—Father Ryan was no longer Father Ryan, but

Monsignor Ryan, a vicar in charge of fifteen parishes in southeastern Massachusetts. Talk about all messed up.

Perhaps this was some sort of weird thinking Garry had going on, and he wasn't remembering things correctly. Could he be delusional? To tell you the truth, I had no idea. Absolutely no idea.

As for me, well, it was out-and-out awful. Father Ryan was someone I not only trusted but in whom I confided. It just couldn't be; I was far too streetwise, and I could read people very well—or at least I thought I could.

I needed to talk to Monsignor Ryan.

So the day after Garry and I talked, on a weekday afternoon, I drove down to where Monsignor Ryan was assigned at the time, St. Joseph Church in Kingston, Massachusetts, a coastal town about twenty miles outside of Boston. I knew that word had gotten back to Monsignor Ryan about what Garry was saying, and that is why I didn't call ahead. In the event that there was some merit to the accusations, I felt that catching Monsignor Ryan off guard would better enable me to get a read on whether his responses to my questions were truthful or not.

I just showed up that day. I knocked on the door of the rectory and Monsignor Ryan came to the door himself. Now, I gotta tell you, with all that was going on, and given that the monsignor knew I was tight with the guy who had come out with the claim against him, the expression on the monsignor's face was not what it would have been if I had made a surprise visit to see him five years earlier. Back then, he would have been all smiles—now he had a look on his face that was a mix of concern, fear, and curiosity.

Monsignor Ryan opened the door and said, "Chris . . . Chris . . . this is great—great to see you," as he reached out and we gave each other a half hug. "Well, c'mon, c'mon in," he said as he motioned me inside. He knew why I was there.

He asked, "What's up, Chris? What brings you here?"

Fuck that. I told you, he knew why I was there.

I came right out and said, "Listen, Father, I'm not going to bullshit you. This whole thing that has come out . . . what Garry Garland is saying about you and all that—well, it is bothering me big time. I just gotta hear from you that this is all bullshit."

Monsignor Ryan looked into my eyes and said, "Well, of course it is nonsense." And then he said, "But let's talk about this," and he walked forward and waved for me to follow. We went into what I guessed was the living room of the house, and he pointed to one of those big, comfy, upholstered chairs, and I sat in it as he sat in the same type of chair that was off to my left and a few feet away.

Monsignor Ryan didn't say anything, not at first. He just sat there and looked over at me—with concern and fear. I was leaning forward with my elbows on my knees, and I was looking at him, and then I looked down while shaking my head and said, "I just don't know, Father. Why would Garry come out with such an accusation and such a tale? I talked with him, and he is very upset—and it didn't look to me like he was making anything up. But I don't want to believe this. I don't want to believe any of it." And then I looked at him and asked, "Why, Father, would he do this?"

The monsignor was spirited in his response, leaning toward me and gesturing with his hands. He said, "I don't know why, Chris. This entire thing has hurt me terribly. I have spent my entire life helping kids and young people. I have given my life to the church. And now this? You have to know that none of it is true. I feel bad for Garry. I don't know why he said what he said. We know—you and I know—that he has had a bit of a tough road over the years. Perhaps this has something to do with it. I can't be sure."

I leaned back and just looked forward. I thought about things for a few moments—moments in which neither of us spoke.

"Okay, okay . . . then you have to tell me this," I said as I looked into his eyes with all the intensity I could muster. "Then you tell me right to my face that you never molested Garry—you never did anything to him. If you can do this, right to my face, then I will believe you. That is all you have to do."

Monsignor Ryan continued to look at me (I wasn't sure if I saw something wavering in those eyes), he didn't turn away, and he said slowly and with an even cadence, "Chris, I never did anything to Garry. I never did anything inappropriate to him. All I did for Garry is what I did for so many of you guys—and that is try to help you."

It was less than convincing, but I said, "Okay, then I believe you. But you do need to know, Father, that this thing could escalate, and the police and the press might get involved."

Monsignor Ryan said he understood, but he had faith it wouldn't come to that.

After Monsignor Ryan made this testimony to me, I figured I had done what I needed to do. I got up and said that I had to get back to Boston. We walked to the door, and we hugged. And then I apologized for showing up and bringing up the matter, and for questioning him, but I said I had to—I just had to. Monsignor Ryan said he understood and that he harbored no hard feelings.

Before I turned and walked toward my car, I said we needed to get together again soon, and that it would be fun. Monsignor Ryan said sure.

Soon enough, I would see Monsignor Ryan again—and the confrontation would be even more unpleasant, far more unpleasant, than the one that played out in that home down along the coast.

❖

Garry Garland hired an attorney a few days after we talked. The attorney he hired, Daniel J. Shea, was a former priest who knew well the culture and internal workings of the church and also despised the church—a perspective and motivation that would help Garry and also hurt him.

On Thursday, March 21, Shea filed a lawsuit on behalf of Garry Garland. He made sure the media knew what was up, and with such a frenzy already in place because of a growing list of other allegations against priests—and given that Garry had once been a star athlete at a local high school—you just had to know that the reporters and editors and producers were all giddy and excited.

With the archdiocese already knowing about the rumors around Monsignor Ryan, and being assailed with accusations, lawsuits, investigations, and microphones and cameras at every turn, it moved swiftly in reaction to the lawsuit, suspending Monsignor Ryan.

Within hours of the archdiocese's decision, Monsignor Ryan was packed and out of St. Joseph's rectory and on his way to a three-story townhouse that his family owned in Chelsea, a gritty, ethnic city that borders Boston on the north. His parents, who had bought the house, were both dead, and his niece was living there at the time.

Filing a lawsuit was the point of no return for Garry. So he must have been telling the truth, right?

Then again, as had been the case throughout his entire career, Monsignor Ryan was held in high regard by his flock, now the parishioners of St. Joseph's. They put together a vigil in support of him, and provided statements to the press in which they said flat out that they were with the monsignor and that they did not believe what was alleged.

This made me feel good. Yeah, Father Ryan didn't do these things.

Then came Palm Sunday, the first day of Holy Week—three days after the lawsuit against Monsignor Ryan and the church was filed.

What happened on Palm Sunday lit and fueled a firestorm.

Garry Garland said that the same night Father Ryan assaulted him at the chancery, he was also violated by another man. That man? Garry said it was Cardinal Medeiros himself—a church leader who had been held in almost saintly reverence by millions. Yes, Cardinal Medeiros was respected and loved—and he was even from the Boston area. The future cardinal had immigrated to America from Portugal when he was a kid and had grown up in the Massachusetts fishing and textile-manufacturing city of New Bedford.

Cardinal Medeiros was known as a gentle and kind man and an outspoken advocate for social justice. In the mid-1960s, when he was a bishop in Texas, he used to say Mass for Mexican migrant workers in the fields.

And what sent people skyward, especially observant Catholics, was that Cardinal Medeiros was not around to defend himself. He had died in 1983.

What a shitstorm. The next day, Monday of Holy Week, the news of Garry Garland's allegations that Cardinal Medeiros had groped his genitals was infuriating people in the streets and in the pews, not to mention radio talk show hosts and newspaper columnists—and they were all firing off heated condemnation.

I hadn't talked to Garry about the matter, but I heard through some people that Garry was receiving death threats because he had accused the cardinal. People, lots and lots of them, were calling Garry a liar, an opportunist who saw the cash compensation that no doubt would come to the accusers.

My head hurt. I had no answers. I had so many questions.

Things got crazier.

Two days after Garry Garland accused Cardinal Medeiros of molesting him, another former Catholic Memorial kid came forward and said that Father Ryan had sexually abused him. I knew this guy as well. His name was David Carney, and he also had Daniel Shea as an attorney. Shea said he was representing yet a third man who said Father Ryan abused him.

Monsignor Ryan made a statement claiming that he knew the men who had made the accusations, but that the accusations were untrue.

I had had enough. I called Mike Daley, a guy I went to CM with. He was a talented basketball player in high school, a tough power forward, a guy I knew from way back. Mike was also smart; he had a good perspective on things and always seemed to have his priorities in order. As well, Mike and his wife, Jane, had three children, all of whom had been baptized by Father Ryan.

And, like me, and like so many other CM kids, especially athletes, he had been close with and admired Father Ryan.

I asked Mike what he thought, and he agreed with me that it just looked bad all through. I said that I was driving up to Chelsea, and that I was going to confront Monsignor Ryan again.

Let me stop here, just for a bit—because you may wonder why, after all those years, I would bother with the matter. Why get involved? Why step into that cesspool? I'll tell you why. It is because the matter just got me so pissed, and it made me feel vulnerable as well. I felt betrayed and a bit foolish. I have made a shitload of mistakes in my life, and I have not always been on the up and up—but I eventually made things right. If Garry and the others are to be believed, what Father Ryan did—who he was—was just such a clusterfuck of hypocrisy, cowardice, selfishness, and evil.

And I had let that clusterfuck into my life—and into the life of my family.

Mike thought it a good idea that he come along with me to see Monsignor Ryan. He thought that whatever Monsignor Ryan said or didn't say, whatever he admitted to or didn't admit to, it would be good to have someone else to back up whatever was said and contended. I agreed.

I must tell you, all through the twenty-minute drive up there, both of us were incredibly edgy. For sure, both of us had been competitive athletes who could handle the cauldron and intensity of pressure—but what we were going to confront that night just might be very, very bad. It just might pull out the underpinnings that had supported so much of what we had believed for so long. It might expose a terrible lie. Fuck, it might reveal someone to be a devil who, for so long, had claimed—and made a stake in life in telling the world—that he worked for God.

We were on our way to confront the past.

Tuesday night, March 23, 2002. Five days until Easter Sunday. And there we were, Mike and I, at the front door of a townhouse in Chelsea. We rang the doorbell and we heard the plodding steps of a man. Then the shout of Monsignor Ryan—"Who is it?" Yeah, you had to know that, with what was hanging over his head, he wasn't going to be opening that door without knowing who was behind it.

I shouted, "Father, it's Chris Nilan and Mike . . . Mike Daley."

Within seconds, the door was open and he was looking at us. His face registered fear and not a sign of anything holy or happy or of a man of the cloth. This was someone who had been slapped and cracked and stomped down with what was being leveled at him. I didn't like anything about being there.

I asked if we could come in, and Monsignor Ryan said sure. As we stepped inside, he said, "So I have to know what this visit is all about."

"Yeah, it is about that," I said.

Father Ryan—or Monsignor Ryan, whatever you want to call him—brought us to the living room of the brownstone. We sat down on chairs; he to my left and Mike to my right. I was going to lead this conversation.

"Father, here we are again," I said. "And I don't know, but it seems really messed up that now we have three guys who say you did things to them—that you messed with and molested them. I mean, now three have said this. Are you going to tell me that all of 'em are lying? Because right now, you have guys being put through the wringer—they are being called liars by you. You got many of your parishioners down in Kingston backing you, which means they are saying that what Garry and David are saying isn't true.

"You always said to tell the truth, and we did tell you the truth. Now it is your turn to tell the fucking truth."

Monsignor Ryan looked at me nervously and then past me to Mike. He put his head down.

"Guys, none of this is true. It is all false."

I was staring at the monsignor, who was still shifting his gaze all around, from me to the floor to Mike to the wall, and I said, "Father, we got three guys now saying that you molested them. Three guys and you're saying there is no truth to any of it. You always told us to tell the truth and to be men of integrity, so I hope you are telling us the truth and you are being a man of integrity. I know one thing: Mike and I are not leaving here until we get the truth."

"I don't know what to say, Chris, but it isn't true. It didn't happen," he replied.

So for about ten minutes we talked. Mike said next to nothing; he was there for verification and support. Monsignor Ryan was halting and nervous; he talked about problems in Garry Garland's life and David Carney's life, and wondered why people do what they do. He talked about how he felt bad for Garry and David, and that there was hysteria out there about priests and abuse and all that.

I let him talk.

I also told him a few times that I still thought things weren't adding up, although I did not come right out and say I thought he was lying. I told him indirectly that I thought he was being less than straight in talking about what may or may not have happened.

And then, after that first ten minutes we were there, Monsignor Frederick Ryan, a vicar in the Catholic Church, admitted he had molested teenage boys.

Some twenty-five years after I had graduated from Catholic Memorial High School thinking that Father Frederick Ryan was just about as stalwart and stand-up a role model for young men as there could be, he told Chris Nilan and Mike Daley he was a fraud, an abuser, a violator of teenage boys. He confirmed that what Garry Garland had said was true, and that what David Carney had said was true.

This was about as rotten and unhappy as it could get.

As the admission came forth, as Monsignor Ryan began to cry and whimper as he told the story, I was lightly muttering lines like, "What the fuck . . . what the fuck." Mike was exhaling loudly as if to get out all the tension and anger in his body. Mike said, "Oh man . . . oh man . . . you got to be fucking kidding me."

Monsignor Ryan tried to explain away what he did; he tried to excuse what he did. In some warped and totally fucked-up manner, which is the only way you can try to excuse that kind of abuse, he talked about how, as a kid growing up in Iowa, he had always wanted to be a popular athlete, but he was not athletic and knew he would never be any type of athlete that would draw attention. He said that when he became a priest, he wanted to hang around with jocks because it fed his ego. It gave him a trumped-up sense of importance. It made him feel like a big man.

Well, being a jock sniffer is nothing new, but when it involves a grown man doing his figurative jock sniffing around adolescent boy athletes, that is very strange and creepy, even if it isn't criminal.

What I considered criminal is what Monsignor Ryan also talked about that night. He said he felt this strong connection to boy athletes, and it got wrapped up in and tied to an attraction he had for them, an emotional and physical attraction that he was almost powerless to control. He said something about how he knew it was wrong, but he did what he did anyway.

He talked about being with boys, getting drunk and molesting them. He went into some detail, which I won't provide here. Let me just say that the specifics were obscene.

Neither Mike nor I needed to hear any more. We didn't want to hear any more.

"You need to make this right," I said to Monsignor Ryan. "You need to clear these guys—you need to remove all the suspicion people have about them. You need to let people know that they are speaking the truth."

"I'll do that . . . I'll do that," Monsignor Ryan muttered as he looked at me, tears streaming down his face. "I'll do that. What do you want me to do? I will do it."

Actually, I was prepared in the event that Monsignor Ryan admitted to abusing the boys. If that happened, I knew exactly what I wanted Monsignor Ryan to do.

"This is what you do, Father: you make a public statement. You get on TV and you say you did it. You admit it. You can never make this thing right, but you can help give back the reputations of these guys who are going through hell because you have lied. I can arrange a TV interview for you with Dan Rea."

Rea had been my agent; he was also a reporter at WBZ-TV in Boston. He and Monsignor Ryan knew each other. When Dan, who was Catholic, was a kid growing up in Hyde Park, he attended Mass at Most Precious Blood Parish, which was in the neighborhood where Father Ryan was a priest.

Monsignor Ryan, still sitting all hunched forward in his chair and sniffling, said, "Yeah, okay, I will do it. I will do the interview."

"Are you sure? Are you absolutely sure?" I asked. And I knew I was looking at the monsignor with total contempt when I spoke. Oh man, I was furious.

"Yes . . . yes . . . absolutely, sure. I will do it. When do you want me to do it?"

"Well, Father . . ." I took out my cell phone. "I want you to do it right now. " With that, I told the monsignor I needed to step outside to make a quick phone call. I left poor Mike sitting there with the predator.

In front of the house, I dialed Dan's number. After a few rings, he answered, and I said, "Dan, do you want to win an Emmy?"

"I always want to win an Emmy," said Dan. "Why, what do you have for me?"

"How about Father Ryan making a confession to you, complete with whatever details you can put on TV, about the boys he molested?"

"Who—are you kidding me? How do you come upon this?"

"I am at his house, along with Mike Daley. Can you do a phone interview with him, now?"

"Yeah, Chris, of course I can, but I want this on camera. I can get back up there and do the interview on Wednesday. Can we do this on Wednesday?"

Wednesday? What the fuck?

"No, we can't do this Wednesday—this thing has a short shelf life," I said. "We could lose the entire confession. We can't wait."

Dan said, "Ah, let me think . . . let me think . . . let me think."

There was a few seconds of silence on the line.

"Okay, I can get back for Tuesday. Call Ryan and ask about Tuesday. Can you do that? Do you think he will hold out?"

I wasn't thrilled. I wanted that fucking interview to get done that night, if possible. But I supposed it could wait until Tuesday. I supposed.

I went back inside and told Monsignor Ryan I would call him the next day to arrange an interview with Dan on Tuesday. Monsignor Ryan said he would do the interview.

With that, Mike and I walked away from the good monsignor and toward the outdoors to get away from this terrible scene and that terrible person. Mike already had the front door open. He stepped out, and I went right after him. We left the door open—and I don't remember Monsignor Ryan saying good-bye to us or anything like that. But as Mike and I walked along the walkway to my car, I did hear the door close behind us.

I was not in the car and driving back to Boston for more than a minute before I called Garry Garland on my cell phone. I got him right away, and I told him Father Ryan had confessed. I told Garry that Father Ryan had gone into detail and was going make a public confession—and not just any public confession, but a confession on TV to a well-known local journalist.

Garry was shocked when I told him, and of course happier than all get-out. He had been taking shit from all sides and from so many, and now he would be vindicated and proven to be telling the truth. Garry thanked me over and over—you could hear him starting to break down. And I understood this—for when the shock was wearing off, he must have felt he had been released from a living hell.

I thought so, too. But as I would quickly learn, Garry was wrong—and so was I.

The next morning, I called Monsignor Ryan. I told him we were all set for the next day, and that—

He cut me off.

"Listen, Chris, I'm sorry. I talked to my lawyer, and he will be representing me, and he told me that I shouldn't talk to anyone. So I'm following his advice."

I was beyond pissed and beyond deflated.

I yelled into the phone. "Nah, you can't do that! You can't do that! You've already messed up so many lives and now you are going to make things even worse, if that is fucking possible. You go to—"

"I'm sorry, Chris."

And then the good monsignor—that blessed apostle of Christ—hung up the phone.

For as long as I had known Garry Garland, he was easy to agitate, and he had that hair-trigger temper (a man after my own heart). He also, of course, had other emotional issues, all of which contributed to unsteadiness and unhappiness. Garry was a smart and hardworking kid—but he was also a bit off.

When Garry found out that Monsignor Ryan had lawyered up and was not talking and that it looked like he would never talk or admit to anything, Garry started to wind up and vibrate with fury and anxiety all rolled into each other. You've heard the term "time bomb"—well, that was the state that Garry was in.

Over the next few days—again, this was Holy Week, and again, this Sunday was Easter—tension and pain continued to roil and mount within Garry Garland. He finally cracked. He cracked with a cry for help. On Holy Thursday afternoon, Garry told his wife and his lawyer he was going to drive to Chelsea, find Monsignor Ryan, and maybe try to hurt him.

Holding a meat cleaver, Garry jumped into his sleek BMW sedan and headed toward Chelsea. Garry's attorney called the Chelsea police and filled them in on what his client had told him. The Chelsea cops raced over to Ryan's residence, and there was Garry, already parked out front and sitting behind the wheel. When Garry saw two cop cruisers approach, he floored the gas pedal and started a chase. The chase didn't last long, maybe a half mile, before Garry pulled over, and cops got out of each of the cruisers, guns drawn, removed Garry from his car, and had him lie facedown on the street. Garry was cuffed and arrested.

As it turns out, Monsignor Ryan was never in any danger. Again, it was Garry's cry for help. If you really intend to do harm to someone, you don't divulge your plans to people who will almost certainly call the police and alert them.

The police found the meat cleaver and some sort of suicide note in Garry's car. Garry was sent to a hospital for psychiatric review. Charges against him were dropped.

Garry, like Carney, ended up being one of the 550 people the Archdiocese of Boston settled with over claims against a list of priests and other church officials, paying out a total of $85 million, without legal admission of liability. I don't know how much money he got out of the case, and I don't care.

Monsignor Frederick Ryan was never charged criminally for abusing any boys. There was not enough solid, concrete evidence to bring a criminal case against him, and the alleged abuse went back two decades and further.

But know this: Monsignor Frederick Ryan admitted to me in person that he molested those kids. He can keep silent all he wants and for as long as he wants, but he is a diddler—and not just a diddler, but a repeat diddler. He is a bad person.

After that final phone call, I did not speak to Monsignor Ryan again. I will not speak to him ever again unless he wants to publicly man up and admit what he did. I don't anticipate this ever happening.

And amid all the upsetting and disgusting revelations about what Father Ryan did, there was one specific practice of his "grooming"—to use a clinical term that is used in describing the conduct of these molesters—of at least one of his victims, that came out. Father Ryan would have the boy over to the chancery and, in his room, would show him some of the hockey memorabilia I had given to him through the years. Father Ryan even had the boy put on a game jersey I had given him.

Father Ryan used gifts from me to him as bait. That's just beyond obscene.

Frederick Ryan is no longer a priest. He is living back in Iowa, where he grew up.

Funny thing: even after Monsignor Ryan admitted to molesting boys, my father—yes, the tough-as-nails Green Beret—defended him, sort of. He talked about all the good things that Father Ryan had done for so many years for kids and others. I told my dad that none of that mattered anymore, and that Father Ryan was a child molester and any good he had done was buried under that terrible fact.

To some, maybe my dad's perspective is not all that surprising. They would know that in Boston, among the Irish Catholics, support for the church can be stubborn and immovable.

39

TOO SOON

KAREN WAS HOLDING THE FAMILY TOGETHER—and our family was doing well despite me. Colleen had just finished her first year in college. Chris had just graduated from Hingham High School and was working. Tara would start junior high in the fall.

I needed to step up a bit—well, more than a bit. I don't know if it was the right thing to do at this point, considering that it hadn't been too long since my stint in rehab, but I decided to start taking classes at the Boston campus of the University of Massachusetts—UMass Boston, as we call it here—to earn my certification as an addiction counselor in the commonwealth.

Karen supported me in this. She supported me in everything that was smart and good for the family and myself. I started courses in the summer 2002 session. Located in the Boston neighborhood of Dorchester, on a peninsula that extends into the Atlantic, UMass Boston has been ranked as one of the best values in education in America. It is a tremendously valuable option for kids from working-class families in the area as well as for adults at all stages of their lives who want to start and finish a degree or earn certification. Over the summer, I took two evening classes a week, each for ninety minutes. I went to every class. I enjoyed them; I was engaged and focused. That summer, things were all right. I was working and going to school, and moving in the right direction. For now.

I was finishing my coursework during the fall semester, and after that I needed to put in three hundred hours of a supervised practicum. With the coursework and successful practicum behind me, I could then take the test. I was into this—I really was.

That fall, I had more good fortune in that Bill Hanson, the legendary hockey coach at Catholic Memorial, asked me to come on board as assistant coach. Hanson, remember, had taken over as coach of CM in my senior year, and since then he had built a dynasty at the school. Now, for sure, prior to Coach Hanson taking over, the Knights were always competitive in a highly competitive league and state for high school hockey. But under Bill Hanson, CM's success entered the stratosphere and the school established itself as one of the top prep programs in the country. CM won Catholic League title after Catholic League title, and also a slew of state titles.

Players that Hanson coached who went on to the NHL were Ted Donato, Paul Stanton, Jim Fahey, and Jim Carey.

Bill and I got along well. A guidance counselor at CM, he knew hockey inside and out, and he never stopped studying the game. Hanson was intense and demanding—and while he wasn't overtly the overly sensitive or warm-and-fuzzy type, he cared deeply about the students and athletes at CM, and not just the hockey players. Right from the first day of practice, I was having fun and knew that I was doing something important—and I also felt I was contributing.

In that CM hockey was, for all intents and purposes, Bill Hanson hockey, Coach Hanson oversaw everything and directly handled the big-ticket items: who was on the team, who was on what line, our game plans. The CM way of hockey was deeply and firmly established. I was appointed to work with the players on fundamentals, and also, on Coach Hanson's direction, to teach or advise players on the particulars of their game.

Naturally, because I had played for CM and in the NHL, I had a fair amount of street cred with the kids. They listened and responded.

I finished up my academic classes in December. I worked with UMass to find myself a facility where I could do a supervised practicum. Together we chose Gosnold on Cape Cod, a treatment center located in Falmouth, Massachusetts, with satellite offices in the eastern part of the state. Gosnold is one of the best-known and most reputable treatment organizations in the region.

Putting in those practicum hours for me was one of the most soul- and character-building experiences of my life. And yet, I look back on it now and wonder if I took on this challenge too early. I question whether so soon after—temporarily—beating my own addiction, I should have been going face to face, literally, with the destruction that drugs and booze do to others.

It was a four-month internship—and that is really what it was, an internship. It was a forty-hour-a-week commitment. I started out at Gosnold as someone who registered and collected information from people entering the program. Just as importantly, I talked with and collected information from members of the families of those entering treatment.

There was a tight, specific protocol I followed, along with specific questions I asked. I would then enter information into a computer database. Again, it was all right in front of you all the time—the pain and hurt. Also in front of you were confusion and terrible uncertainty.

For the first two weeks, I almost exclusively focused on the intake process. So much of what I entered into the computers, and so much of what I heard and saw on the faces of those entering the program and their families, were emotions and experiences I knew intimately. I was also supervised as I studied and learned the administrative processes involving the keeping of records and information on each person receiving treatment at the center.

After two weeks, I started sitting in on group sessions, which were led by a certified counselor. When the sessions were over, I sat with the counselor as she reviewed her notes, and she asked questions of me, which I answered. We discussed what had gone on in the session, what my thoughts were on certain people, and what they needed to do to successfully complete the program. It was intensive education.

My remaining time at Gosnold involved shadowing counselors and sitting in on one-on-one counseling sessions and group sessions. The counselors at Gosnold were super-dedicated, and they were diligent and committed to providing the direct interaction and tutoring I needed. About halfway through the four months, I was asked to develop my own courses of treatment based on individuals enrolled at Gosnold. After I drew up the treatment plan, a counselor would go over it with me, pointing out areas in which the plan was good and areas in which my suggestions needed to be reworked.

Counselors posed questions to me, giving me hypothetical cases to which I had to respond with answers and treatment options.

There were also many sessions in which I sat with counselors and another person going through his practicum, in which we watched videos of real-life sessions—both group sessions and individual—and the video would intermittently be shut off, and we would discuss what we just saw.

I successfully completed my practicum. All that remained was to pass the state certification exam. I studied hard for the exam, and I thought I knew everything I needed to know. Yet I took the test, and I failed by two points. I was deflated.

Now, most people would say, "Okay, so you didn't pass. Just sign up for the next test and go at it again." That would be the right approach. Then again, I often had attitude, and I didn't do what I should do. I didn't sign up to retake the test. It has been a decade since I took the test, and I still haven't retaken it.

40

TREADING WATER

BEGINNING IN THE SUMMER of 2004, and over the next three years, my grounding was shaky. I did not have steady employment— I made NHL-related appearances and helped Bill Hanson coach CM hockey during the winter. I started drinking and doing pills again. And I caroused and saw a lot of Mary.

I never turned down a request to participate in a philanthropic or charity event. So in this way, at least, I was a contributing citizen and doing some good.

But Karen was concerned about how our children viewed me. I was just, as I like to say, treading water—and you can only tread water for so long before you go under.

In early June 2005, Karen found out about Mary. It wasn't through an intercepted email, text message, or voicemail. It was just that there were nights when I didn't come home and so many absences I didn't want to talk about. Karen confronted me and asked me if I was having an affair. At first, I denied it; and then a minute later I admitted it. Karen was beyond furious and upset. She ordered me out of the house—and told me to stay gone.

I left our home in Hingham and went to live with Mary in her apartment in Boston. I stayed in touch with Karen and Colleen, Chris, and Tara. I took the kids out to eat or would visit with them.

Karen had no issue with me stopping by to see the kids.

Sometime in October, after pitching the idea to Karen over and over, she took me back and we resolved to make another go of it. I think, though, that my past actions and irresponsibility and selfishness had poisoned things too much. When you add in the fact that I continued to get drunk and get high, well, it could never work. By the following spring, it was over. I moved out of the house again in April 2006, and moved back in with Mary. Karen filed for divorce, which became official the following September.

If I haven't already emphasized this enough, I want to make sure I reassert it here: The end of our marriage was because of me and no one else. Karen is a wonderful woman, and was a great wife, and she remains the best of mothers. Karen stood by me in dark times and supported me in my efforts to get back on track. But my efforts were lacking—and ultimately, a good marriage is about strong cooperation and excellent teamwork. Starting not long after I left the NHL, I was not cooperative or any type of teammate in our marriage. I was a nasty addict.

Karen and I remain close, and we still have the strongest bond in our shared love of and commitment to Colleen, Chris, and Tara. They are our gift to each other. We love them fiercely, and their presence and our participation in their lives will always be a saving grace.

As my marriage was in its death throes, Mike Daley, the CM basketball player who was with me when Monsignor Ryan admitted to me the despicable things he had done, introduced me to Alan Stone, a very bright, energetic lawyer—a graduate of Tufts University and Boston College Law School. Alan was sort of an entrepreneur—he had run a legal recruiting firm since 1982, and in 2005 he founded the Worcester Tornadoes, a minor-league baseball team.

Alan was in the process of starting another company—a video-conferencing company called Vizzitt Corporation. Alan was looking for someone who had some cachet in the Boston area and could help with business development. Vizzitt would offer corporate videoconferencing services as well as a videoconferencing product marketed to schools—one in which pro and college athletes had conversations about important issues with high school students.

In September 2006, Alan hired me for a sales position, and for the techie aspects of the biz he hired a super-smart kid named Jack Speranza, who had just graduated from Purdue University with a degree in engineering. We had an office in Newton, just outside of Boston. I had a paycheck now, which was great—and even though I was still drinking and consuming opioids, I was able to make it to work and, for the most part, stay off chemicals during the workday.

We tried to make a go of it with Vizzitt. We actually had some demonstration projects that we ran with local high schools. I managed to get a verbal commitment from about a hundred retired pro athletes, almost all hockey players, to be a part of Vizzitt if we got it up and going. But we never did. After sixteen months, Alan Stone hit the off switch on Vizzitt. I couldn't really blame him.

I had been working at Vizzitt for six months when, in early spring, I received a phone call from Mark Napier of the NHL Alumni Association. Mark asked me if I would like to be part of a group of ex-NHL players who were going to Afghanistan to meet with Canadian and American troops stationed there. I said sure.

CHRIS NILAN

That trip to Afghanistan, and four more I would make over the next six years, were among the most important and rewarding things I would ever do. Accompanying me on some of those trips were Mark Napier, Bob Probert, Dave "Tiger" Williams, Ron Tugnutt, Yvon Lambert, and Réjean Houle.

It goes without saying that such events are humbling and put things in perspective. It was our priority to honor and give whatever comfort we could to the soldiers. We brought the Stanley Cup with us, and the soldiers would pass it around and have their photos taken with it. We played ball hockey with the troops—and I must tell you that some of the games got quite spirited and a bit physical.

These young men and women have the best attitude and are simply the best all around. I wish I had their discipline. If Bob Probert were here now, I bet he would say the same thing.

I had just returned from my first visit to Afghanistan and was in Ottawa sitting at a table in a restaurant. Also at the table were Bob (sitting next to me), Gaston Gringas, Steve Shutt, and Jimmy Mann. We were in Ottawa to play a five-game NHL alumni series. Anyway, while we were sitting, someone asked me a question, and as I was answering, Bob interupted. This happened again, and I turned to Bob and said, "Just fucking relax." He didn't like that, and he pushed me and jumped up and threw a punch at me. I retaliated, and we slugged it out for a few seconds before the guys jumped in and separated us.

41

SPIRALING DOWNWARD

EARLY IN 2008, I commenced a stretch that just had to end with me six feet under. No, I didn't want to kill myself. But without a job again, I had more time to ingest the poisons. I didn't really care anymore. So maybe I was in some sort of prolonged suicide attempt. Maybe.

When the high school hockey season arrived, I was not behind the Catholic Memorial bench anymore. I had decided not to continue coaching. Now I couldn't even get that right.

I was living with Mary, and I was a junkie.

I came oh-so-close to not making it to 2009.

It was early in December 2008; it was about seven in the morning and I was out of drugs. I couldn't score any more from doctors or other contacts in Boston. So a friend, Jimmy, and I jumped in Mary's Cadillac SRX and we headed north, into Vermont, and up Interstate 89 to Montreal. I was sick from withdrawal, but I was fully awake.

At 11 a.m., we crossed into Canada. About ten minutes later, as we were on the highway passing through the town of Henryville, an eighteen-wheeler crossed into my lane. I pulled my vehicle over to the oncoming side of the highway, and the draft from the big rig, combined with the torque I had imposed on my truck, pushed the SRX across the other lane and onto and down a slight embankment next to the road. My truck rolled over once. I was not buckled in—about an hour earlier when we stopped to take a piss, I had gotten back behind the wheel without buckling up—and at some point I was launched into the rear of the vehicle and through the back window.

I woke up lying on my side; Jimmy was shaking me lightly. Blood spilled into my eyes from a cut on my forehead. Jimmy seemed all right; then again, he had been wearing his seat belt. So let that be a lesson to everyone: wear your seat belt.

Soon enough, the police, paramedics, and an ambulance arrived. I was placed on a stretcher and put in the ambulance and taken to the hospital in Saint-Jean-sur-Richelieu. Jimmy rode in the back of the ambulance with me, along with the paramedics.

I didn't get charged with anything, because I didn't have any drugs or booze in my system. I sat there in the emergency room for a half hour. My head ached, and I had glass in my hair and some embedded in my skin. Jimmy said his shoulder was in pain. Finally, I told Jimmy we were getting out of there. We walked out the front door of the hospital and got ourselves a cab and had it bring us to Montreal, which was forty kilometers away.

We were dropped off at a bar in downtown Montreal sometime in the afternoon. After a good eight hours of drinking, we grabbed a room at the Château Champlain. In the morning, I visited a doctor who gave me OxyContin. With the drugs in hand, I hired a limo to take us back to Boston.

42

THE SECOND STINT

IF AN ADDICT IS FORTUNATE, he not only has that "Saul on the road to Damascus" moment—that full-bore kick in the teeth and whoop upside the head—but he also is able to respond quickly and in a healthy manner to that revelation. It was the lightning bolt of the Holy Spirit that resulted in Saul changing his ways; for me, maybe, just maybe—I do believe in God and his saints, after all—there was something of divine inspiration connecting with me as well.

I was regularly snorting eighty milligrams of Oxy a day. Again, I obtained the pills through doctors and sometimes through street pushers. You may wonder how doctors could still prescribe me pain medication; well, you see, I was still playing in a lot of NHL events, after which I would see a physician and explain that I had aggravated an old injury (and my extensive injury history was public knowledge) and was hurting and needed relief. This tactic worked over and over.

I don't know exactly what enabled me to see that death was only one bad trip away. But two weeks after the car accident, I had an episode of life-saving clarity.

Basically, my friends and family figuratively, and literally, put me in front of a mirror and told me that death would be calling any minute now. Only a few grains of sand remained in the upper half of the hourglass.

A great family and great friends. And this realization started me thinking hard about the pain I dumped on them every day I lived like this. I was living with Mary, and she was going through hell.

So one afternoon, I spilled out of the bed in the apartment I shared with Mary. I crawled and half walked and half stumbled to the dresser, where I had left my cell phone. I grabbed the phone and, while sitting on the floor, my back and head against the dresser, I started thumbing through the contact list. I found Dan Cronin and gave him a call. Thank God he answered. I said right out that I was in mortal trouble—the worst type of trouble, and that I needed help, yesterday. He immediately got the ball rolling to locate the right treatment facility. Dan also received clearance from Brian O'Neill for the NHL to pay for my treatment and for any travel associated with the program.

Within two hours, Dan called me back. He said he had arranged for me to be an inpatient at Astoria Pointe, a facility in Oregon that had an excellent track record of success, which employed a holistic method and the twelve-step Alcoholics Anonymous and Narcotics Anonymous programs of detoxing and healing people, and then getting and keeping them on a path of healthy living. Astoria Pointe is located in the town of Astoria, which is on the coast and at the most northwestern point in Oregon. It is hilly and just across the Columbia River from Washington state.

So there I was again. It was February 5, 2009, and I was doped up pretty good as I sat in a plane headed west. I understood that if I didn't make this flight, I wouldn't live much longer.

I arrived late in the afternoon at Portland International Airport. Astoria Pointe had sent a car to pick me up—and as the sun was setting, we started out on the long drive of almost 100 miles to Astoria Pointe. I understood that Astoria was a beautiful place—the type of place people don't want to leave and to which people want to move. The center itself afforded very nice views of the ocean, hills, and Columbia River. It was dark, though, when we arrived at Astoria Pointe, so I would have seen little that night of the surroundings.

It wouldn't be for a week, actually, that I would see the outside of Astoria Pointe or even much of anything outside of one big room at the facility. That was because for seven days I was in what is called a "detox room." That's right: similar to what I underwent at Steps in California, I was in a sort of solitary-confinement cell with a bed and an adjacent private bathroom. During this period, I was given a steady stream of detox meds. I could read or watch TV, but I could not have any contact with anyone outside of Astoria Pointe. I was very groggy and calm, and I stayed that way for the week.

In fact, I was in so much of a daze that I walked into the edge of a door, giving myself a deep cut on the brow line that needed seven stitches to close.

After detox, it was on to the next phase, which lasted thirty days. During this phase, I had a roommate, a great guy from the West Coast who was partially of Native-American descent. Again, during this period, there was radio silence—no phoning, email-ing, or texting anyone in the outside world. Astoria Pointe was a bit more "earthy, crunchy" and spiritual in its approach than was Steps. During those thirty days, we were woken up every morning at seven, and my roommate and I and about twenty other patients— men and women—sat in a circle and had what was called morning meditation. So we sat there and read from Daily Reflections, a book of inspirational and instructive passages that AA has put out. After fifteen minutes of reading and reflecting in silence, the counselor directing and proctoring the group would ask if anyone wished to share with the group his or her thoughts on something they had read or anything else.

Each patient had a counselor assigned to him or her. This counselor was the direct point of therapy and the direct monitor of how a patient was doing.

At eight-thirty we went to a small cafeteria for breakfast. The food at Astoria Pointe was actually quite good.

After breakfast, starting at nine, we began our series of one-hour group classes. There were about eight people in each class. You stayed with the same group of people from class to class. Each group had a letter attached to it; you were in either Group A or Group B, and so on. Each group had six classes a day. Classes had focuses such as art therapy; sex, love, and relationships; relapse prevention; and staying positive.

Lunch was at twelve-thirty.

Late in the afternoon every day, there was a group therapy and talking session—again, about six to eight people participated in each session like the classes—in which you could share your feelings and thoughts and all that. I usually kept quiet. After the group part of the session was over, you met individually with your assigned counselor.

During those thirty days, we went on chaperoned mini–field trips that took us away from the center a few times a week. I remember we went to a bowling alley and to a park and to the beach.

You are probably wondering how I was able to handle this environment, in which my life was so tightly controlled and in which my freedom was so stringently regulated. Here I was, Knuckles Nilan, someone who was spontaneous and bristled at authority and being told what to do. So I must have been out of my mind at Astoria Pointe, right? Actually, no. I finally recognized—in major part because of the help I was provided in rehab—that there was a mountain of bad decisions and choices I had made. I had to face reality—and the reality was that my life had been one of self-destruction. I knew I had to suck it up or annihilate myself.

There was also a sort of exclusive and special group at Astoria Pointe that was called DIG—an acronym for Deeper Issues Group. It was a bit mysterious, this DIG. If you had been at the center for at least six weeks, members of DIG could invite you into the group. And you had to be invited. I received an invitation to join DIG, and I accepted. DIG got together at five in the afternoon, after the classes and group sessions everyone attended. There were fifteen people in DIG as well as a counselor. Those sessions got very intense—a lot of deeply personal and, quite frankly, unsettling experiences were discussed. A lot of pain got out. I opened up a bit more in DIG than I did in other parts of the Astoria Pointe program. What was kind of weird about DIG was our discussions about individuals outside the group and whether they were of the right stuff to be invited in to DIG. I didn't much like those discussions because they were, in a way, about passing judgment. I was at a point in my life when judgments passed on me were almost all negative—albeit earned.

At quarter of six in the evening every day, immediately after DIG, everyone in the center would congregate in the main living room and have MEPS—another acronym. MEPS involved each person saying out loud how he or she was feeling mentally, emotionally, physically, and spiritually—hence the initials. After MEPS we had dinner.

Every night, we had the option of attending AA or NA meetings, to which center staff would drive us. One night a week, there was an AA meeting in the common room of Astoria Pointe.

When you completed half of your scheduled stay at Astoria Pointe, what had been your daily schedule seven days a week became your Monday-through-Friday routine. You would have more free time on weekends, and the center took groups of us to a local lake for cookouts or to a park for hikes and general relaxation.

Also, after your first six weeks at Astoria Pointe, on weekends you could have your family in for a visit. These visits were also an opportunity, if the patient requested and family members agreed, for patient and family to have sit-down sessions together with the patient's counselor.

It was four weeks into my stay at the facility that I noticed a young woman, twenty-something, walking down the corridor with a counselor. She was waifish, pretty, with shoulder-length blonde hair. She had her arms crossed in front of her, holding on to herself; her eyes darted from side to side. Obviously, this was a new patient— and just as obviously, she was very nervous.

Over the next few weeks, we would see each other here and there. We said hi to one another. I could tell something was there.

I had been participating in the DIG sessions for a month when we had a new member: the pretty girl with blonde hair. I found out her name was Jaime. It was difficult not to notice her. She was very pretty, and she smiled easily and radiated good energy. Yeah, she caught me looking at her—and truth be told, I wanted her to catch me looking at her.

I had only a couple weeks to go before finishing my rehab. Jaime had six weeks left in her stint. This was her first time in rehab. Like me, she had an addiction to opioids. My addiction, the choices I made, and my selfishness had ruined my marriage. As Jaime explained, she was living in Hawaii (where she grew up), and she had been engaged to be married, but her fiancé, a dedicated triathlete, said that unless she got treatment for her addiction, the marriage could not happen. So Jaime came to Astoria Pointe.

Within days of Jaime starting DIG sessions, her fiancé visited her. And it was during this visit that she told him she couldn't go through with the marriage. In many ways, it was immensely sad.

It is against the rules, and an accepted violation and taboo, for people in rehab to become involved romantically with one another. It just can't happen, for many reasons. First off, you gotta figure that the focus of a person needs to be on getting clean and getting well. And then you have the potential, for people who are sick and emotionally vulnerable, for the push and pull of the heart to make things worse.

I felt something for Jaime, and I thought she might feel something for me. But all we did was exchange comments in DIG and have a few conversations in the common area of Astoria Pointe. This broke no rules.

We might not have broken any rules, but the staff were aware of our chemistry. Indeed, one of the counselors, a woman, called Jaime in to talk about the matter. She told Jaime there were palpable emotions being transmitted between Jaime and me, and it was dangerous and it threatened to prevent a successful treatment outcome for both of us.

Jaime and I were issued a "no contact" order. And it meant just that—we were not to talk to one another, and we were not to be in the same room together. During meals, we had to sit on opposite sides of the room. We were both removed from DIG.

Yes, I was still involved with Mary, but I felt the relationship was going to end. I guess there is no way to sugarcoat it; I had met someone else—someone I was falling for. I talked every other day with Mary on the phone, and she and I both knew something was different. I felt terrible about putting Mary through this, but I also felt terrible about living another lie.

In the final week of my stay at Astoria Pointe, the center set me up at a sober house on the campus of the facility. It was an all-male home I would share with three other recovering addicts. During my two-month stay at the home, I would be subject to random drug tests and I would be required to attend meetings on campus.

Immediately after arriving at the sober house, I flouted the no-contact order and enlisted an emissary to deliver a greeting card in which I had written a note to Jaime. Over the next couple weeks, I had a card delivered to her every day. We also managed to talk on the phone several times. What we didn't know was that Jaime's roommate was secretly gathering information on our clandestine relationship, and she fed the info to the staff at Astoria Pointe.

Armed with the information, the administrators kicked me out of the sober house, and Jaime was called in for a meeting before several counselors. At the meeting, the counselors shared all sorts of information about me with Jaime, including that I had girlfriend back home (true), to whom I had given a big diamond ring (true), and to whom I was engaged (not true). And, then—and this really ticked me off—Jaime was told that there was something very dark and bad in my background, that they would not share with her. WTF?

I was fortunate in that I had an immediate housing option after getting the boot. While in treatment, I had become friends with a recovering alcoholic, a local resident, who attended meetings at Astoria Pointe. His name was Jim McCulley; he was in his early sixties and was tall and lanky with a tanned, weathered face and a smoker's light growl for a voice. Jim was a great guy who shared my passion for fishing.

Jim knew about my predicament. He lived with his wife in a small home on the Pacific Ocean. Next to the house he had a garage, over which was an apartment. Jim offered the apartment to me at a more-than-reasonable rate. When I heard it was a garage, I kind of thought, I don't know . . . But then he showed it to me, and it was a pretty nice setup: a studio apartment with its own kitchen, living room, and bathroom, and a big window through which you could see the ocean. I decided it could work.

Jaime had two more weeks in rehab when I set up home above the garage. And, of course, I managed to stay in touch with her. One afternoon, we talked in person in downtown Astoria. I explained everything to her about Mary and told her the rest was up to her.

Jaime was in the final two days of her on-site treatment, and she was told that there were no openings at local sober houses, but that she could stay on campus until one became available.

I would provide Jaime with another option. You see, anticipating her finishing up at Astoria Pointe, I had rented a cabin along the Nehalem River. It was a very nice cabin in a beautiful place. I was able to get in touch with Jaime and tell her that, when she got out, I wanted her to come over to the cabin for dinner, which I would make for her. It would be our first date.

Of course, someone at Astoria Pointe ratted out the offer. Again, Jaime was hauled in front of the tribunal. She was told I had relapsed (again, not true) and that she should think very carefully about being in that cabin with me, because in the event that I wanted to do something she didn't want to, I would force my plan on her.

Please, the only people who need to fear me physically are guys with big mouths.

Jaime admitted to indecision, but she chose to follow her heart and come over for dinner. It couldn't have been a better backdrop—a mild early-July night, amid all that natural majesty. It was just right.

Jaime grew up in the fishing village of Kona in Hawaii, and her father was a fisherman. I knew that her favorite meal—one she had had often throughout her life—was grilled fresh fish with salad and rice, so that is what I made. I also included raw oysters on the menu (read from this what you will).

After dinner, we sat and talked and listened to music. And we kissed for the first time. It was a wonderful evening—and morning—all around.

43

MORE TROUBLE

STAYING SOBER and on a smooth, flat, sunlit path was not going to be easy.

Jaime stayed with me for three days. I had not asked her, but I knew I wanted her to live with me. Yes, I know—but oftentimes I can't find the brakes and don't know how to stay off the accelerator. I called Jim and asked him if it would be all right for Jaime to share the apartment with me. He said sure. So I asked Jaime if she would move in, and she said yes.

Right after Jaime said she would move in with me, I called Mary and told her I was going to move on, but I neglected to mention that it was because there was someone else in my life. It was only after Jaime and I had been together a little more than a year that I talked in person with Mary and told her the reason I chose to end it with her. It was one of the most difficult conversations of my life, and I can only imagine how much it sucked for Mary.

Moving on meant that Jaime and I would get domestic. But before this big step, Jaime was going to Billings, Montana, for a couple weeks to visit her father, who was now living there. I was going back to Boston to see my family and meet up with friends. While in Boston, I got into a bit of trouble.

❖

It's not the way I like to make the news. You can go online and read versions of it. Here, I will tell you my story—the true story.

While on my visit back to Boston, I met up with my longtime friend Jimmy McGettrick. We went shopping at the South Shore Mall in Braintree. I bought several items of clothing at a few stores in the mall. We went into Lord & Taylor, and while in there, I saw some bathing suits and took three into a dressing room to try them on. Before I did so, I handed Jimmy three bags containing clothes I had bought at the other stores. So I was in the dressing room when I heard Jimmy and some other guys yelling. It sounded like a fight.

I immediately pulled on the shorts I had been wearing when I entered the store—with $1,000 in cash and a credit card with a high limit in one of the pockets—and ran out of the dressing room to see what was going on. Through the front window of Lord & Taylor, I could see Jimmy, just outside the store, wrestling on the sidewalk with what looked like two security guards. Well, I knew what to do—I ran to help Jimmy. And when I got there, I cracked both these security guards, knocking both down.

Jimmy got disentangled from the guards and was shouting something about those guys demanding to see what was in the bags he was holding—bags that held nothing but clothing paid for in full. Those asshole guards came back at me, and I knocked both of them down again—with some help from Jimmy. But then, another guard jumped on my back, taking me by surprise, and I went down. Jimmy and I still could have handled these three, but it didn't come to that because two cops were there only seconds later, and Jimmy and I were arrested for disorderly conduct. I also had a shoplifting charge thrown at me because I left the store with merchandise I hadn't paid for.

In the back of the cruiser, on the way to the police station, Jimmy filled me in on what had happened. When I tried on the bathing suit, he walked outside of the store, and the security guards followed him and demanded to check his bags. He told them to fuck off, which is probably what I would have done. They tried to forcibly inspect the bags and Jimmy resisted—and a fight broke out.

The case against Jimmy and me got dismissed. We both had to pay court costs, though.

❖

I flew from Boston to Montana and met up with Jaime, and we rented a car and drove back to Oregon. We lived together in the garage apartment and attended local meetings of Alcoholics Anonymous and Narcotics Anonymous a few times a week. Jaime got a part-time job as a waitress. In addition to the meetings I attended with Jaime, I filled my days with reading, walking, and a daily dip in the frigid Pacific.

In January 2010, Jaime and I moved out of Jim's apartment and into a small house we rented in Ilwaco, Washington, a shipping village about fifteen miles north along the coast from Astoria. It is beautiful country—that entire area. Soon, Jaime left her waitressing gig and got a job handling the front desk during the day at a hotel in Cannon Beach, Oregon—across the Columbia River and south of Astoria. Cannon Beach is a quaint, artsy town, and as the name suggests, it's also on the Pacific Ocean. Jaime was doing her job well, and the owner of the hotel told her that if she would move to Cannon Beach, she would be promoted to assistant manager.

So in the summer of 2010, we moved yet again, to an apartment about a half mile from Jaime's workplace.

I fell in love with Jaime, and she with me. It seemed that things were going to be all right. Yet, as I would soon be reminded, love doesn't cure all or prevent all pain. Soon enough, I was again drinking and taking pills. I cringe when I think about how easily I went back down that road—and I cringe more when I consider that I took Jaime with me.

I made a big mistake not getting a job. Working would have helped me by giving me structure and keeping me busy. I had too much time on my hands, I had too many doubts about the future, and I harbored so much pain about what I had done and put people through. You would think that the pain and doubt that had come as a result of my drug use would be all the incentive I needed to stay away from them—but no.

The relapse started one afternoon with me drinking a couple beers. Then it all went downhill . . . so, so fast. That same night, when Jaime came home, she drank beer with me. The next day, I went on the hunt for pills, and I quickly found them. I got myself a nice stash of Oxy, and I started to gobble them. I had enough for both Jaime and me, and at the end of her workday, she also took some pills.

You might ask whether we had a big discussion about going back into the junk that nearly killed us. Well, in our case, it wasn't like that. We didn't do much talking; we just took the drugs. We weren't strong enough, we weren't committed enough, and we had a biological predisposition to needing those chemicals that, at least at this point, we were largely, but not totally, powerless to resist. It owned us, the addiction. We could fight it, but we chose not to. We chose to give in and surrender—and grab a hold of what made us feel good in the moment but destroyed the future.

I bought Oxy on the street, and I also located a source that had it couriered to me, regularly. We had plenty of pills. One day, I snorted thirty 8-milligram tablets of OxyContin.

This relapse became just about as bad as it could get. I say "just about" because neither of us died, which surely this would have been the worst, and just as surely this was the path we were on.

All this started happening in the summer of 2010. A year after we joined each other outside of rehab and in sobriety, we were junkies again. Opioids are that gripping, and that grip is that relentless. It is embedded in the core of your mind and body and just keeps pulling on you.

I don't know how Jaime did it, but while she was on the drugs she continued to hold that job at the hotel. She went to work every day, and she did her job every day. Fairly remarkable, from my point of view.

We were just surviving, not much more. We would have been homeless without Jaime's job. We weren't eating much, and we both lost weight. I am not sure how long we could have lasted, but something happened in early December 2010 that saved both our lives.

That something was Jaime and her ability to do what, at that point, I couldn't: leave the drugs and make a run, and maybe a final effort, to avoid total destruction—hers and mine.

On December 8, 2010, I boarded a plane in Seattle, bound for Toronto, where I was going to take part in an NHL alumni game—an appearance that Mark Napier had set up for me. I was going to make a little money for my participation, which I needed, and of course I still loved being on the ice as well as meeting up with former teammates and guys I had played against.

I would be staying at a budget hotel just outside of Toronto and planned to be in the area for about a week before going back to Washington. On the four-hour flight to Toronto, I was in a semiconscious state induced and maintained by Oxy and rum and Cokes. Whatever I did feel felt great.

When I arrived in Toronto, I was met by a friend from my playing days in Montreal (not a hockey player), whose name I won't mention. Waiting for us in his car was a small hill of pain pills. We drove around and popped some pills, and then we made it to a bar, where we drank and did more pills.

That night, in the game, played before a sold-out crowd in a small rink fifty miles outside of Toronto, I skated—literally and figuratively. I don't remember much about it. After the game, I met up with my friend again and we went out and drank and did more pills. He dropped me off at the hotel where I was staying, and I remember waking up in my room sometime the next afternoon to the sound of my cell phone ringing. I picked it up; it was Jaime. Her voice was shaky—she was crying. Well, this jolted me from my stupor, and I asked her what was going on. What she told me she had done would set my life in turmoil—shake it up and down, throw a massive bolt of fear, adrenaline, and anxiety through me.

Jaime said she was back in Hawaii, where she was from, and . . . Back in Hawaii?

As I lay there in bed with my heart racing, Jaime told me she couldn't live the life we had been living anymore. She said if she kept it up she would be dead, and I would be dead too. She explained that she would be staying at her mom's house, and that she had just signed on for intensive outpatient treatment with her former physician, Dr. Kevin Kunz, a general practitioner and certified substance abuse counselor. Jamie had responded well under his care a few years prior, and she believed he could provide the support she needed so she could do well again.

Jaime said that leaving Washington and going home, to her family and to her doctor, and to that wonderful, beautiful, and healing island, were all necessary. She told me that she loved me and wanted to be with me and no one else. She told me, though, that the only way we could be together again is if we were both clean and sober. It was the only way.

Oh man, this hurt; it hurt so, so bad. I was confused and afraid. I didn't know what would be my plan of action.

Jamie asked me straight out if I would commit to getting clean. And, you know, I didn't even have to think; I blurted, "Yeah, definitely—I love you. I will do this."

What came next was difficult. Very difficult. I didn't return to Washington. Instead, I flew to Boston and continued with hotel life, renting a room in a low-cost motel near the water in the town of Hull.

I stayed in touch with Jaime, and she filled me in via Skype, email, and the phone about her recovery and how she was getting clean. Meanwhile, I continued to do drugs—lots of drugs. I lied to Jaime and told her I was clean and getting better, but that wasn't the truth. And she knew it; it became particularly apparent to her when we talked on Skype.

Maybe in April—or it could have been May—I did what I said I would never do: I shot heroin. I continued to shoot it almost daily for the next two months. And every day, I was in contact with Jaime. Now there was no more lying, no more pretense; I was annihilating myself, and Jaime was begging me to stop.

Then I disappeared from Jaime for a day or two at a time. She told she was going crazy, and she told me to get help. I said I would, but I didn't.

One morning, I woke up sitting on the toilet with a needle in my arm attached to a syringe of heroin.

Heroin is the final step before you die.

❖

Jaime was clean and healthy, and her future was bright. Yet she stayed with me. Why? I can give you many reasons, but I know our connection was cosmic and that we loved each other. Maybe, just maybe, some sort of karma, some sort of fate, was in play that could possibly result in showing others that, at the brink of death and nearing the end of the most destructive behavior, salvation and good health are still attainable. I am not sure.

Finally, in late May, Jaime offered me what I now know was my final chance to live. She invited me to come to Hawaii, to stay with her and see her doctor, and get clean alongside her while she continued her sobriety. And she gave me an ultimatum; even as she told me she loved me and that she did not want to be with anyone else, she said that when I got off the plane, she would know if I was on anything. And if I was, she would turn around and walk away, forever.

The day before I flew to Hawaii, in early June, I stopped using for the first time in eight months. What came next was physical torture; it was out-and-out awful. But I brought it on, and I faced it and fought well.

That long plane trip to Kona was painful, but I was committed fully to what I had signed on to do.

When the plane landed, as it was taxiing, I called Jaime and she picked up the phone, excited. Yes, she was at the airport. She had shown up. She was waiting for me at the gate.

Now, while it is my style to get emotional, it isn't my style to act all sappy—and there is a difference. But when I got off the plane and looked out there, at the crowd of people waiting for the passengers, and I saw Jaime among them, waving and smiling, beautiful and tanned, I was in meltdown mode. Even as physical agony washed through me, I felt intense emotional comfort. We hugged for a long time, and both of us cried.

As you may imagine, Jaime and I needed some "personal" time together. We drove right to an oceanfront studio apartment that Jamie had rented for me.

But a stint of hellish detox was still in front of me. I was going to get clean without chemical assistance—just through guts, meetings, therapy, and Jaime's companionship.

Those first two weeks were hell, but they were necessary if I was to have a future—of any kind. I met with Jaime's doctor twice the first week, and twice the second week. I went to an NA meeting every day—sometimes twice a day. And every day, there was Jaime to help keep me moving toward sobriety. There is absolutely no way I could have done it without her.

After two weeks, that awful withdrawal was no more.

I stayed in Kona for a month—for two weeks at the apartment and after that at Jaime's mother's house. Jaime was totally healthy and doing great; she had a full-time job at a property management company. Over the final two weeks, I continued to get better, I continued the meetings, and I saw Dr. Kunz three more times.

I also spent a lot of time at the beach. Let me tell you, Hawaii, the beach, and the ocean pack an incredibly potent punch when it comes to healing. Oh man, that place is good for your soul.

At night and on the weekends, Jaime and I planned the next step—the first step of our lives together. I told her that at this point in my life, having next to no money (save for my NHL pension, which

I hadn't touched yet) and having had far more defeats and down periods since retiring from the NHL, Montreal was the place that held the most opportunity for me. More than that, though, it offered the best opportunity for both of us as a couple. And we certainly wanted to remain a couple.

While getting and staying clean in Hawaii, I had talked to many people in Montreal, and I came to appreciate more than ever before the affection and warmth that the people of the city felt for me. I knew that I could make a serious go of it up there.

As for exactly how I would make a living, I started to plan and map out appearances I could make in which I would deliver anti-bullying talks to young people. I felt I was well qualified and highly credible in this area, for I had become famous as a fighter, but I was never a bully. I stuck up for people who were bullied on and off the ice. I knew that teachers, school administrators, and students in Canada would be interested in hearing what I had to say.

Also, among the people with whom I had been talking in Montreal was a longtime friend, Mitch Melnick, the highly popular sports radio host. Mitch's show, *Melnick in the Afternoon*, on TSN Radio 690 is a favorite of radio listeners in Quebec and Ontario. Mitch told me he could get me some regular paying gigs making appearances on his show.

In early July 2010, I flew back to Boston. Two months after that, I met Jaime at Logan Airport, where she had just arrived from Kona. She had two suitcases with her—that was it. A week later, in Boston, Jaime and I got into a car a friend had lent me. We had with us those two suitcases of Jaime's and my stash of clothes and other personal items. Between us, we had $600 in cash—no other money.

We began driving—to Montreal, where we would start a new life together.

EPILOGUE

AS I WRITE THIS, I'm back on track—and I am fully aware of the ever-present potential to go off track and give in to a biological pre-disposition—or longing, weakness, call it what you will—and for my life to fall apart, and for me to hurt and disappoint others.

For sure, this awareness, and my understanding of the chemical, mental, and environmental nature of addiction, is a first line of defense against relapsing. So are the fortitude and intensity that enabled me to have a successful thirteen-year career in the NHL and to stay clean for more than four years now.

I am busy, and this helps me stay healthy. My partner in keeping busy—and in life—is Jaime. I probably wouldn't be alive today with-out her—and I surely would not have arrived at this productive and healthy stage in life without her love and friendship.

Montreal is our home. Again, I must say I love Montreal and its people. They have all been so good to me.

Jaime and I live in a house in a quiet neighborhood in the city. We share the house with our two best buddies—our dogs Bhodi, a golden retriever, and Kona, a Saint Bernard.

Every weekday afternoon, I am on the air for three hours on TSN 690, the leading sports-radio station in Montreal. From noon until one, I co-host, along with Tony Marinaro, *The Intermission Show*. Then, from one until three, I host my own show, *Off the Cuff with*

Chris Nilan. Things are going well with both shows, with each receiving strong ratings.

Every month, I deliver about four to six speeches to groups. I speak primarily on two subjects: bullying, and my battles with alcohol and drugs—what I learned from these conflicts and healthy strategies to remain sober or return to sobriety.

When I talk about bullying, my audience will be young people, anywhere from third or fourth grade up through high school. In discussing staying sober and resisting chemicals, the age demographic is broader. I speak to high school and college kids, with the intent of educating and advising them and preventing a problem from happening in the first place; I also talk to people of all ages who are alcoholics and addicts, whether they are now in the grips of the disease and are using or are clean.

I can help in many ways.

I am featured in the movie *The Last Gladiators*, which was produced and directed by Academy Award–winning director Alex Gibney. The movie, which opened in theaters across Canada in February 2013, tells my story and the story of other top contemporary NHL enforcers. *The Last Gladiators* has received positive reviews. *Sports Illustrated* declared, "If fans embrace *Slap Shot* as the *Casablanca* of hockey films, then *The Last Gladiators* is *Apocalypse Now*." Sportsnet proclaimed, "With apologies to *Slap Shot*, whose cult status is ironclad and whose replay value is off the charts, *Gladiators* just might be the best hockey film made yet."

I have a website, KnucklesNilan.com, which Jaime administers and updates. There, you can send me questions, learn more about me, and find photos and video clips of me from today and my playing days. You can also contact me through the site with appearance inquiries. As well—and this part of my business is growing steadily—you can purchase items through the site from my own Knuckles brand of clothing as well as Montreal Canadiens memorabilia, including a replica of the home jersey I wore when I played for the Habs. All items can be autographed, and personalized, on request.

I continue to visit hospitals in the Montreal area.

I skate in Canadiens and NHL alumni games and at other old-timers' events. Most of my exercise now, though, is spinning and lifting weights a few times a week. My joints still creak a bit, but I'm not stopping and trying not to slow down.

I will always be a Boston kid at heart. All of my family still lives in the Boston area. And I visit there frequently.

I maintain a strong and positive relationship with my ex-wife, Karen, who is still a nurse and whose boyfriend is a great guy. Our three children—Colleen, Chris, and Tara—are now adults, and are doing great, with young families of their own. Karen and I, grandparents, love our children and grandchildren fiercely.

I am fortunate that my mother, Leslie, and my father, Henry, in their late seventies, are in good health and still living in the house where I grew up in West Roxbury. In 2013, they celebrated their sixtieth wedding anniversary.

My two sisters, my brother, and their families live in towns south of Boston.

I remain remorseful for the pain I have caused my family and my friends, and I seek every day to atone and make amends for these injuries.

As I write this, Jimmy Bulger—Whitey Bulger to most of the world—was recently convicted on a laundry list of charges, including eleven murders. In the spring of 2012, I visited with Jimmy in the Plymouth House of Correction, where he was being held awaiting trial. It was weird, this meeting, with Jimmy in an orange prison jumpsuit, sitting across from me on the other side of a glass partition. Jimmy told me he was being charged with many crimes for which he was not responsible, and that this was because he was the last of his gang to be caught, so it was a convenient way for the authorities to tie up loose ends. Jimmy was particularly upset about the charges that he killed two women. He told me he had done a lot of bad things, but that he did not, and could not, kill a woman.

Among the crimes of which Jimmy Bulger was convicted was murder.

On August 13, 2013, days after he was convicted, Bulger made a statement that he would willingly part with the more than $800,000 the feds had confiscated from his apartment in Santa Monica, and with any other material possessions, but he would fight to hold on to the Stanley Cup championship ring. Now, here's the thing: I never gave Jimmy Bulger a Stanley Cup ring. I gave my Stanley Cup ring to my father; when Jacques Lemaire found out about this, he had a replica made for me. I made a statement to the press, setting the record straight.

Jimmy Bulger is eighty-three years old and will no doubt live out his days behind bars.

❖

I still believe in God, even though I don't talk or visit with Him enough. I believe I am blessed, and that I have been given more chances than I deserve. And I think that everything that has happened is for a reason—it is part of a plan, maybe a plan set out and orchestrated by a force far stronger than and beyond and above me. Just maybe.

In my mid-fifties now, with so much good accomplished, and so much bad and destruction behind me, I can see clearly a path with the potential for me to make immense contributions, helping, healing, and achieving.

Staying on the path will not be easy. It will be a battle.

Yet, I know this: when I am committed, strong, and healthy, fighting and battling are what I do best.

Chris "Knuckles" Nilan
Montreal
August 2013